D1052817

Gabriel García Márquez

Also by Ilan Stavans

Fiction
The One-Handed Pianist
The Disappearance

Nonfiction
A Critic's Journey
The Hispanic Condition
Art and Anger
The Riddle of Cantinflas
Knowledge and Censorship
    (with Verónica Albin)
Imagining Columbus
The Inveterate Dreamer
Octavio Paz: A Meditation
Bandido
On Borrowed Words
Spanglish
¡Lotería! (with Teresa Villegas)
Dictionary Days
Resurrecting Hebrew
Love and Language (with Verónica Albin)

Anthologies
Growing Up Latino (with Harold
    Augenbraum)
Tropical Synagogues
The Oxford Book of Latin American Essays
The Oxford Book of Jewish Stories
*Becoming Americans: Four Centuries of
    Immigrant Writing*
Mutual Impressions
Wáchale!
The Scroll and the Cross
*The Schocken Book of Modern Sephardic
    Literature*
Lengua Fresca (with Harold
    Augenbraum)

Cartoons
Latino USA (with Lalo Alcaráz)
Mr. Spic Goes to Washington (with
    Roberto Weil)

Translations
Sentimental Songs by Felipe Alfau

Editions
The Collected Stories by Calvert Casey
The Poetry of Pablo Neruda
Collected Stories by Isaac Bashevis
    Singer (three volumes)
Encyclopedia Latina (four volumes)
Selected Writings by Rubén Darío
I Explain a Few Things by Pablo Neruda
Cesar Chavez: An Organizer's Tale
Spain, Take This Chalice from Me by
    César Vallejo

General
The Essential Ilan Stavans
Ilan Stavans: Eight Conversations (with
    Neal Sokol)
Conversations with Ilan Stavans
Collins Q&A: Latino History and Culture

Gabriel García Márquez

The Early Years

Ilan Stavans

palgrave
macmillan

GABRIEL GARCÍA MÁRQUEZ

Copyright © Ilan Stavans, 2010.

First published in 2010 by
PALGRAVE MACMILLAN®
in the United States—a division of St. Martin's Press LLC,
175 Fifth Avenue, New York, NY 10010.

Where this book is distributed in the UK, Europe and the rest of the
world, this is by Palgrave Macmillan, a division of Macmillan Publishers
Limited, registered in England, company number 785998, of Houndmills,
Basingstoke, Hampshire RG21 6XS.

Palgrave Macmillan is the global academic imprint of the above
companies and has companies and representatives throughout the world.

Palgrave® and Macmillan® are registered trademarks in the United
States, the United Kingdom, Europe and other countries.

ISBN: 978–0–312–24033–2

Library of Congress Cataloging-in-Publication Data

Stavans, Ilan.
    Gabriel García Márquez : The Early Years / Ilan Stavans.
       p. cm.
    Includes bibliographical references and index.
    ISBN-13: 978–0–312–24033–2 (hardcover)
    ISBN-10: 0–312–24033–3 (hardcover)
       1. García Márquez, Gabriel, 1928– 2. Authors, Colombian—
    20th century—Biography. I. Title.

PQ8180.17.A73Z9355 2010
863'.64—dc22
[B]   2009025896

A catalogue record of the book is available from the British Library.

Design by Newgen Imaging Systems (P) Ltd., Chennai, India.

First edition: January 2010

10 9 8 7 6 5 4 3 2 1

Printed in the United States of America.

To Alison,
amor e inspiración

The invention of a nation in a phrase.

—Wallace Stevens

Contents

Acknowledgments

This biographical exploration has been a decade in the making. The idea was first suggested to me around 1998 by my friend Gayatri Patnaik, my editor at Routledge at the time. Since then I've traveled around the globe to meet extraordinary people and engaged them in dozens of interviews. In Colombia, with the helpful guidance of Eduardo Maireles, I journeyed, with paused dedication, across *la ruta garciamarqueana*, visiting Aracataca, Riohacha, Santa Marta, Sucre, La Ciénega, Barranquilla, and Cartagena. I learned just how much literature matters in a region of the world plagued by illiteracy. The effigy of Gabriel García Márquez, known to everyone as Gabito, is everywhere—literally and symbolically. He is seen as a redeemer, a man whose statue is held in equal honor to that of another messianic figure: Simón Bolívar, *El Libertador*.

First and foremost, I wish to thank García Márquez for the way he has refined his talent in his oeuvre, pushing it to its limits. As I relate in the preface, I was dumbstruck when I first read him as a twenty-one-year-old in my native Mexico. It suddenly became clear to me that words have magic: when used meticulously, they are able to conjure alternative universes, some more appealing than our own.

My wholehearted *gracias* to Cass Canfield Jr. of HarperCollins, friend and editor extraordinaire, who throughout the years encouraged me to pursue the writing of this biography. I spent marvelous hours with him talking about his passion for *One Hundred Years of Solitude*. Thanks to Airié Stuart of Palgrave for her patience and insistence. It is due to her, in large measure, that I've focused my whole attention on this endeavor. Jill Kneerim at Palmer & Dodge believed in the project. Steve Wasserman, at the *Los Angeles Times Book Review*, asked me to reflect, at different times, on a number of García Márquez's books, as did Oscar Villalón at the *San Francisco Chronicle* and Jim Concannon at the *Boston Globe*. Thanks to Henry Louis Gates Jr. and Mike Vásquez for opening the doors of *Transition*, to Henry Finder at the *New Yorker*, Laurence Goldstein at the *Michigan Quarterly Review*, Fidel Cano Correa at *El Espectador*, Martin Levin at the *Globe and Mail*, Karen Winkler at the *Chronicle of Higher Education*, and Erica González at *El Diario*.

I appreciate the openness and *la calidad humana* of my dear Hugo Chaparro Valderrama in Bogotá and Juan Fernando Merino of *El Diario* in New York. The Colombian photographer Nereo López-Meza regaled me with a fiesta of images of García Márquez's coastal landscapes and his journey to Stockholm. I am all the better as a result of the guidance I received in Barranquilla from Meira Delmar as well as from Heriberto Fiorillo, who hosted me at La Cueva; Iliana Restrepo, who was in charge of *la ruta garciamarqueana* in Cartagena; Rafael Darío, director of the Casa Museo García Márquez, who was generous with his time and knowledge as he took me around in Aracataca; the welcoming Jaime García Márquez at the Fundación Nuevo Periodismo in Cartagena; the wonderful Elkin Restrepo in Medellín; and the erudite Juan Gustavo Cobo Borda in Bogotá, where Claudia Leyva and Piedad Bonnett made me feel comfortably at home.

I'm honored with the friendship of Harold Augenbraum at the National Book Foundation, Jonathan Galassi at Farrar, Straus, and Giroux, and Max Rudin at the Library of America. I felt a kindred soul in Gregory Rabassa, with whom I discussed in detail issues of translation. I've enjoyed the numerous conversations I've entertained with scores of people in and beyond García Márquez's circle. I've had dialogues with Isabel Allende, Fernando del Paso, Augusto Monterroso, Antonio Muñoz Molina, Álvaro Mutis, Elena Poniatoska, and John Updike. I appreciate the support of Gloria Gutiérrez at the Carmen Balcells Literary Agency in Barcelona; Donald Yaes in California; Alberto Blanco, Angelina Muñiz-Huberman, and Alejandro Springall in Mexico City; Ali White in Vermont; Edith Grossman and Silvana Paternostro in New York; Jesús Díaz and Martín Felipe Yriart in Madrid, Spain; Alicia Agnese-Milia and Héctor Urrutibéheity in Houston, Texas; Isaac Goldemberg and Daisy Cocco de Fillippi at Hostos Community College; Alberto Fuguet and Iván Jaksic in Santiago, Chile; Alberto Manguel in Paris; Antonio Benítez-Rojo at Amherst College; Francisco Goldman at Trinity College; Caryl Phillips at Yale University; Edmundo Paz-Soldán at Cornell University; John King at University of Warwick; and Tomás Eloy Martínez at Rutgers University.

Verónica Albin read the manuscript in different versions, offering insightful suggestions. With insistence as well as undiminished cordiality, Marie Ostby, Leah Carroll, and Yasmin Mathew shepherded it through production.

I have benefited enormously from, and made use of, the foundational work done by journalists and scholars who came before me and whose contribution I used as a compass, particularly Jon Lee Anderson, Gene H. Bell-Villada, Eligio García Márquez, Jorge García Usta, Rita Guibert, Jacques Gilard, Luis Harss, Gerald Martin, George R. McMurray, Dasso Saldívar, Mario Vargas Llosa, Ernesto Volkening, and Michael Wood. I tested my ideas with my students at Amherst College in the courses on *One Hundred Years of Solitude* I taught, intermittently, from 2001 to 2009. Their intelligence and dedication always inspires me.

My beloved parents Abraham and Ofelia Stavchansky in Mexico City allowed me to use their house as my headquarters. My mother even functioned as a liaison with the García Márquez entourage. *Mi corazón está lleno.*

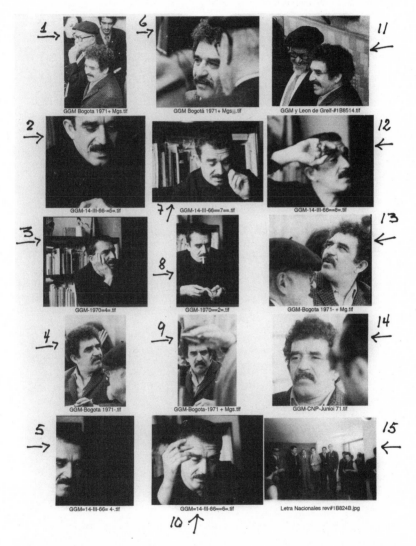

Gabriel García Márquez

Preface

This book is the story of how Gabriel García Márquez—a middle-class *costeño* from Colombia's Caribbean coast, a law-school dropout with strong literary aspirations, whose career in journalism included stints at some of the major newspapers of Barranquilla, Cartagena, and Bogotá, and whose left-leaning views put him at odds with the dictatorship of General Gustavo Rojas Pinilla (1953–57)—came to write a masterpiece that, almost in a single stroke, reconfigured the cultural map of Latin America in the second half of the twentieth century.

I remember vividly the rainy afternoon in my native Mexico City when I first read *One Hundred Years of Solitude*, finishing it in a dizzying twenty-four-hour session. It was April 1982, and I was in my early twenties. I had had an aversion to books (I was the outdoorsy kind) until I discovered the novel as a literary genre, and, specifically, the work of the so-called *El Boom*, writers from Latin America who belonged to my father's generation (most of whom were born between 1909 and 1942), whose narratives were still hypnotizing the world. But no book by this cadre of myth-makers (the term was coined by the British man of letters V. S. Pritchett) compared remotely to *One Hundred Years of Solitude*, a veritable lesson in what a friend described as *lo neobarroco*, the neo-baroque style that defined the literature from the region. I didn't just read it; I devoured it.

I was on my bed, near the window. I remember going to the bathroom twice. And I recall reaching chapter eighteen, with only two more to go before the end, as the sun began to rise. I was dumbstruck. Could a novel really be this good?

We retain forever the memory of the moment when certain books imposed themselves on us because nothing feels the same afterward. That afternoon I went to Librería Gandhi on Avenida Miguel Ángel de Quevedo, a favorite haunt of mine, bought every García Márquez title I could find, and binged on them for weeks. I was impressed by the carefully constructed Caribbean reality of despair. The Colombian author, it seemed to me, was looking at my own milieu, *el mundo hispánico*, with fresh eyes. What fascinated me in particular was that he wasn't an urbane, cosmopolitan intellectual like my other role model, Jorge Luis Borges, whose oeuvre revolved around philosophical conundrums.

In my opinion, there are only two novelistic masterpieces written in Spanish whose influence radically revamped our understanding of Hispanic civilization: Cervantes's *Don Quixote* and García Márquez's *One Hundred Years of Solitude*. *Don Quixote* accomplished it with its mordant critique of a seventeenth-century Iberian empire. It offered an Erasmian celebration of free thought defined by misadventures abroad and a zealous Catholic Inquisition at home and across the Atlantic. The masterful *One Hundred Years of Solitude* is a sweeping genealogical narrative about an entire continent and its people: its corrupt politicians, its religious aspirations, its gender disparity, and its natural and historical calamities. Like Cervantes's opus, which is purportedly written by a Moor, García Márquez's novel is presented as a palimpsest: a manuscript drafted by a gypsy. What is one to make of the fact that such fringe social types in the Spanish-speaking world are the creators of the two literary pillars on which it stands?

García Márquez, then a little-known novelist, wrote the book over an eighteen-month period, in seclusion, in Mexico

City, not too far from where I lived. Released in Buenos Aires in 1967 by Editorial Sudamericana, it was the most important novel ever to be published in the Americas. It follows the fanciful Buendía family of Macondo, a small, forgotten town on Colombia's Caribbean coast, over the course of more than a century (in spite of the title), from the mythical foundation of the town to its demise. The cyclical structure of the plot, its omniscient, third-person narrative, and the magical nature of the incidents chronicled fill the book with biblical resonances. At its core is the most basic of biblical curses: incest. The Buendías are born of incest and forever condemned by it. There is language that recalls the Tower of Babel, sibling rivalries like those of Cain and Abel and Joseph and his brothers, larger-than-life imperial figures such as Colonel Aureliano Buendía, who bring to mind the kings of Israel, as well as magical illnesses such as an epidemic of insomnia and disasters like a rainstorm of butterflies that are reminiscent of the plagues.

Symmetrically divided into twenty unnumbered chapters of approximately eight thousand words each, it includes a cast of three dozen characters delineated with great confidence. Pick your favorite: Remedios the Beauty, whose elegiac loveliness enables her to ascend to heaven; Úrsula Iguarán, the Buendía matron, on whose shoulders the endurance of the family lies; the seventeen Aurelianos fathered by José Arcadio Buendía; the foreboding prostitute Pilar Ternera; rebellious *niñas* such as Santa Sofía de la Piedad; Indian servants; and the turcos, Middle Eastern immigrants.

The novel is about memory and forgetfulness, about the trials and tribulations of capitalism in a colonial society, about European explorers in the New World, about the clash of science and faith, about matriarchy as an institution, about loyalty, treason, and vengeance in the political arena, about the path that a rivulet of blood takes after a tragic death, about the flora and fauna of the Caribbean, about mishaps in urban planning, about the fancifulness of names in Spanish-speaking culture (Quick: how many Aurelianos are there?), about the difference between official and popular history, about intelligence and stupidity not as counterparts but as extensions of each other. It manages to build a self-sufficient Leibnitzian universe, one paralleling our own. Personally, I can't think of a more luminous, if demanding, read.

The legend of how García Márquez's book came to be is in itself enchanting. He and his wife Mercedes were driving to Acapulco, on the Mexican Pacific coast, when suddenly he was visited (like Samuel Taylor Coleridge, who, after an opium dream, shaped "Kubla Khan") by the muse of fiction. He turned the car around and isolated himself in his Mexico City study until he finished the manuscript. In his description of the experience, he comes across less as an artist than as a scribe, as if *One Hundred Years of Solitude* had been dictated to him from first to last. The English translation by Gregory Rabassa is superb, maybe even better than the original. García Márquez has said as much. He even called Rabassa "the best Latin American writer in the English language."

Reading *One Hundred Years of Solitude* got me hooked on literature, prompting me to understand its metabolism: how it works, why it matters, who produces it and who reads it, what the connection is between history and fiction, between what is true and what is a lie. It inspired me to become a cultural critic. As I've traveled through life, intellectually as well as existentially, I've always had my copy of the novel nearby. It has been a center of gravity, my raison d'être as a reader.

It is clear that contemporary literature owes much to García Márquez: his visions, his discipline.

But he transcends literature: García Márquez was a crucial protagonist in the major events of the second half of the twentieth century, in Colombia in particular and in Latin America in general. From the 1948 riots sparked by the assassination of presidential candidate Jorge Eliécer Gaitán, known as *El Bogotazo*, to Fidel Castro's Communist Revolution in 1958–59, from *El Boom* itself to the neo-liberal economic policies that defined the eighties, from the emergence of a fresh type of journalism to the war against the Colombian drug cartels, from a new Latin American cinema to the project of simplifying Spanish orthography, García Márquez has been a larger-than-life force.

Biography as a literary genre wasn't as popular in the Spanish-speaking world as it has been in its English-language counterpart. Not until the seventies did publishers invest in biographies as marketable items. This reluctance was due, in part, to the Latin American psyche. Latin Americans are not fond of confessing their sins in public. The act of revealing oneself is rather private. Not surprisingly, the heirs of the estates of political and cultural luminaries tended to shy away from allowing the secret lives of the departed made accessible to the public. This doesn't mean that biographies were inexistent prior to that time. The seventeenth-century Mexican nun Sor Juana Inés de la Cruz, for instance, wrote a denunciatory letter defending her behavior from calumnies propagated by her male superiors in the Catholic Church. But these scant biographies are the exception to the rule.

In recent decades, literary biographies written in Spanish have multiplied in the hands of Iberian publishers. There are several on Borges, a couple on Mario Vargas Llosa, and one on García Márquez himself. None strike me as rigorous enough. In English, there is a handful on Borges, among others. I have written this book as a biographical investigation with an English-language reader in mind. I wouldn't have embarked on it had I not become aware of the pleasures the genre provides in the hands of practitioners like Leon Edel, whose multivolume life of Henry James is a tour de force—better even than James's own tranquil life at his desk.

The traditional biographer—like James Boswell whose meticulous work ethic is derived from a Protestant sensibility—is eager to record everything, including minutiae, to squeeze the meaning out of a subject's every thought and action, to dissect a person's behavior for the sake of posterity. In a sense, the methodical biographer is akin to a vampire, sucking the subject's blood. Or better yet, like a *dybbuk*, inhabiting his body and soul, walking, eating, and dreaming with him at all times. These images may be grotesque, but they are not altogether inaccurate. By choice, the biographer doesn't quite surrender his own self in order to become someone else. What he does is gather all the possible ingredients of another person's existence and retrace his journey from one point to another. Needless to say, the biographer's subjectivity is constantly in question. It is his vision of *el otro*, the suspect's path as interpreted by the fastidious detective. The best meditation I know on the biographer's quest is Julio Cortázar's novella *The Pursuer,* about the impossible attempt to pin down a fictional jazz master whose profile resembles that of Charlie Parker.

Other biographies are punctilious in their delivery of even the most anodyne detail. My quest is not to accumulate facts, for data isn't knowledge. I am most interested in the background to *One Hundred Years of Solitude:* what prompted it and what were the conditions under which it was gestated? In other words, I am after the raw material of literature. Where does a writer find his inspiration? How does he transform life into fiction? My interest is at once on García Márquez's personal travels and in the historical backdrop against which that traveling unfolded.

This biography of Gabriel García Márquez covers a little over four decades, from his birth in 1927 in the small

Caribbean coastal town of Aracataca in Colombia to 1970, when Rabassa's English translation of *One Hundred Years of Solitude* was released by Harper & Row in the United States, three years after its explosive publication in Latin America. I trace the author's journey against the tapestry of the principal historical, ideological, and cultural events that shaped Latin America during that period. He lived in almost a dozen places, mostly for extended periods, including Aracataca, Barranquilla, Bogotá, Cartagena, Barcelona, Paris, and Mexico. For most of that time García Márquez was, to a large extent, an unknown newspaper reporter and columnist, as well as a screenwriter. He was astoundingly prolific, publishing sundry pieces, sometimes at a bi-weekly rate, if not more often. He built an enviable reputation as an imaginative journalist. But it was in García Márquez's short fiction—stories and novellas, some of which were first published in periodicals—where his true talent emerged. In these pieces the fabulous universe of Macondo and its inhabitants slowly took shape. Equally significant was the way in which he devised a carefully calibrated style (in the words of a reviewer, with García Márquez, every sentence is a surprise and the surprise is, in general, "really an extension of our knowledge or feeling about life, and not simply a trick") and plots that were unique to his native environment. It wasn't until after he turned forty that his fortune radically changed, though not always for the better. García Márquez is known to have resented the merciless scrutiny fame brought to his private life. My narrative concludes at that point.

In writing this biography, I follow García Márquez almost at every turn of his journey. I pore over his journalistic efforts in newspapers, such as *El Heraldo* (Barranquilla), *El Independiente* (Bogotá), *El Universal* (Cartagena), *El Tiempo* (Bogotá), and *El Espectador* (Bogotá), and magazines like *Elite* (Caracas). These took the form of news reports, political, social, and cultural commentary, travel writing, and chronicles of exceptional events, such as the miraculous survival of a sailor lost at sea for twenty-eight days. This account, serialized as "The Story of a Shipwreck," scandalized Bogotá in the mid-fifties.

I explore his connection with *El grupo de Barranquilla,* a cadre of dilettantes (writers, photographers, dancers) who orbited around Ramón Vinyes, known as *El sabio catalán,* or the wise Catalan, with whom he forged a lasting friendship. Some of them, such as Álvaro Cepeda Samudio, Álvaro Mutis, and Plinio Apuleyo Mendoza, are essential to understanding García Márquez's Colombian footing and his transition to the European, Cuban, and Mexican periods. I study his connection to the Cartagena intelligentsia. I survey his sexual escapades and focus on his courtship of Mercedes Barcha Prado, his lifelong wife, whom he met at a high-school dance when he was nineteen and she thirteen. I examine his debt to William Faulkner and the influence Borges had on his oeuvre. I scrutinize the writer's block he experienced in the early sixties and his discovery of Juan Rulfo's fiction, which triggered the creative output that resulted in *One Hundred Years of Solitude.*

I consider the camaraderie he forged with other Spanish-language writers, including Carlos Fuentes, Mario Vargas Llosa, and, to a lesser extent, Julio Cortázar, a connection that benefited them as a group in marketing terms but was put to the test by polarizing ideological issues in the late seventies. Unlike his literary colleagues, García Márquez was a *costeño* with an acute sense of place, someone who had traveled far beyond his humble origins without ever truly leaving them behind.

A crucial aspect in García Márquez's early years is his collaboration with Mexican filmmakers. Starting with his friendship with Mutis—who in turn was an acquaintance of Luis Buñuel—he slowly created partnerships with directors, producers, and actors that allowed him to be involved in a number of important movie projects, the most significant of which were *El gallo de oro* and *Tiempo de morir*. The impact of these experiences on García Márquez seemed enormous. Not only are screenplays and other cinematic collaborations an essential component of his oeuvre but, to a large extent, his style was shaped by his exposure to the screen, both as spectator and screenwriter.

In short, *One Hundred Years of Solitude* is my aleph. I quote from it to shed light on García Márquez's life and vice versa. I'm enthralled by the way it isn't only a novel; it is a *bitácora*, an account of the most decisive events in Colombia until the sixties. It is also a retelling of the Bible, a summation of the painful colonial past of Latin America, and an autobiographical chronicle of García Márquez's friendship with important figures of the time. I pay as much attention to its inception as I do to the *rezeptiongeschichte*. I cover how the book is received in Mexico, Colombia, and Argentina, but especially in the United States, where García Márquez's posthumous reputation was forever cemented with the publication of Rabassa's translation.

To intellectuals in Latin America, García Márquez is a polemical figure. A close friend of Fidel Castro, for years he defended the Cuban Revolution against charges of censorship, corruption, and xenophobia. For scores of young writers, his influence has been both a blessing and a curse. Such is the power of his fiction that successive generations of writers have lived under his shadow, constantly asked to produce narratives with a magical realism bent, even when this style is alien to them. This love-hate relationship is palpable as a reaction to what has come to be known as Macondismo, a concept—or better, a full-fledge ideology—understood to be an index of continental, national, and regional validation. To be a Macondista is to celebrate Latin America as "undecipherable, beyond the code, and as a place whose very disjunctions are, in and of themselves, identifying characteristics."[1] The ambivalence is tangible in the literary movement known as McOndo, which came about in the eighties and promoted the work of young voices, such as those of Alberto Fuguet and Edmundo Paz-Soldán. The movement's name was a refutation of Latin America as a geography populated by Macondos: provincial towns in the middle of the jungle, besieged by epidemics of insomnia.[2]

The McOndista narratives were defined by hyper-realists à la Raymond Carver. They were about urban life, included a dose of crime and drugs, made constant references to popular culture, and addressed issues of globalization and sexuality. In an essay published in Salon.com, entitled "I am not a magic realist!" Fuguet stated: "Unlike the ethereal world of García Márquez's imaginary Macondo, my own world is something much closer to what I call 'McOndo'—a world of McDonald's, Macintoshes and condos. In a continent that was once ultra-politicized, young, apolitical writers are now writing without an overt agenda, about their own experiences. Living in cities all over South America, hooked on cable TV (CNN *en español*), addicted to movies and connected to the Net, we are far away from the jalapeño-scented, siesta-happy atmosphere that permeates too much of the South American literary landscape."

Parricide is an essential part of the process of growing up. The classics are references in opposition to which younger writers define themselves. However, García Márquez's towering reputation has only heightened with time. Will there come a period when his aesthetics are totally eclipsed? I believe that, like Cervantes, his standing is secure for the ages. While he will surely continue to be attacked, *One Hundred Years of Solitude* is an irreplaceable piece in the Latin American cultural puzzle. It contains the DNA of its people.

A word about names and the sequential approach I take. To keep my objective distance, I refer to my subject as García Márquez and not as the overly familiar Gabo, or even the diminutive Gabito. I also avoid referring to the author as

Márquez, as many in the English-speaking world are wont to do. Such simplification is an outright aggression to Hispanic onomastics. People in Spanish-language countries often have not one but two or three names. The popular singer José Antonio Jiménez doesn't go by José, nor is he known as Tony. Likewise with patronymics: Mario Vargas Llosa isn't Llosa to his readers in Lima. García Márquez always uses his two last names, the former referring to his paternal heritage, the latter to his maternal one. To drop one of them is a sign of laziness. I have respected the way names are articulated in interviews and newspaper clippings.

As for the chronology of events, I follow the biographer's mantra that a life lived and a life narrated must parallel each other. In other words, I move from García Márquez's childhood until the success of *One Hundred Years of Solitude* in a linear fashion. I deviate from it only to give a general picture—historical, social, and cultural—of the environment in which García Márquez moved. And I interrupt the sequence when discussing the reception of his work in the English-speaking world. For instance, *La hojarasca* appeared in Spanish, in book form, in 1955, but the English translation was published only in 1972. To avoid needless repetition, I discuss the volume's reception in Spanish and in English in the same section.

In October 1982, several months after my discovery of *One Hundred Years of Solitude* in a reading marathon that began one rainy April afternoon, I read the triumphant headline of the daily newspaper *Unomásuno*: "*¡Gabo gana el Nobel!*" The Swedish Academy in Stockholm had awarded García Márquez the Nobel Prize in Literature. The jubilation in Mexico City was uncontainable. There were special book editions. Literary supplements published entire issues dedicated to his odyssey, with comments by luminaries splashed everywhere. A new novel, *Chronicle of a Death Foretold*, had been released the year prior and was still topping best-seller charts.

His prize made Latin America feel proud. García Márquez was the fourth Latin American to be awarded the Nobel Prize in literature. Prior to him the recipients were Gabriela Mistral, Miguel Ángel Asturias, and Pablo Neruda. They were recognized for giving voice to the people through their art. García Márquez was singled out "for his novels and short stories, in which the fantastic and the realistic are combined in a richly composed world of imagination, reflecting a continent's life and conflicts." Seldom does the prize feel right, not only in the writer of choice but in the time of choice. That year, it most certainly did.

It was then that I came to recognize a phenomenon I call *Gabolatría:* the unstoppable need to adore García Márquez. This unofficial biography isn't one of its vicissitudes. Unlike hundreds of adulatory exercises published in the Hispanic world, where literary criticism doesn't thrive as a democratic activity and, thus, hagiography continues to be one of the cheap forms of reverence, this biography doesn't shy away from presenting an analytical view of García Márquez's life and career. After all, the task of the critic, as Mathew Arnold once put it, is to look at art as a manifestation of the complex forces that define us all the time.

Chapter 1

Aracataca

In an anthology entitled *Los diez mandamientos* (The Ten Commandments), published in Argentina in 1966 and edited anonymously, Gabriel García Márquez, then a thirty-nine-year-old novelist, journalist, and screenwriter from Colombia, appended to his contribution, a story composed six years prior that would become a classic, *"En este pueblo no hay ladrones"* (There Are No Thieves in This Town), a self-portrait that is unique in its autobiographical value. The self-portrait reads:

> My name, sir, is Gabriel García Márquez. I'm sorry: I don't like the name either, because it is a bunch of common places I haven't been able to identify for myself. I was born in Aracataca, Colombia, almost forty years ago and I'm not sorry about it yet. My zodiac sign is Pisces and my wife is Mercedes. Those are the two most important things that have happened to me in life, because thanks to her, at least until now, I've been able to survive by writing.
>
> I'm a timid writer. My true vocation is that of a magician, but I became so clumsy while trying to do a trick that I have had to find refuge for my solitude in literature. In any case, both activities lead to the

only thing I've been interested in since childhood: to continue to be loved by my friends.

In my case, to be a writer is an outstanding merit because I'm quite a brute when it comes to writing. I've had to apply myself to an atrocious discipline in order to finish half a page in eight hours of work; I fight head on with each word and almost always it is the word that ends up winning, but I'm so stubborn I've been able to publish four books in twenty years. The fifth one, which I'm writing now, is coming out even slower than the others, since I have very few free hours left from so many creditors and a case of neuralgia.

I never talk about literature, because I don't know what it is, and, besides, I'm convinced the world would be the same without it. Instead, I know it would be completely different if the police didn't exist. I think, therefore, that it would have been more useful to humankind if instead of being a writer I had become a terrorist.[1]

Written amid his self-imposed seclusion in Mexico City, in the study he described as *La Cueva de la Mafia* (the mafia cave), this impressionistic mini-essay displays García Márquez's usual sarcasm toward literature as a serious yet treacherous profession. It reveals his penchant for meticulous, carefully chosen words. But the most valuable component of these four mirror-like paragraphs is their autobiographical voice: García Márquez describes his name as a conundrum and his profession as a curse. He is a writer, he argues, not out of choice—he would have preferred to be a *prestidigitador*—but out of necessity. Magic is what he professes to like most: the art of creating illusions with a simple sleight of hand, the capacity to make the supernatural natural and vice versa. While García Márquez tells the reader that he struggles with words, he won't stay away from them for too long, for they are one of the only things he has: words and friends. Words are friends, of course, and through words he wants to achieve a single result: to be loved by those he loves.

Finally, in his mordant self-portrait García Márquez wonders if instead of having become a writer, it would have been more useful for him and for humankind had he been a terrorist. That is the writer's ultimate dream: *si en vez de escritor fuera terrorista,* to be a saboteur, to be remembered for reformulating the rules of the game. The word choice is ominous, but he isn't being literal. He isn't referring to the use of violence with the intention of coercing society. Instead, he embraces metaphor as a form of persuasion: in subtle, tangential, enchanting ways he is ready, through literature, to unsettle the establishment.

Gabriel García Márquez was born in the small town of Aracataca, on Colombia's Caribbean coast, on a hot and humid Sunday, March 6, 1927, at 9 A.M., as a rainstorm was descending on the coast. Rumors circulated for some time that the actual place of his birth had been Riohacha—the capital of the province La Guajira, where his mother had spent most of her pregnancy—but those proved untrue. For years his birth date was mistakenly given as March 6, 1928. The Library of Congress in Washington still quotes that date, as do scores of reference volumes.[2] The confusion stems from various factors. There were no official papers like a birth certificate issued and his was a large family. Furthermore, the author himself seems to have nurtured this misunderstanding.

His immediate younger sibling, Luis Enrique, once said that for years he "believed he had been born on September 8, 1928, after his mother's nine-month pregnancy. But it happened that in the year of 1955, Gabito wrote *The Story of a Shipwrecked*

Sailor in *El Espectador* and had complications with the government of [General Gustavo] Rojas Pinilla. So he had to leave the country, for which he needed a certain document, and I don't know why but Gabito ended up as having been born on March 7, 1928, that is, the same year I was born, something that leaves me in a difficult situation: either I am the only six-month old that weighed four kilos of whom there had been any notice, or I am almost his twin. He never rectified that date."[3] Eventually, the truth was uncovered as myriad biographers from the nineties onward, among them Dasso Saldívar and Gerald Martin, corroborated the information.[4] In March 2007, celebrations took place worldwide to commemorate his eightieth birthday and the fortieth anniversary of the publication, in June 1967, of his magnum opus, *Cien años de soledad (One Hundred Years of Solitude)*.

He arrived after an eight-month-long pregnancy, and weighed 9.3 pounds at birth. Three years later, on July 27, 1930, García Márquez was baptized by Father Francisco C. Angarita at the Iglesia de San José of Aracataca. The baptism had been delayed because García Márquez's parents, Gabriel Eligio García Martínez (Sincé, 1901–Cartagena, 1984) and Luisa Santiaga Márquez (Barrancas, 1905–Cartagena, 2002), were not based in Aracataca. Luisa had lived there but after the couple met, they were exiled from the town by her parents, Nicolás Ricardo Márquez Mejía (Riohacha, 1864–Santa Marta, 1937) and Tranquilina Iguarán Cotes (Riohacha, 1863–Sucre, 1947), who didn't look favorably upon their liaison. Another reason for the delay may have been the family's ambivalence toward institutionalized Catholicism, an ambivalence later embraced with enthusiasm by García Márquez and connected to his left-leaning political views. It is manifested in the presence of the hypocritical town priests that populate his fiction from the stories *"La siesta del martes"* (Tuesday Siesta) and *"Un hombre muy viejo con unas alas enormes"* (A Very Old Man with

Enormous Wings) to the novella *La mala hora* (In Evil Hour) and, of course, *One Hundred Years of Solitude*.

Known colloquially as Cataca, Aracataca, in the Magdalena Department, is an unremarkable town dotted with one-story houses. While most are made of masonry, a number sport the humble tin roofs characteristic of dwellings in this tropical Caribbean climate, where the temperature at mid-afternoon can rise above 110°F. The lush vegetation, with its stunning hues of emerald, grows chaotically everywhere. Humidity quickly integrates new buildings into the environment, staining them with pervasive mildew.

Founded in 1885 and established as a municipality in 1912, the town is located approximately fifty miles south of the capital of the Department, Santa Marta. Aracataca is on the banks of the non-navigable Aracataca River that flows from the Sierra Nevada de Santa Marta range into the Ciénega Grande. To the north, it borders the municipalities of Zona Bananera, Santa Marta, and Ciénega, to the east is the César Department, to the south lies the municipality of Fundación, and to the west is El Retén and Pueblo Viejo.

The Aracataca municipality has a population of approximately 50,000, living in about three dozen barrios mired in poverty. Between the two world wars, the drop in world prices for bananas and the establishment of plantations in other parts of the globe were just two developments that forced the main employer, the United Fruit Company, to downsize. Colombian plantations on the Caribbean coast were abandoned, settlers left, and unemployment skyrocketed, resulting in the financial collapse of the region.

To understand García Márquez's universe it is important to visualize Aracataca. The town, as in other Caribbean regions, has an agricultural economy that is based on banana, plantain, yucca, tomato, sugar cane, cotton, rice, oil palm, and livestock, including cattle, horses, mules, and pigs. The weather is marked by relentless humidity, the result of tropical rains that might be sudden or else prolong themselves for days on end. Gerald Martin describes it as the hottest and wettest place in the entire zone. He suggests that in 1900 Aracataca had a population of a few hundred. By 1913 it had risen to 3,000 and by the late 1920s it had perhaps 10,000.[5]

Commerce is largely unstructured, and the principal means for transporting goods is by land. The town is bisected by Highway 45, which leads to the Colombian Andean region. It is crowded with buses, taxis, and minivans. The railway, which played a predominant role during the banana bonanza and is an important motif in *One Hundred Years of Solitude*, is no longer used as a means of public transportation but rather to transport coal from La Loma to the port of Santa Marta.

The accident of birth defines one's *weltanschauung*. The location of Aracataca in the northwestern region of South America as well as the lower edge of the Caribbean basin always made García Márquez feel like he was part of two worlds. He perceived himself as a citizen of a manglar at once belonging to a continent and a constellation of islands. "The Caribbean taught me to look at reality in a different way," he pronounced, "to accept the supernatural as part of our everyday life." He stated, "...the Caribbean is a distinctive world whose first work of magical literature was *The Diary of Christopher Columbus*, a book which tells of fabulous plants and mythological societies. The history of the Caribbean is full of magic—a magic brought by black slaves from Africa and by Swedish, Dutch and English pirates who thought nothing of setting up an Opera House in New Orleans or filling women's teeth with diamonds. Nowhere in the world do you find the racial mixture and the contrasts that you find in the Caribbean."

García Márquez added: "I know all its islands: their honey-colored mulattas with green eyes and golden handkerchiefs round their heads; their half-caste Indo-Chinese who do laundry and sell amulets; their green-skinned Asians who leave their ivory stalls to shit in the middle of the street; on one hand their scorched, dusty towns with houses which collapse in cyclones and on the other skyscrapers of smoked glass and an ocean of seven colours. Well, if I start talking about the Caribbean there's no stopping me. Not only is it the world which taught me to write, it's the only place where I really feel at home."[6] This viewpoint serves as a map to understand his oeuvre. Early in his career García Márquez enjoyed being grouped with Latin American writers as much as he did with his Caribbean counterparts. In the article *"Caribe mágico"* (Magical Caribbean), García Márquez wrote of a common language beyond words that is spoken by everyone in the Caribbean, about a unifying aesthetic worldview. He wrote about immigrants from abroad who descended on the region, adapting to its customs. This group included Henri Charrière, author of *Papillon,* who prospered in Caracas as a restaurant promoter as well as in other less worthy enterprises.[7]

García Márquez is the eldest of the eleven children of Gabriel Eligio García Martínez and Luisa Santiaga Márquez; he has one half-sibling born of one of his father's extramarital escapades. Gabriel Eligio García Martínez was originally from a town in the Bolívar Department. In the early twenties he moved to Cartagena, where he enrolled at the university. But his stay in the classroom didn't last long, because he needed to support himself. At the time, the nation's Atlantic region was experiencing an enormous boom in banana plantations. The United Fruit Company, a major corporation that traded in tropical fruit, especially pineapple and banana, was incorporated in 1899 as a result of the merger between Minor C. Keith's banana-trading concerns and Andrew W. Preston's Boston Fruit Company. It penetrated the markets of Latin American countries, such as Colombia, Ecuador, and the West Indies, where it became a monopoly. Currently known as Chiquita Brands International, it continues to export products to Europe and the United States.

Banana plantations in the Third World were a loci of contradictions. They became great magnets for agricultural laborers from different parts of the world—Spain, Italy, Syria, Lebanon, and Palestine. García Márquez writes about this immigration in his early work, the novella *La hojarasca*, translated into English as *Leaf Storm*. It was the banana boom that brought to Aracataca electricity, its first orchestra, the avenue named Camellón 20 de Julio, a church, as well as a weekly lottery game. But the United Fruit Company's exploitation of both natural and human resources resulted in accusations of neocolonialism. The term "banana republics," coined by the short-story writer O. Henry, is intimately associated with the presence of the United Fruit Company in Latin America. The local, regional, and national governments in countries such as Colombia sided with their corporate patrons against the native population, resulting in clashes that left numerous victims.

The sense of injustice from decades of exploitation by the United Fruit Company is still palpable in the area. Many years later, people in restaurants, on the street, and in elementary schools continue to talk about the excesses of the banana boom and the system of abuse established by the corporation, which has left deep scars. In *One Hundred Years of Solitude* García Márquez describes, in patient detail, the agricultural, social, political, and economic transformation that took place and how mores were ruled by greed and the thirst for power. The United Fruit Company occupies an infamous and prominent place in Latin American literature. From the thirties onward, a slew of writers depicted the changes it brought in a sharply critical tone. Pablo Neruda, in a famous poem included in *Canto*

General (1938–1949), in the section "The Sand Betrayed," refers directly to the United Fruit Company.

Other Latin American writers like Miguel Ángel Asturias of Guatemala, Carlos Luis Fallas of Costa Rica, Ramón Amaya Amador of Honduras, and Álvaro Cepeda Samudio of Colombia condemned the company in their work. In 1950 the prolific American novelist Gore Vidal wrote *Dark Green, Bright Red*, set in a fictional Central American country where the corporation supports a military coup. The infamous place the United Fruit Company has in literature is but a thermometer of the region's popular hatred toward it.

Spanish explorers led by Rodrigo de Bastidas first set foot in the Caribbean littoral of Colombia in 1499. (The country's name comes from Christopher Columbus.) In the beginning of the sixteenth century, Vasco Nuñez de Balboa started colonizing the territories, which were populated by indigenous tribes, including the Muisca, Chibcha, Carib, Quimbaya, and Tairona. The process of colonization led to the creation of the Viceroyalty of New Granada, comprising modern-day Colombia, Venezuela, Ecuador, and Panama. The fever for independence that swept across Latin America in the nineteenth century reached New Granada in 1819. Internecine wars and secessions fractured the newly independent nation, as Venezuela and Ecuador broke away. What is now modern Colombia and Panama emerged as the Republic of New Granada. The new nation experimented with federalism as the Granadine Confederation of 1858 before the Republic of Colombia was finally founded in 1886.

By the time the United Fruit Company arrived in the region, at the close of the nineteenth century, bipartisan divisions had resulted in civil clashes, the most famous of which was the Guerra de los Mil Días, the Thousand-Day War (1899–1902). One of the most popular military figures of the war was General Rafael Uribe Uribe, on whom García Márquez is said to have based Colonel Aureliano Buendía, one of the central forces moving the plot of *One Hundred Years of Solitude*. His identical last names may have inspired García Márquez's playfulness with names in a book that has more than a dozen Aurelianos.

Born in Valparaíso, in the Antioquia Department, in 1859, General Uribe Uribe died in Bogotá in 1914, after being hacked to death by envoys sent by his foes. The general was a lawyer, journalist, and one of the most radical members of the Liberal Party. He played a major role in the civil war of 1895, in which he was defeated by General Rafael Reyes in the Battle of La Tribuna. Although he made his escape forging the Magdalena River, he was captured in Mampox and imprisoned in Cartagena's Cárcel de San Diego. He was eventually pardoned and was elected to the House of Representatives. Uribe Uribe was an acerbic critic of the political process known as Regeneration, which advocated a strong central government and the restriction of civil liberties, advocated by two presidents: Rafael Núñez (1880–1888) and Miguel Antonio Caro (1892–1898).

General Uribe Uribe was a federalist. He founded the newspaper *El Autonomista*. In 1898 he said: "Colombia is divided, so to speak, into two nations: Bogotanos and provincials, the latter being the victims of the former...For it is here [in Bogotá] that the politicians have always hatched the wars we provincials have had to fight for them to further their fortunes, while they stay here enjoying themselves, chatting delightfully among enemies."[8] In *One Hundred Years of Solitude*, Colonel Aureliano Buendía—a liberal military figure impatient with himself, involved in seditions, civil wars, and truces, active in politics, and ultimately essential in a peace agreement known in García Márquez's novels as the Treaty of Neerlandia—is closely patterned after General Uribe Uribe, under whose command García Márquez's maternal grandfather, Nicolás Márquez Iguarán, fought against the conservative forces.

As a child, García Márquez heard about General Uribe Uribe's adventurous life from his grandparents and even studied his military tactics in school. The general was a leader of the October 20, 1899 uprising that triggered the Thousand-Day War. He commanded the Liberal troops during the Santander military campaign between October 1899 and August 1900, and defeated the Conservatives at the Battle of Bucaramanga. He then went to the city of Cúcuta, where he joined forces with Liberal Benjamín Herrera. En route to Ocaña, his troops were ambushed and the confrontation resulted in the Battle of Peralonso. The battle ended the following day with the general's triumph over the Conservatives. General Uribe Uribe then became an advocate of peace, although he continued his military enterprise. On June 12, 1902, the Colombian government ended the armed conflict by pardoning the Liberal rebels who began to demobilize. The general surrendered in the Hacienda Neerlandia in October of that year.

General Uribe Uribe was not the only source of inspiration for García Márquez. The story of his parents served as the blueprint for his novel *Love in the Time of Cholera*. As a young man, Gabriel Eligio García Martínez benefited from the economic boom brought by the United Fruit Company and found a job as a telegraphist in Aracataca. It was there that in 1924 he met Luisa Santiaga Márquez Iguarán, the belle of the town. She belonged to a family who had lived in Aracataca since 1910. Her parents viewed the arrival of outsiders to the region with suspicious eyes even though they themselves had settled in Aracataca after a twenty-two-month exodus from Barrancas, in La Guajira, through Riohacha, Santa Marta, and Ciénega. They acquired a good property near the central plaza.

Luisa Santiaga returned Gabriel Eligio's love, but her parents, Colonel Márquez Iguarán and his wife, Tranquilina Iguarán Cotes, were adamantly against the relationship. The young man was part of *la hojarasca*, the immigration that came as a leaf storm, and he was an illegitimate child, which to them meant that he was a low-life. They forbade the couple from seeing each other. But Gabriel Eligio and Luisa Santiaga persevered in their courtship. In response, her parents sent her away to stay with various friends and acquaintances in the Bolívar Department.

They soon discovered that Gabriel Eligio kept in touch with her via telegraph, sending messages to the various localities where she lived. Furious, her parents arranged to have him transferred to Riohacha. The young couple's love only increased. Many not only supported them but urged her parents to reconsider and allow them to be together. Her parents finally agreed to a wedding, on the condition that they stay in Riohacha and not return to Aracataca. Gabriel Eligio and Luisa Santiaga were married in the Santa Marta cathedral on June 11, 1926. According to various sources, it was the news of Luisa Santiaga's pregnancy that softened her parents. They invited the couple to return to Aracataca, so that Luisa Santiaga could give birth there.[9] Until the end of his days, Gabriel Eligio never learned to like the place—he called it *"un moridero de pobres,"* the place where poor people die—but he agreed. García Márquez was born in the big house that belonged to his grandparents.

Aracataca, Riohacha, La Ciénega, and other places in the area were infused with folklore and a history of colonialism. As García Márquez grew up, he absorbed all their details into his personal memory. He took in the history he learned from the textbooks he used at school, the stories he heard from his grandmother and others, and daily conversations. For instance, he discovered that the year after he was born, banana workers went on strike in La Ciénega, a town in the region where Aracataca is, north of Magdalena, twenty miles from Santa Marta in the Magdalena Department, and the second largest population center in the Department. Workers in the area's plantations went on strike in December 1928. They demanded written contracts, eight-hour days, six-day weeks, and the elimination of food coupons. The strike became the beginning of a labor movement that turned into the largest of its kind in Colombia. It involved members of the Communist and Socialist parties, as well as radical members of the Liberal Party. An army regiment from Bogotá was deployed by the government in support of the United Fruit Company, whose capital was deemed essential to the economy, to crush the strike. The strategy was to portray the strikers as subversive, law-breaking thugs.

On a Sunday, right after Mass, soldiers with machine guns were positioned on the roofs of the low buildings at the corners of the main square and streets were blocked off. A crowd of some 3,000 workers and their families had gathered to hear the governor speak. After giving the crowd a five-minute warning along with the order to evacuate the plaza, the army opened fire on them. General Cortés Vargas, who issued the order to shoot, later said that he had given the order because he had information that U.S. warships were poised to land troops on Colombian coasts to defend American personnel and the interests of the United Fruit Company.

The exact number of dead has never been established. General Vargas claimed there were only forty-seven, although the reports put the numbers higher. The episode was an integral component of García Márquez's childhood. "I knew the event as if I had lived it," he wrote in his memoir *Living to Tell the Tale*, "having heard it recounted and repeated a thousand times by my grandmother from the time I had a memory: the soldier reading the decree by which the striking laborers were declared a gang of lawbreakers; the three thousand men, women, and children motionless under the savage sun after the officer gave them five minutes to evacuate the square; the order of fire, the clattering machine guns spitting in white-hot bursts, the crowd trapped by panic as it was cut down, little by little, by the methodical scissors of the shrapnel."[10]

One Hundred Years of Solitude includes a scene memorializing the event: The strikers test the government forces. Soldiers begin shooting without warning, and then the bodies are taken away in a train. The following day, nobody is able to remember anything. García Márquez said that the massacre in the square, as he depicted it, was "completely true, but while I wrote it on the basis of testimony and documents, it was never known exactly how many people were killed. I used the figure three thousand, which is probably an exaggeration. But one of my childhood memories was watching a very, very long train leave the plantation supposedly full of bananas. There could have been three thousand dead on it, eventually to be dropped in the sea. What is really surprising is that now they speak very naturally in Congress and the newspapers about the 'three thousand dead.' In *The Autumn of the Patriarch*, the dictator says that it doesn't matter if it's not true now, because sometime in the future it will be true. Sooner or later people believe writers rather than the government."[11]

The strike is the topic of another Colombian novel by García Márquez's close childhood friend, Álvaro Cepeda Samudio: *La casa grande* (The Big House), originally published in 1954 (thirteen years before *One Hundred Years of Solitude*). It is unclear if Cepeda Samudio, who was born in 1926, witnessed the massacre. García Márquez includes a scene in the novel in which a child on his father's shoulders watches the shooting. Some literary historians see this as an homage to Cepeda Samudio. In a foreword in the English translation of *La casa grande*, García Márquez writes: "This manner of writing history, arbitrary as it might seem to the historian, is a splendid lesson in poetic transformation. Without distorting reality or playing loose with the serious political and human aspects of the social drama, Cepeda Samudio has subjected it to a kind of purifying alchemy and has given us only its mythical essence, which will remain forever, far longer than any man's morality, justice, and ephemeral memory. The super dialogues, the straight-forward and virile richness of the language, the genuine compassion aroused by the character's fate, the fragmentary and some-what loose structure which so closely resembles the pattern of memories—everything in this book is a magnificent example of how a writer can honestly filter out the immense quantity of rhetorical and demagogic garbage that stands in the way of indignation and nostalgia."[12]

The siblings who followed García Márquez were born in different places, depending on where their parents were stationed. They include Luis Enrique (Aracataca, September 8, 1928), Margarita, aka Margot (Barranquilla, November 9, 1929), Aída Rosa (Barranquilla, December 17, 1933), Ligia (Aracataca, August 8, 1934), Gustavo (Aracataca, September 27, 1935), Rita del Carmen (Barranquilla, July 10, 1938), Jaime (Sucre, May 22, 1940), Hernando (Sucre, March 26, 1943), Alfredo Ricardo (Cartagena, February 25, 1946), and Eligio Gabriel (Bogotá, November 14, 1947). The family is close knit and shies away from publicity, although through the years they have agreed to speak with researchers. Silvia Galvis spent several years interviewing the siblings for a volume entitled *Los García Márquez,* which is composed of ten stand-alone personal essays based on extended conversations in which each sibling gives his or her version of what it was like to grow up together. His siblings include an engineer, a journalist, a businessman, a consul, a fireman, and a nun, the latter an ironic career choice given the anti-clericalism that defines García Márquez's *weltanschauung.*

Jaime, the second child, was an engineer who, at García Márquez's request, became director of the Fundación Nuevo Periodismo in Cartagena. The story of Eligio, the youngest, born in Sucre in 1947, is moving. His full name was Eligio

Gabriel, and he grew up in his famous brother's shadow. He once remarked, "there are different versions surrounding my name. The one I've heard most frequently is that when I was born my father held me in the air and said: 'He is exactly like me; this one is a García and needs to have my name.' Until that moment none of his children was called exactly like him: Gabriel Eligio. But when I was about to be baptized, my mother wondered how they could call me Gabriel if there was already a Gabito. Then my father, who disliked complications, responded: 'Alright, then let's call him Eligio Gabriel.' It's that simple and I believe it is true because my father was that way, never allowing to get too entangled in things." He added, "Gabito has his own version, obviously, and it is that when I was born he had already left the house, that's why my mother said: 'We called him Gabriel and he left, but we need to have a Gabriel at home.' "[13]

In 1966, Eligio enrolled at the Universidad Nacional to study theoretical physics, but he decided that he preferred to write. He struggled; each time he published something, everyone asked him if he was related to the famous author of *One Hundred Years of Solitude*. He opted to use a shortened version of his name, Eligio García, as his pen name. Toward the end of his life he made peace with this and reverted to using his full name: Eligio García Márquez. He achieved peace in other ways. Beginning in 1974 he lived in Paris and London, where he worked as a correspondent for several Colombian periodicals, such as *El Espectador*. He was the editorial advisor of the magazine *Cromos*, and served as the general editor of his brother's magazine, *Cambio*. In 1978, Eligio published the novel *Para matar el tiempo* (To Kill Time), and in 1982, a collection of interviews with Latin American writers and a companion volume to the movie adaptation of *Chronicle of a Death Foretold*, directed by Francesco Rosi. Shortly before his death on June 29, 2001, he released a book he had been working on for years, *Tras las claves de Melquíades,* an impressionistic study of how *One Hundred Years of Solitude* came to be.

García Márquez spent the first eight years of his life in his maternal grandparents' house in Aracataca. His relationships with them were decisive. He called his grandfather Papalelo. "My grandfather was stocky, with a florid complexion, and the most voracious eater I can remember. He was the most outrageous fornicator, as I learned much later on."[14] It was his grandfather, who died in 1937, when the author was around ten years old, who took young García Márquez to the town of Ciénega to visit the Goleta that could go to Barranquilla.

In contrast, he had an intimate connection with his grand-mother, from whom he learned the art of storytelling. The manner in which she related an outrageous anecdote in all seriousness, without a hint of surprise, was something he was accustomed to as a child but didn't understand until much later—when he decided that telling stories was what he enjoyed most in life and what he wanted to do for a living. "What was most important," García Márquez reminisced about Tranquilina Iguarán Cotes, "was the expression she had on her face. She did not change her expression at all when telling her stories, and everyone was surprised. In previous attempts to write *One Hundred Years of Solitude,* I tried to tell the story without believing in it. I discovered that what I had to do was believe in them myself and write them with the same expression with which my grandmother told them: with a brick face."[15] His grandmother, who was the inspiration for Úrsula Iguarán, arguably the most important female character in his magnum opus and the novel's center of gravity, was prone to exaggeration, a device he later used with great skill as a narrator: "For example, if you say that there are three elephants flying in the sky, people are not going to believe you. But if you say that there are four hun-dred and twenty-five elephants flying in the sky, people will probably believe you."[16]

"The strange thing," García Márquez later told his friend Plinio Apuleyo Mendoza, "was that I wanted to be like my grandfather—realistic, brave, safe—but I could not resist the constant temptation to peep into my grandmother's territory."[17] García Márquez's relationship with women was crucial in his upbringing. In *Living to Tell the Tale*, he writes: "I believe that the essence of my nature and way of thinking I owe in reality to the women in the family and to the many in our service who ministered to my childhood. They had strong characters and tender hearts, and they treated me with the naturalness of the Earthly Paradise."[18] A wide constellation of females, from relatives to servants, surrounded him. There were his five aunts: Tía Elvira Carrillo, his grandfather's illegitimate child and his mother's half-sister; Tía Francisca Cimodosea Mejía, known as La Cancerbera; Tía Mama, a beloved cousin who had grown up with his grandfather and who raised García Márquez in Aracataca; Tía Wenefrida Márquez, his grandfather's older sister; and Tía Petra Cotes, who died at the age of one hundred in the Aracataca home while sitting on a rocking chair in a hallway filled with begonias.

There were other women, too, such as Tía Margarita Márquez Iguarán, his grandmother's sister, who died of typhus at the age of twenty-one and is arguably the model for Remedios the Beautiful, although the actual name may come from yet another aunt, Remedios Núñez Márquez, his grandfather's eighth natural child. Such abundance of female models in his childhood marked him forever. In *One Hundred Years of Solitude* it was the Buendía women who grounded the family and safeguarded the collective memory. They were at the helm, raising the next generation, while the men explored the world, fought wars, and built their reputations. Women defined the home: what was morally acceptable and what wasn't, what everyone's diet was, who was a welcome visitor, and so on.

These home-bound women stood in sharp contrast to another type of woman: the intrusive mistress who often stole a family man away through concupiscence. Just as in *One Hundred Years of Solitude,* in García Márquez's family husbands were constantly bringing home their out-of-wedlock offspring. Aside from his three children with Tranquilina Iguarán Cotes, Nicolás Ricardo had a total of nine illegitimate children. And García Márquez's own father, Gabriel Eligio, had four: Abelardo García Ujueta, Carmen Rosa García Hermosillo, Antonio García Navarro, and Germaine (Emy) García Mendoza.[19]

And there were the maids, with some of whom García Márquez was physically intimate. One was Trinidad, the daughter of one of the workers in the family home. In his autobiography, García Márquez describes how she took away his innocence, as he put it. Trinidad was only thirteen. Suddenly music started to play from a nearby house. She held him so tightly that "she took my breath away." He explains, "my intimacy with the maids could be the origin of a thread of secret communications that I believe I have with women and that throughout my life has allowed me to feel more comfortable and sure with them than with men."[20]

García Márquez's relationship with his own mother, however, was more distant.[21] Her seriousness defined her in his eyes. He once said, "perhaps it comes from having gone to live with her and my father when I was already old enough to think for myself—after my grandfather died." As a result of his parent's itinerant life, which meant moving the family from one place to another, he didn't live with his parents "under the same roof for very long because a few years later when I was twelve, I went off to school, first to Barranquilla and then to Zipaquirá. Since then we've really only seen each other for brief visits, first during school holidays and after that whenever I go to Cartagena—which is never more than once a year and never for more than a couple of weeks at a time. This has inevitably made our relationship distant."[22]

Luisa Santiaga, while a somewhat peripheral female figure in García Márquez's family constellation, was the family anchor. In March 1952, at the age of twenty-five—after having lived in the big cities of Barranquilla, Cartagena, and Bogotá— García Márquez returned to Aracataca with his mother to sell his childhood home for $7,000 to a couple of old peasants, or *campesinos*, who had recently won the lottery. That sentimental journey served as the opening episode in *Living to Tell the Tale* and was an invaluable narrative viewpoint from which to relate his foundational past. Luisa Santiaga was nothing if not practical. The character based on her in *Love in the Time of Cholera* is romantic but down to earth. And García Márquez has suggested that Úrsula Iguarán has some of his mother's features.[23]

In spite of its seriousness, this relationship was more grounded than the one García Márquez had with his father. Gabriel Eligio didn't come from Riohacha to Aracataca to visit García Márquez until several months after he was born, in large part because his in-laws had made it so difficult for him to be with Luisa Santiaga. The families made peace and he eventually came back, but after a period working as a telegraphist, he left town again to become a homeopathic doctor. This and his future departures, all apparently related to work, turned Gabriel Eligio into a ghostlike figure in García Márquez's childhood.

In an article entitled *"Vuelta a la semilla,"* published on December 21, 1983, García Márquez wrote, "Contrary to what many writers good and bad have done across history, I have never idealized the town where I was born and where I spent the first eight years of my life. My memories of that time—as I have repeated so often—are the most clear and real I have, to the point that I'm able to evoke as if it was yesterday not only the appearance of each of the houses that are still preserved, but even to spot a crack that didn't exist during my childhood." García Márquez argued that trees always live longer than people and he believed that the trees in Aracataca were able to remember us, perhaps even better than we remember them. Yet, in spite of the similarities between Aracataca and Macondo, García Márquez remarked that every time he returned to his birth town he had the impression that it resembled less and less the fictitious one, with the exception of a few external elements, such as the unrelenting heat at two in the afternoon, its white and burning powder, and the almond trees that line its streets. On June 25, 2006, due to the international attention García Márquez had brought, there was a referendum to rename the town "Aracataca-Macondo," although it failed due to a low turnout.

It's been almost a century since García Márquez was born, and Aracataca has hardly changed. He is its only famous child and claim to glory. One dramatic transformation in recent years, not only in Aracataca but in the entire region, is the rise of a tourist trade that attracts hordes of people who love his books. García Márquez isn't directly involved in these efforts. Local agencies, government-run as well as private, in Aracataca, Riohacha, Barranquilla, and, primarily, Cartagena, decided to capitalize on the attention the writer had brought to the region. In order to understand the phenomenon (literature as a magnet for tourism), I took a tour. I boarded a bus in Barranquilla that took me to Aracataca. The poverty I saw was moving. I spoke with local merchants, students, politicians, waitresses, journalists, policemen, and librarians, among others. They talked about the lack of financial support from the federal government, which remembers the town only when there is a García Márquez anniversary—an event that always brings an influx of tourists.

Aracataca, as I discovered, now parades tourists to some of the sites where García Márquez spent his childhood. Some of them are now even makeshift museums. There is, for instance, the *Casa del telegrafista*, behind the town church, where his father worked as a telegraphist. The visitor is able to see some of the early twentieth-century tools he used. The place is decorated with yellowed news clippings about the future Nobel laureate, his parents' romantic liaison, and the publication of major works such as *One Hundred Years of Solitude* and *Love in the Time of Cholera* among some sculptures and drawings by local talent. Given the site's extraordinarily limited resources, most of the items on display are exposed to the elements—humidity being foremost among them—and are in a slow state of decay.

There is Doctor Antonio Barbosa's pharmacy, where Gabriel Eligio would leave messages for his beloved Luisa Santiaga. Pharmacists play a curious role in García Márquez's oeuvre. In the primal landscape of the Caribbean, à la Gustave Flaubert, they are the promoters of scientific knowledge in society. And there is the Iglesia de San José, where García Márquez was baptized, the Calle de los Camellones, where he played on his way to and from school, and the train station, where a yellow train arrived at 11 A.M. every day, a scene that is depicted in *One Hundred Years of Solitude*. García Márquez attended preschool and the first grade at a local Montessori school. The school was established by María Elena Fergusson, a teacher from Riohacha who taught him how to read and who first ignited his incipient interest in poetry. Years later, he confessed that as a child one of his favorite characters was Sleeping Beauty.

According to García Márquez, the most famous house in Aracataca belonged to the parochial priest Francisco C. Angarita, who baptized him and his entire generation. Father Angarita was famous for his irascible mood and his moralizing sermons. As a child, García Márquez didn't know that Father

Angarita had taken a very concrete and consequential position in support of the strike of the banana workers in 1928, and the priest was also an informant for Jorge Eliécer Gaitán, the lawyer and later left-wing political figure martyred during *El Bogotazo*, who represented the case of the workers after the massacre.[24] But for purposes of this biography, unquestionably the most important site in Aracataca is García Márquez's family home.

"My most constant and vivid memory is not so much of the people but of the actual house in Aracataca where I lived with my grandparents," he once said. "Every single day of my life I wake up with the feeling, real or imaginary, that I've dreamt I'm in that huge old house. Not that I've gone back there, but that I *am* there, at no particular age, for no particular reason—as if I'd never left it."[25]

The family home, now known as the Casa Museo Gabriel García Márquez, has been reconstructed to satisfy tourists' needs. The *campesino* couple who bought the house from García Márquez sold it to another family, who in turn sold it to the municipality, which planned to turn it into a museum. While changing hands, a large portion of the house was demolished to make room for a more modern structure. When the municipality finally bought it, a group of researchers studied the architecture of the town in the early decades of the twentieth century and analyzed the foundation of the house. Thanks to this endeavor, García Márquez's family home is now restored to its original condition.

A plan of *la casa*, recreated by architects Gustavo Castellón, Gilver Caraballo, and Jaime Santos, is in the town's Casa Museo García Márquez. Looking at it, the structure of the Buendía home in *One Hundred Years of Solitude* becomes more concrete. It is located on Carrera 5, also known as Avenida del Monseñor Espejo, a street graced and perfumed by acacia and almond trees. Built on a rectangular piece of land, the house consists of three independent structures. To the left is García Márquez's grandfather's office. As one enters the building, there's a patio that lies adjacent to a visitors' room. Behind the grandfather's office is a garden with a fragrant jasmine tree. Beyond the garden is the grandparents' bedroom. There is also a pantry, the kitchen, and another patio. Then come a few surprises: a room containing statues of saints, a room for suitcases, a silversmithing workshop, a hallway flanked by two chestnut trees and filled with begonias, and a carpentry shop. I found the latrine at the back of the property.

One of the most stunning scenes in *One Hundred Years of Solitude* takes place in chapter seven, when José Arcadio Buendía's son, the eldest child and the sibling of Colonel José Arcadio Buendía and Amaranta, dies mysteriously. This remains one of the only—*the* only?—unsolved mysteries in *One Hundred Years of Solitude*. Expelled from the family home, José Arcadio Buendía moves into another house with Rebeca.[26] One September afternoon, he comes home, greets Rebeca, who is taking a bath, goes to his room, and soon after a gunshot is heard. But when his mother, Úrsula, enters the room, she doesn't find a weapon, nor does she find a wound on her son's body. Immediately after the gunshot, a trickle of blood spills out from the victim onto the street. García Márquez's description is superb:

A trickle of blood came out under the door, crossed the living room, went out into the street, continued on in a straight line across the uneven terraces, went down steps and climbed over curbs, passed along the Street of the Turks, turned a corner to the right and another to the left, made a straight angle at the Buendía house, went in under the closed door, crossed the parlor, hugging the walls so as not to stain the rugs, went on to the other living room, made a wide curve to avoid the dining room table, went along the porch with the begonias, and passed without being seen under Amaranta's chair as she gave an arithmetic lesson to Aureliano José, and went through a pantry and came out in the kitchen, where Úrsula was getting ready to crack thirty-six eggs to make bread.[27]

In a 143-word segment (in the Spanish original the total is 149) that pays homage to the luminous imagery of French novelist Boris Vian, the victim's blood goes from one end of town to the Buendía family home in search of its origins. Readers of the novel and visitors to the Casa Museo in Aracataca will note the accuracy with which García Márquez describes not only the town streets but each and every one of the rooms in the house. But what's truly tantalizing is the metaphor built by the trickle of blood: unquestionably, in *One Hundred Years of Solitude* the house represents the foundation. And for the writer, the actual place where he spent his childhood is *el origen*.

It has been said that had García Márquez never left Aracataca in 1936, when his parents took him to live with them in Sucre, he would never have become a writer.[28] By then his parents had had other children. His departure from the family home—and the enclosed environment in which he had been nurtured by his grandparents and the many women there—felt like a break. The house had allowed him to remain in his fantasy world within an adult habitat. His relationship with each of the people in the family home, and with the town as a whole, was seared in his mind forever. Leaving Aracataca was equivalent to being expelled from paradise.

Chapter 2

Apprenticeship

On November 9, 1929, García Márquez first visited Barranquilla—a major industrial port city on Colombia's Caribbean coast with a population of approximately 250,000, where his parents were living at the time—to see his newborn sister Margot, the third child. He was only two years and eight months old, but he remembered the changing colors of the traffic lights. On December 17, 1930, his grandmother took him on his second trip to Barranquilla, where he met his second sister, Aida Rosa. Barranquilla was commemorating the centennial of Simón Bolívar's death, and García Márquez recalled seeing a group of airplanes doing pirouettes in the sky, particularly a little black plane *"como un gallinazo enorme,"* like an enormous vulture, drawing circles in the air.

In 1934 his parents returned from Barranquilla to Aracataca to live with his maternal grandparents. Along came two more siblings, Margarita and Ligia. García Márquez's parents were concerned about the parochial nature of the town's school. He had gone to a Montessori school, where his teachers were nothing if not devoted and where he fell in love with reading. But Gabriel Eligio and Luisa Santiaga wanted their offspring to have access to a better educational system, so they established themselves in Sucre. Eventually the family moved to Barranquilla's Barrio Abajo neighborhood, where they lived from 1937 to 1939.

In school the boy fell in love with drawing. García Márquez would make doodles and show them to adults. One of his favorite books at the time was *The 1001 Nights.* When drilled by Father Angarita, who wanted to make sure the young didn't waste their time on dull readings, García Márquez told him of his passion for this book. He had an uncensored adult edition that didn't suppress "scabrous episodes." "It surprised me to learn," he later said, "that it was an important book, for I had always thought that serious adults could not believe that genies came out of bottles or doors opened at the incantation of magic words."[1]

The importance of this Persian classic in his oeuvre cannot be overestimated. There are many connections between this anthology of folktales and stories and *One Hundred Years of Solitude.* The narrator of *The 1001 Nights,* Scheherazade—which in Persian means "townswoman"—must survive by telling a story to her husband, the sultan Shahryar, each night. The sultan has a penchant for killing spouses who don't entertain him properly in the evening. There are similarities between Scheherazade and Melquíades, the Bedouin in García Márquez's magnum opus, a larger-than-life, ghost-like character who dies only to come back again and who drafts the saga of the Buendía family in scrolls. His narrative foretells events and frames the genealogical epic within, roughly, a hundred years. Melquíades and the Wandering Jew are mythical figures who appear in the novel. García Márquez shaped his novel as a compendium of folktales. Different subplots acquire a life of their own as the overarching story unfolds, but they are all connected by the characters' relationships with the Buendía family.

Another book that greatly influenced García Márquez at the time was the Bible. This was never fully acknowledged, given his anti-clerical views. But in a deeply Catholic country such as Colombia—notwithstanding its exposure to African culture brought to the Caribbean coast by the slave trade in the sixteenth century—biblical narratives are ubiquitous not only in Sunday sermons but in popular culture and other forums. There were constant biblical references in music, newspapers, and other media. Local politicians invoked characters from the Bible to make a critical point. This influence is important because *One Hundred Years of Solitude* is shaped like a Bible story, complete with natural disasters, famine, and wars. Incest is at the heart of the Buendía curse. That curse is behind the concept of the Chosen People: like the people of Israel after Abraham is called by God to leave his home in *Genesis* 12:1–2 in search for a new land where he will become the patriarch of a great nation, one susceptible to scorn, the Buendía family is destined for glory as well as infamy.

During that period García Márquez discovered other children's stories that were typical of the reading of bookish boys and young adults: the folktales recounted by the Brothers Grimm, *The Three Musketeers* and *The Count of Monte Cristo* by Alexander Dumas, *Around the World in Eighty Days* and *Voyage to the Center of the Earth* by Jules Verne, *The Hunchback of Notre Dame* by Victor Hugo, and *The Black Corsair, The Mystery of the Black Jungle, Sanmdoka the Great, The Tigers of Mompracem,* and *The Pirates of Malaysia* by Emilio Salgari. Álvaro Mutis, García Márquez's friend, whom he met in Barranquilla in 1949, often talked about finding the inspiration for his ubiquitous character, Maqroll el Gaviero (Maqroll the Lookout) in the adventure novels of Verne and Salgari, which he read as a young adult. Salgari also inspired other Latin American writers, from Jorge Luis Borges to Carlos Fuentes. His anti-imperialist views likely resonated among Spanish-language authors who were wary of American influence in the Southern hemisphere. Salgari, unlike Verne, appears to have gone unnoticed in the United States.[2]

Then, of course, there was *Don Quixote of La Mancha*, a book to which García Márquez's own masterpiece has often been compared, not because they are similar in plot or cast or characters but because each has come to be seen as a testament of the time in the Spanish-speaking world. The juxtaposition of reality and fiction is at the core of Cervantes's two-part novel, originally published in 1605 and 1615, approximately three and a half centuries before *One Hundred Years of Solitude*. García Márquez's reading of it, in his own words, "always deserved a different chapter." He had an instinctive dislike for the novel and he wasn't shy about saying so. "The long learned speeches of the knight errant bored me, I did not find the stupidities of the squire all that amusing, and I even began to think it was not the same book that people talked so much about."

But his secondary school teacher, Maestro Juan Ventura Cassalíns, had recommended it highly, and the respect García Márquez had for the teacher meant that he needed to give *Don Quixote* a second look. He did so, but felt as if he were swallowing it "like spoonsful of purgative." García Márquez added: "I made other attempts in secondary school, where I was obliged to study it as a requirement, and I had an irremediable aversion to it until a friend advised me to put it on the back of the toilet and try to read it while I took care of my daily needs. Only in this way did I discover it, like a conflagration, and relish it forward and back until I could recite entire episodes by heart."[3]

In 1939, the family moved to Sucre. A year later, García Márquez started middle school at the Colegio San José. It was at the heart of the city, adjacent to the church. He had lived away from his parents for the first eight years of his life and later while he was in high school, which meant that he was largely absent from the family household. This is how his siblings remembered him during that period. They received word of his interests, of who his friends were, but always from a distance. This remoteness would characterize his relationship with his family. They were constantly amazed by his achievements. In some instances this translated to devotion, while in others it generated envy. After he had achieved glory, he became a source of financial support for his family, at times buying someone an apartment or paying another's medical bills.

As a child, García Márquez was curious. His transcripts from elementary and secondary school show an attentive student devoted to his courses. He was shy, taciturn even. He was known to have no interest in athletic activities. While at the Colegio San José, he met Juan B. Fernández Renowitsky, who would later become a prominent journalist and editor of *El Heraldo*. In 1941, García Márquez went home to Sucre because of health problems. Upon his return to the Colegio San José, he wrote his first narrative exercises for the school magazine, *Juventud*, a modest endeavor promoted by Jesuits to help students develop their talents.

The middle-class status of the García Márquezes, however, were at peril. The family was by that time in a deep financial crisis. Gabriel Eligio was barely able to make ends meet. This prompted García Márquez to return home once again in January 1943. He had two options: stay home with his six siblings or find a way to complete his high school education. He decided to travel to Bogotá with some letters of recommendation in hand to seek a scholarship from the Ministerio de Educación. He wanted to do his *liceo*, known elsewhere in the Spanish-speaking world as *bachillerato*, the equivalent of high school, in the country's capital. He felt he needed more space for himself and a chance to see the world from a broader perspective.

Bogotá, located almost at the geographic center of Colombia, generated in him both nervousness and anticipation. While there he received a scholarship to the prestigious all-boys school

Liceo Nacional de Varones de Zipaquirá; it marked his rising status as a student.

Zipaquirá—in the Cundinamarca Department, some twenty to thirty miles from Bogotá but now considered part of the metropolitan area—was known for its salt reservoirs and grand cathedral. (The name Zipaquirá means in Chibcha, the language of the Muisca Indians, "The Land of the Zipa," Zipa being the territory's king.) It was there, in high school where García Márquez first reflected on political issues. Years later, he recalled that "the place was full of teachers who'd been taught by a Marxist in the Teachers Training College under President Alfonso López's leftist government in the thirties. The algebra teacher would give us classes on historical materialism during break, the chemistry teacher would lend us books by Lenin and the history teacher would tell us about the class struggle. When I left that icy prison I had no idea where north and south were but I did have two very strong convictions. One was that good novels must be a poetic transposition of reality, and the other was that mankind's immediate future lay in socialism."[4]

During that period, García Márquez discovered the writers of the Spanish Golden Age, including Félix Lope de Vega y Carpio, Francisco de Quevedo y Villegas, Luis de Góngora y Argote, Pedro Calderón de la Barca y Henao, and Tirso de Molina. For centuries this literary constellation had exercised enormous influence on the Spanish Americas, establishing the way poetry was written, in a baroque, self-conscious style. He discovered their sonnets, villancicos, and redondillas and tried his hand at poetry. None of those early literary efforts survive.

Just as he was finishing high school (García Márquez graduated from the *liceo* at the age of nineteen on December 12, 1946),[5] love struck during a ball in Sucre, where he met thirteen-year-old Mercedes Barcha Prado. Born in Magangué on November 6, 1932, Mercedes was the eldest daughter of a family of Mediterranean immigrants. Her great-grandfather was Syrian, and her grandfather was from Alexandria, Egypt. Her father was an Arab businessman who ran pharmacies and grocery stores. García Márquez asked Mercedes to marry him immediately after the ball, although the marriage would not take place until more than a decade later, after he had lived not only in other Colombian cities but in Rome, Paris, and London and had traveled extensively throughout Europe. Years later he told his friend Plinio Apuleyo Mendoza, "Looking back, I think the proposal was the metaphorical way of getting around all the fuss and bother you had to go through in those days to get a girlfriend."[6]

Love is the quintessential ingredient in García Márquez's oeuvre and it might well have been at that point, in his late teens, when he first recognized its depth and scope. "I believe one thing," he told a reporter decades later in Havana, "all my life I have been a romantic. But in our society, once youth is gone, you are supposed to believe that romantic feeling is something reactionary and out of style. As time passes and I grew older, I came to realize how primordial these sentiments are, these feelings."[7]

Mercedes was from the Bolívar Department, where the Roman Catholic Diocese has a see. It was one of the places where García Márquez's father had been a telegraphist. Her Mediterranean beauty hypnotized him. He couldn't stop dreaming about her. She reminded him of an Egyptian goddess, an image that long remained with him. In the eighteenth chapter of *One Hundred Years of Solitude* he pays tangential tribute to Mercedes. The last Aureliano, after a long seclusion, leaves the house twice. On his second outing, "he had to go only a few blocks to reach a small pharmacy with dusty windows and ceramic bottles with labels in Latin where a girl with the stealthy beauty of a serpent of the Nile gave him the medicine the name of which José Arcadio had written down on a piece of paper."[8]

According to transcripts dated February 25, 1947, García Márquez enrolled in the Universidad Nacional in Bogotá to study law. He did it mainly to please his parents. Coming as he did from a town of barely 20,000 people, the metropolis seemed colossal to him. But size wasn't necessarily a synonym of depth. He perceived it as "a distant, gloomy city where an unrelenting drizzle had been falling since the beginning of the sixteenth century." He told his friend Plinio Apuleyo Mendoza that "the first thing I noticed about the somber capital was that there were too many men in too much of a hurry, that they all wore the same black suits and hats as I did, and that there wasn't a woman to be seen. I noticed enormous Percherons drawing beer wagons in the rain, trams which gave off sparks like fireworks as they rounded the corners in the rain, and endless traffic jams for interminable funerals. These were the most lugubrious funerals in the world with grandiose ornate hearses and black horses decked out in velvet and black plumed nosebands, and corpses from important families who thought they had invented death."[9] In the seventh section of *One Hundred Years of Solitude*, García Márquez describes an army of lawyers all dressed in black suits who do little else but cater to the status quo.

Was García Márquez ready to become a lawyer? It is difficult to ascertain the extent of his commitment. His studies bored him to death. In *Living to Tell the Tale*, he quotes George Bernard Shaw: "Since very little I had to interrupt my education in order to go to school." Judging from the recollections of his siblings, the exact sciences weren't his forte.[10]

According to the same transcripts, during his first year he did well in all his courses, except statistics and demographics. Boredom appears to have taken the upper hand; García Márquez's transcript for the second year reveals him to have been frequently absent, which resulted in the failure of various courses.[11] Years later he would say that instead of attending classes, he read novels. In other words, it was the educational system that disappointed him; his interest in knowledge— especially in literature—remained strong.

His passion for literature (which he called the *"sarampión literario,"* the literary chickenpox) dates to this time. He read the European classics. "My literary education began [then]," he told a journalist. "I would read bad poetry on the one hand, and Marxist texts lent to me secretly by my history teacher, on the other. I would spend Sundays in the school library to stave off boredom. So, I began with bad poetry before discovering the good. Rimbaud, Valéry..."[12] García Márquez enjoyed "popular poetry, the kind printed on calendars and sold as broadsheets. I found I liked the poetry as much as I loathed the grammar in the Castilian text which I did for my secondary school certificate. I loved the Spanish Romantics—Núñez de Arce, Espronceda."[13]

Although poetry was an essential component in his literary apprenticeship, it seldom makes an appearance in his oeuvre. On occasion—in *Love in the Time of Cholera, Of Love and Other Demons,* and his autobiography—García Márquez includes quotes from favorite masters he had read in his youth. Decades later, after he had achieved international renown, García Márquez, in collaboration with Surrealist painter Roberto Matta, published in Cuba a calendar that included riddles he'd written about fruits. There's hardly any more evidence. Still, his discovery of poetry was auspicious. "My most salacious form of entertainment (at the time) was to sit, Sunday after Sunday, on those blue-paned trams that took you back and forth from the Plaza Bolívar to the Avenida de Chile for five cents—desolate afternoons which seemed to promise nothing but an interminable string of other empty Sundays to come. I'd spent that entire journey of vicious circles reading books of poems, poems and poems, getting through about one slim volume for each city block, until the first street lamps would light up in the never-ending rain. Then I'd roam the silent cafés of the old town searching for someone who'd take pity on me and discuss the poems, poems, poems I'd just read."[14] Those volumes of poetry were by writers who, as Plinio Apuleyo Mendoza put it, were politically committed and sought to produce a literature that was clear and accessible to "the simple people." Among them were Rubén Darío, Juan Ramón Jiménez, and Pablo Neruda.

To a large extent, García Márquez's understanding of literature was shaped by his discovery of Franz Kafka's writings. "I must have been around nineteen (on other occasions, he said he was seventeen) when I read *The Metamorphosis*," García Márquez recalled in 1982. The transformation of Gregor Samsa astonished him. He remembered the first line with astonishing precision: "'As Gregor Samsa awoke one morning from uneasy dreams he found himself transformed in his bed into a gigantic insect.' 'Bloody hell!' I thought. 'My grandmother used to talk like that.' I said to myself, 'I didn't know you could do this, but if you can, I'm certainly interested in writing.'" He decided to read the most important novels ever written.[15]

Kafka had a significant impact on García Márquez's generation, but it took some time for the Czech Jewish author, who died of tuberculosis in 1924, to gain a presence in Latin America. The translation of *Die Verwandlung* that García Márquez read has been at the heart of a heated debate for years. For some time, it was believed to have been done by the Argentine man of letters Jorge Luis Borges, who had been infatuated with Kafka since 1938. He translated the parable "Before the Law" for the journal *El Hogar*, and, as critic Efraín Kristal notes in his book *Invisible Work: Borges and Translation*, the Argentine also included a number of his renditions of Kafka in the famous *Anthology of Fantastic Literature*, which he edited with his friends Adolfo Bioy Casares and Silvina Ocampo.[16]

However, Borges himself cast doubt on having translated *The Metamorphosis*. The novel was first translated into Spanish in 1925, a year after Kafka's death, and published in *Revista de Occidente*, the intellectual magazine based in Madrid and edited by the Spanish philosopher José Ortega y Gasset. The translator was probably Galo Sáez, although others attributed it to Margarita Nelken. In 1945 that translation was published in book form by the Editorial Revista de Occidente, in a series called *Novelas extrañas* (Strange Novels). Borges purportedly translated *The Metamorphosis* in 1938 for Editorial Losada in Buenos Aires, in a series entitled *"La pajarita de papel,"* the paper bird.[17]

Which translation did García Márquez read? It is impossible to know. What is unquestionable is that it was a trigger. Years later, he said that he wouldn't have been able to write his early story, *"La tercera resignación"* (The Third Resignation)— dated September 13, 1947, when he was twenty—had he not read Kafka's novel. The story, which first appeared in English in the *New Yorker*, is García Márquez at his most self-conscious. It chronicles the impressions of a nameless narrator, much like Gregor Samsa, as he lies in his coffin, a man "ready to be buried, and yet he knew that he wasn't dead. That if he tried to get up, he could do it so easily."[18] The middle-class angst and the bizarre condition in which the protagonist finds himself seem to be an homage to Kafka's narrative.

García Márquez claimed that "Kafka, in German, told stories in the exact same way my grandmother did."[19] While Kafka's absurdism resonated with many in Europe, especially after World War II, his initial reception in the Spanish-speaking world was mixed—in spite of the enthusiasm of Borges, García Márquez, and a few others. There are ardent followers of Kafka in the Americas (Calvert Casey, for instance), but they aren't numerous. And then there are writers, such as the Uruguayan Felisberto Hernández (1902–1964) who are

Kafkaesque without necessarily being Kafkian, i.e., they might not be aware of the debt they owe to the author of *The Castle,* yet it is obvious.[20]

Equally significant, although for the opposite reasons, was García Márquez's relationship with Borges himself. Born in 1899 in Buenos Aires of British and Argentine stock, the author of "The Circular Ruins," "The Garden of Forking Paths," "Funes the Memorious," and other fictions was a Europeanized poet and essayist known, until the late fifties, only among a small cadre of intellectual devotees. A voracious reader, Borges's cosmopolitanism and his disdain for politics often put him at odds with the Latin American left. Borges was of a diametrically different ideological mindset. While he opposed, even ridiculed Argentine dictator Juan Domingo Perón, he was an intellectual dandy in the tradition of Oscar Wilde. He had little interest in the indigent. His view of the world was based on philosophical disquisitions and metaphysical constructions.

Emir Rodríguez Monegal, a Uruguayan critic and Yale professor who befriended both Borges and Neruda and wrote biographies of each (rather mediocre ones, filled with psycho-analytic interpretations), once asked Borges, sometime in the seventies, if he had heard of *One Hundred Years of Solitude,* a book that everyone was talking about. Borges, with acumen, said he had never heard of it. Except that with Borges it is always difficult to know if he was being honest. Had its author not been a left-leaning intellectual, had it been written elsewhere on the globe, maybe even in the nineteenth century, the Macondo saga would probably have hypnotized the Argentine man of letters. But the model of the writer as an artist engaged with the world that García Márquez represented was antithetical to Borges.

The English novelist Graham Greene—author of *The Power and the Glory, Our Man in Havana,* and other books—was another strong influence on García Márquez. Ironically, it was through Greene that García Márquez learned to appreciate his own environment. "Greene taught me how to decipher the tropics, no less. To separate out the essential elements of a poetic synthesis from an environment that you know all too well is extremely difficult. It's all so familiar you don't know where to start and yet you have so much to say that you end by understanding nothing. That was my problem with the tropics. I'd read Christopher Columbus, Antonio Pigafetta and the other chroniclers of the Indies with great interest. I'd also read Emilio Salgari and Joseph Conrad and the early twentieth century 'tropicalists' who saw everything through Modernist spectacles, and many others, but always found an enormous dichotomy between their visions and the real thing. Some of them fell into the trap of listing things and, paradoxically, the longer the list the more limited the vision seemed. Others, as we know, have succumbed to rhetorical excess. Graham Greene solved this literary problem in a very precise way—with a few disparate elements connected by an inner coherence both subtle and real. Using this method you can reduce the whole enigma of the tropics to the fragrance of a rotten guava."[21]

But the most significant literary influences on García Márquez, at least according to critics, were three writers from the United States: John Dos Passos, Ernest Hemingway, and William Faulkner. He admired the three for dramatically different reasons. Dos Passos studied the infrastructure of capitalism in all its excesses. Hemingway had a succinct, almost telegraphic style. His language was simple yet polished. But it was Faulkner who left the deepest, most defining mark on him. The novels *Sartoris, As I Lay Dying, The Sound and the Fury,* and *Absalom! Absalom!* showed García Márquez the capacity of literature as a tool for revisiting history, and, through history, society as a whole. Macondo as an autonomous reality, with its geographical boundaries, its vegetation, and its genealogical lines, was inspired by Faulkner's Yoknapatawpha County, which was modeled after Lafayette County, Mississippi.

Unquestionably, there are similarities between Faulkner's native state of Mississippi in particular and the Deep South in general, and Macondo and Colombia. The loss the South experienced during the American Civil War and the depth and breadth of the trauma left by numerous victims is comparable to the aftermath of Colombia's Thousand-Day War and successive civil wars. Faulkner received the Nobel Prize for Literature in 1949, a year after the assassination of Liberal Party leader Jorge Eliécer Gaitán in Bogotá. Spanish translations of Faulkner's stories had appeared in literary magazines and cultural supplements, and Spanish translations of books were published in the late thirties. (Borges translated *The Palm Trees*.)[22] Throughout the forties, he was read with reverence in intellectual circles.

Juan Carlos Onetti, whose readings of Faulkner defined him, once described how he discovered the Nobel laureate's oeuvre.

The recollection speaks not only for Onetti but for an entire generation of starstruck Latin American readers.

One afternoon, after I left the office where I worked, I stopped by a bookstore and bought the last issue of *Sur*, a magazine founded and supported by Victoria Ocampo...Looking back, when I remember that I opened the issue on the street, for the first time in my life I encountered the name of William Faulkner. An unknown writer had written the introduction, which was followed by a story poorly translated into Spanish. I started reading while continuing to walk, beyond the world of passers-by and automobiles, until I decided to enter a café to finish the story, happily forgetting that someone was waiting for me somewhere. I reread it again and the bewitchment increased. It increased and every critic agrees that it is enduring.[23]

On September 13, 1947, at the age of twenty, García Márquez published his first short story, *"La tercera resignación"* (The Third

Resignation), in the evening newspaper *El Espectador,* one of Bogotá's most important dailies. It appeared on page eight, in the section *Fin de semana* (Weekend) edited by Eduardo Zalamea Borda. It would be the first of eighteen short stories he would write before publishing his first book, *Leaf Storm.* A little over a month later, his second and third stories, *"Eva está dentro de su gato"* (Eve Is Inside Her Cat) and *"Tubal Caín forja una estrella"* (Tubal Caín Shapes a Star), were published in the *Fin de semana* supplement.

García Márquez wrote for long hours, secluded from everyone else, on a typewriter. In an article entitled *"El amargo encanto de la máquina de escribir,"* he discussed the difference between writing in longhand and typing. He suggested that the former had an aura of mystery but that the latter was the inevitable outcome of modern life. "Truth is that everyone writes in whatever way possible, because the hardest thing of this arduous business isn't how one handles tools, but the way one succeeds in putting one word after another."[24]

Although it is essential to recognize the value of translation in García Márquez's literary education, it would be wrong to suggest that all the influences on his oeuvre were foreign. All artists are shaped by their provenance, and García Márquez was no different. Equally important, if only for its aesthetic consistency, was the work of Colombian authors. García Márquez responded to nineteenth-century romantic and naturalistic novels, but he sought ways to create something fresh and different, to be a new voice that would allow Colombian literature to be viewed beyond its regional confines and to be embraced by the international literary community.

The Colombian novel is defined by its geography. The coastal narrative of *One Hundred Years of Solitude* belongs to a tradition shared by other Caribbean nations. Not surprisingly, García Márquez is often compared to baroque authors such as Alejo Carpentier and José Lezama Lima. That coastal tradition is represented by Juan José Nieto's novel *Ingermina* (1844). As Raymond Leslie Williams, a scholar of the Colombian novel, has mapped it out, other national traditions include the narrative based in the interior highlands, such as Eugenio Díaz's *Manuela* (1858) and Eduardo Caballero Calderón's *El buen salvaje* (1963); the Antioquian tradition, evident in Tomás Carrasquilla's *Frutos de mi tierra* (1896) and Manuel Mejía Vallejo's *El día señalado* (1964); and the Cauca tradition, encompassing works that range from Jorge Isaac's *María* (1867) to Gustavo Alvarez Gardeazábal's *El bazar de los idiotas* (1974).[25]

While studying law at the Universidad Nacional in Bogotá, a crucial moment took place that served as a catalyst in García Márquez's apprenticeship as a writer. In 1948 the populist Jorge Eliécer Gaitán, a charismatic, immensely popular leader of the Liberal Party and a presidential candidate, was assassinated during a riot in Bogotá; he was fifty years old. García Márquez remembers that day as a watershed moment in his life.

Trained in the law at the Universidad Nacional, Gaitán had been mayor of Bogotá and minister of education. Gaitán was killed during a period known as *La Violencia,* in which violent clashes between liberals and conservatives resulted in the death of several hundred thousand people. In a speech he gave the year he died, Gaitán said, "If I am killed, avenge me!"

The events took place on April 9. The nation's capital was hosting the Pan-American Conference, which was devoted to trade issues, although politics occupied center stage. President Mariano Ospina Pérez was at a meeting with the secretary of state of the United States, General George Marshall.

Gaitán and a few colleagues left his office at around 1:05 P.M. Witnesses heard three gunshots, then a fourth. Gaitán was hit in the back; the bullet tore though his lungs. Another lodged in the back of his head. He lay on the ground for at least ten minutes before being taken in a black taxi to the

Clínica Central, five blocks away. He reached the clinic at around 1:30 P.M. A historian described the scene: "There was an inexorable finality about what had happened. The leader was gone for all who witnessed the shooting. It mattered little that he had been rushed to a clinic, where doctors would try to save his life. The assassination had been on everyone's mind. It was too predictable. His death was inevitable. He was too dangerous and too feared by the leaders of both parties."[26]

The assassination was a pivotal event in modern Colombian history. In Bogotá the news quickly spread. People screamed, *"¡Mataron a Gaitán! ¡Mataron a Gaitán!"* and took to the streets in anger. Radio broadcasters cautioned Bogotanos to stay home. The minister of the interior went on the air to deny that Gaitán had been shot. But to no avail. People marched to the *palacio* on Calle Real. Revolution was in the air, but no one was at the helm. A crowd of workers and middle-class folks carried off the body of Gaitán's alleged assassin. There is still confusion regarding the true identity of the perpetrator.

The role of the media was critical. Radio station *Últimas noticias*, managed by Gaitán supporters, made the following broadcast minutes after the assassination: *"Últimas Noticias con ustedes. Los conservadores y el gobierno de Ospina Pérez acaban de asesinar al doctor Gaitán, quien cayó frente a la puerta de su oficina abaleado por un policía. Pueblo ¡a las armas! ¡A la carga!, a la calle con palos, piedras, escopetas, cuanto haya a la mano. Asalten las ferreterías y tomen la dinamita, la pólvora, las herramientas, los machetes..."* An English translation: *Últimas Noticias* is broadcasting to you. The conservatives and Ospina Peréz's government have just assassinated Doctor Gaitán, who collapsed in front of his office after being gunned down by a policeman. People, take arms! Be ready to battle! Go on the street with sticks, stones, muskets, anything at hand. Assault the hardware stores and take away the dynamite, the gun powder, the tools and machetes.

The broadcast instructed people to make Molotov cocktails. The crowd on Calle Real was organized, but in other parts of the city it was amorphous, massive, and dangerous. People shouted, "Down with the Conservative government!" On the Plaza de Bolívar, busses were set on fire. President Mariano Ospina Pérez believed "the republic would fall into the hands of rioters whose prime objective was control of the nation's government."[27]

Gaitán's assassination was known as *El Bogotazo*, the period preceding the event as *la convivencia*, in which people with opposing ideological views—liberal and conservative—tried to coexist. *El Bogotazo* led to a long spell of violence. "Gaitán had taken his followers from a life in which they were excluded from the decisions that affected them to another in which they felt they participated in those decisions," a historian recounted. "His death thrust them instinctively back to the sacrosanct old hierarchies and to their lowly, deferential, and reviled place in society. As the crowd lost contact with the *convivialistas*, the old anonymous world with distant and sporadic leaders materialized again. The actions of the crowd in Bogotá on the afternoon of April 9 were a sign of the people's refusal to return to the past, to retrace the distance already traveled. But the crowd could not undertake the rest of the journey without Gaitán. How was it suddenly to take power? The idea was never even there. Unwilling to move back and unable to move forward, the anger and frustration of the rioters had only one outlet: the destruction of a society in which they could no longer live. From the feeling of loss that enveloped Gaitán's followers at the moment of his death, from the sense of pride and cohesion that he had offered them, and from the hatred he had shown for the *convivialistas*, the crowd delivered the courage, and the need, to destroy."[28]

The riots during *El Bogotazo* lasted ten hours. They started in Bogotá and quickly spread to the rest of the country. Stores were looted; goods were stolen and fenced at cheap prices.

The death toll reached 200,000, and approximately one million were injured. *La Violencia* raged for a decade, until 1958. In the article "Bogotá 1947," about the book *Mafia: Historias de caleños y bogotanos* by Gonzalo Mallarino, García Márquez described the day he first set foot in Bogotá at the age of thirteen: "...it was a somber January afternoon, the saddest of my life." He added that the greatest heroism of his life, and of his generation's, was having been young in Bogotá at the time. He would jump on the trolleys on Sunday and go from Plaza Bolívar to Avenida de Chile. Sometimes he would meet a random person, usually a man, and they would have coffee together and chat until midnight.[29]

During the riots, García Márquez's boarding house burned down and the Universidad Nacional closed. A penciled statement in his transcript reveals that he transferred to the Universidad de Cartagena. "I realized that literature had a relationship with life that my short stories didn't," García Márquez said later. "And then an event took place that was very important with respect to this attitude. It was *El Bogotazo*, on April 9, 1948, when a political leader, Gaitán, was shot and the people of Bogotá went raving mad in the streets. I was in my *pensión* ready to have lunch when I heard the news. I ran toward the place, but Gaitán had just been put into a taxi and was being taken to a hospital. On my way back to the pension, the people had already taken to the streets and they were demonstrating, looting stores, and burning buildings. I joined them. That afternoon and evening, I became aware of the kind of country I was living in, and how little my short stories had to do with any of that."[30]

García Márquez's entry into journalism took place shortly afterward. He decided to leave Bogotá after witnessing the riots. While he understood the causes that had led to the mobilization of the masses, he was shocked and frightened by the anarchy. He needed to leave the nation's capital, to gain perspective by looking at things from afar. He decided to go to Barranquilla first, but the university there was closed. After some time he made his way to Cartagena, a thriving coastal city with deep colonial roots where Afro-Colombian culture thrived. It was a bold move. These two cities, Bogotá and Cartagena, dramatically different in their metabolism and in the way García Márquez approached them, would allow him to come to terms with his own literary talents.

Chapter 3

Mamador de gallos

"When I was later forced to go back to Barranquilla on the Caribbean, where I had spent my childhood," García Márquez later recalled, "I realized that that was the type of life I had lived, known, and wanted to write about."[1] Being a participant of *El Bogotazo* convinced him that the responsibility of a writer was to bear witness, to use words to describe the dramatic transformations taking place in a journalistic fashion.

Once in Barranquilla, García Márquez started writing a daily column and some editorials for the newspaper *El Heraldo*. Its offices were located on a street known for its underworld bar, which people referred to as *Calle del Crimen* (Crime Street). He lived in "one of those hotels for casual customers which are really brothels."[2] The newspaper paid him three pesos per column and another three per editorial. At the time, according to his friend Germán Vargas Cantillo, whom he had just met, García Márquez worked intensely, "after midnight, on an insurmountable novel, *La casa* [The House], which he never finished nor did he publish with that title, but it's unquestionable that in that novel, which we called *el mamotreto*, the huge thing, there were probably, in essence, a few of the stories and some of the novels for

which he would later be known among readers and critics."[3]
But progress was slow. He wasn't quite sure what the plot
was about, how to approach it, and what narrative perspective to take. He struggled with it, often feeling disappointed.
Did he have to accept that the project needed to be aborted?
The material was germinating within him but, although he
refused to acknowledge it, the novel wasn't quite ready to
acquire its final shape.

He was twenty-two, frustrated, and anxious. Eager to
test his talent, he spent late nights at the office of *El Heraldo*
and began another novel that would eventually become *La
hojarasca* (Leaf Storm). García Márquez wrote the manuscript
in a hurry. He was broke. "When I hadn't got the one-fifty
to pay for the room," he later said, "I used to leave the manuscript...as a deposit with the hotel doorman. He knew that
I valued those papers highly. A long time afterwards, when I
had already written *One Hundred Years of Solitude*, I came across
this doorman among the people who would came to see me or
ask for an autograph. He remembered everything."[4]

There is much debate among critics regarding exactly
where García Márquez wrote *Leaf Storm*. For years the writer
himself suggested that he had composed it in Barranquilla
among friends, but there were two versions of the novel. The
first was likely written in Cartagena between the end of 1948
and the beginning of 1949, while García Márquez was working
at *El Universal*. He held a deep affection for Cartagena, but he
told an interviewer that he harbored some reservations about
its people *"porque son cachacos,"* because they were too similar
to the people in Bogotá. The second and final version, in his
own words, was written in Barranquilla.[5]

His technique in *Leaf Storm* is reminiscent of some of his
idealized masters: Virginia Woolf, James Joyce, and Faulkner.
Its structure resembles the shifting viewpoints used by Faulkner
in *As I Lay Dying*, although, unlike Faulkner's narrators, who

aren't always identifiable, García Márquez had only three unnamed ones: an old man, a boy, and a woman. From Wolf and Joyce he assimilated a modernist bent, which is palpable in this novel as a style but is more evident in his first stories published in newspapers, such as "The Third Resignation," "Bitterness for Three Sleepwalkers," and "Dialogue with the Mirror," later collected in *Ojos de perro azul* (Eyes of Blue Dog) (1973). Such is the impact of the Modernists on him that many of these stories, when read today, don't feel like having been written by García Márquez. Perhaps he even nurtures a distaste for them, as if they were his bastard children. Is that why these stories have never appeared in English in a separate book as *Eyes of Blue Dog* but, instead, were integrated to the volume *Collected Stories* translated by Gregory Rabassa that Harper & Row released in 1984?

Trying to publish the book was a nightmare; for years he and others believed that his *opera prima* was cursed. It took him five years to find a publisher. He sent it to Editorial Losada, the prestigious publishing house in Buenos Aires, but the Spanish critic Guillermo de Torre, who worked for Losada (and was Borges's brother-in-law), sent him a rejection letter that stung him deeply. Not only did de Torre say that *Leaf Storm* wasn't for Losada but he advised García Márquez, in spite of the manuscript's poetic quality, not to pursue literature and to concentrate on other things. At least de Torre "recognized something in me that now gives me a lot of satisfaction," García Márquez expressed as a form of consolation, "a definite feeling for poetry."[6]

In 1955, *Leaf Storm* finally was published in Bogotá by the editor Samuel Lisman Baum, with a probable print run of a thousand copies (although the published book included a colophon that announced a printing of four thousand copies). Its cover image was by the Cartagena painter Cecilia Porras. Dedicated to Germán Vargas, *Leaf Storm* was priced at five pesos. But the book was full of typographical errors! García Márquez was beside himself. He and a group of friends decided to buy the entire print run. Among those who helped in this endeavor was Eduardo Zalamea, who took—in exchange for half the royalties for a novel he had published with Lisman Baum—about five hundred copies of *Leaf Storm.*

The embarrassment of the ubiquitous typos didn't stop García Márquez from enjoying his success. This was his first published book, and the critical response in Bogotá, Barranquilla, and Cartagena was positive (the first review was by Eduardo Zalamea, under the pseudonym of Ulysses, in *El Heraldo*). *Leaf Storm* announced many of García Márquez's literary themes, in particular his interest in immigrants. In *One Hundred Years of Solitude,* the presence of immigrants is represented by the Street of the Turks, a catch-all term for those who had come to Colombia's Caribbean coast from different parts of the Ottoman Empire, including Turkey, Syria, Egypt, and Greece. Another prominent element in *Leaf Storm* that is later amplified in García Márquez's oeuvre is natural disasters, such as plagues.

His fascination with these flare-ups of nature may be traced to what he saw as a child in Aracataca and from his readings of the Bible, the Greek tragedies, and other classics. "Beginning with Oedipus," he reminisced, "I've always been interested in plagues. I have studied a lot about medieval plagues. One of my favorite books is *A Journal of the Plague Year* by Daniel Defoe, among other reasons because Defoe is a journalist who sounds like what he is saying is pure fantasy. For many years I thought Defoe had written about the London plague as he observed it. But then I discovered it was a novel, because Defoe was less than seven years old when the plague occurred in London. Plagues have always been one of my recurrent themes—and in different forms."[7] (In an interview in the Cuban newspaper *Gramma,* García Márquez was asked what he wanted to

die of: "Love would be good," he replied, "but not from AIDS.
As a subject, love in the time of AIDS would never interest me
because AIDS is a plague that is much related to one's behavior. It's not like cholera or other plagues that are uncontrollable
dangers, they cannot be evaluated, they creep up on you even
if you don't move, shut away in your home...")[8]

Leaf Storm was published in Colombia during a time of
political repression. After Gaitán was assassinated in 1948, the
country was mired in political instability. On June 13, 1953,
General Gustavo Rojas Pinilla seized power in a coup d'état
supported by both Liberals and Conservatives, as well as the
United States. Rojas Pinilla had been a delegate to the United
Nations, and he was supportive of American opposition to communism. A year before the coup, the Conservative government
of Laureano Gómez promoted him to the rank of general of
the Armed Forces of Colombia. His rule heralded a period of
military repression and the restriction of civil liberties which
lasted until 1957.

At the time, García Márquez was a strong proponent of
socialism. In his words, he wanted "the world to be Socialist
and I believe that sooner or later it will happen."[9] As an
engaged intellectual, he was committed to the cause of change.
Yet *Leaf Storm* didn't seem to present a clear ideological stand.
According to his friends, the book condemned repression but
it didn't expose anything. García Márquez felt guilty about it.
His progressive loyalties were apparent, but his writing was
less a tool for transformation than a source of enjoyment, at
least on the surface. He responded that, while he sympathized
with the socialist cause, he opposed what in the Soviet Union
was described as "committed literature." He believed that when
writers became tools for government-sponsored plans, the aesthetic effect was deadly. "Far from accelerating any process of
raising consciousness," García Márquez argued that this type
of literature "actually slows it down. Latin Americans expect

more from a novel than an exposé of the oppression and injustice they know all too well. Many of my militant friends who so often feel the need to dictate to writers what they should or should not write are, unconsciously perhaps, taking a reactionary stance inasmuch as they are imposing restrictions on creative freedom. I believe a novel about love is as valid as any other. When it comes down to it, the writer's duty—his revolutionary duty, if you like—is to write well."[10]

Years later, in 1972, when the English translation of *Leaf Storm* by Gregory Rabassa was published in the United States, Alfred Kazin reviewed it in the *New York Times Book Review:* "Unlike the subtle but timid Borges, who comes out of a library and may be remembered as the Washington Irving of Latin America, Márquez—born in 1928 [*sic*]—reflects the incessant ironies of post-imperialist national development. He has extraordinary strength and firmness of imagination and writes with the calmness of a man who knows exactly what wonders he can perform. Strange things happen in the land of Márquez. As with Emerson, Poe, Hawthorne, every sentence breaks the silence of a vast emptiness, the famous New World 'solitude' that is the unconscious despair of his characters but the sign of Márquez's genius."

Kazin understood that García Márquez was not a Protean romantic of the time when it seemed that *all* the world would soon be new. Instead, he is a "dazzlingly accomplished but morally burdened end-product of centuries of colonialism, civil war, and political chaos; a prime theme in all his work is the inevitability of incest and the damage to the gene pool that at the end of his great novel produces a baby with a pig's tail. *Leaf Storm* was Márquez's first book, begun when he was 19...In each of these stories Márquez takes a theme that in a lesser writer would seem 'poetic,' a handsome conceit lifted out of a poem by Wallace Stevens but then stopped dead in its narrative tricks. Márquez manages to make a story out of each of these—not too ambitious, but just graceful enough to be itself. He succeeds because these are stories about wonders, and the wonders become actions."[11] Kazin concluded: "I am guessing but I wonder if the outbreak of creative originality in Latin America today, coming after so many years of dutifulness to Spanish and French models, doesn't resemble our sudden onrush of originality after we had decided really to break away from the spell of England."[12]

To illuminate the way dialogue works in *Leaf Storm*—he ascribes so little of it, yet when it is present its strategic location in the narrative makes it resonate loudly—it is useful to bring to mind a response García Márquez once gave to an interviewer. Dialogue, he stated, "doesn't ring true in Spanish. I've always said that in this language there's a wide gulf between spoken and written dialogue. A Spanish dialogue that's good in real life is not necessarily good in a novel. So I use it very little."[13]

The five years it took for *Leaf Storm* to be published were constructive. During this time García Márquez perfected the art of *mamar gallo*, a Colombian expression meaning to tease, to kid, to make clownish jokes. Although his newspaper job was demanding, he started writing short stories on the side and publishing them in the Sunday magazine. Around 1949, García Márquez met a group of writers, artists, and intellectuals, mostly male who, like him, were *mamadores de gallo*. The cadre was eventually known as *El grupo de Barranquilla* and included Germán Vargas Cantillo, a journalist, literary critic, and newscaster born in Bucaramanga, Colombia in 1929, Álvaro Cepeda Samudio (Barranquilla, 1926), and Alfonso Fuenmayor (Barranquilla, 1915).

One of *El grupo de Barranquilla*'s collaborations was the making of a short film, the production of which has become legendary in Colombian intellectual circles. It was an eleven-minute, black-and-white short called *La langosta azul* (The Blue Lobster). Directed by three members of the group—Álvaro

Cepeda Samudio, cinematographer Luis Vicens, a Catalan bookseller who founded the first cinema club in Bogotá, and painter Enrique Grau—it was filmed at the end of 1954 in Puerto Salgar with a 16-milimeter Boller movie camera. Some additional footage was taken in early 1955 by Cepeda Samudio, and the short was edited by Vicens.

Almost everyone involved in *La langosta azul* contributed money for its production. In spite of the lore that surrounds the project, the truth is that García Márquez was only a peripheral participant in the endeavor. It appears that his involvement may have been used to attract publicity for the film. *La langosta azul* may be classified as science fiction, in the tradition of such films as *The Andromeda Strain* and *Invasion of the Body Snatchers*. In that sense, it's a fascinating experiment. After all, Latin America isn't known for its embrace of science fiction. The number of novels, stories, films, and TV shows that belong to that genre is insignificant. A *gringo*, or foreigner (played by photographer Nereo López-Meza), arrives in a small Caribbean coastal town with a suitcase full of lobsters, one of which is blue and has atomic power. As the gringo wanders around town, the blue lobster is lost. Most of the film features the search for the blue lobster; this allows the camera to explore the tropical landscape. In the end, a strong wind blows the lobster away.[14]

The short has a similar feel to some of the surrealist projects of André Breton, Tristan Tzara, or Salvador Dalí. It is loosely reminiscent of Luis Buñuel's *Un chien andalou* (Andalusian Dog) and *L'age d'or* (Golden Age), although *La langosta azul* has a narrative that is far less discombobulated and its intent is not to scandalize but to entertain. The plot is supposedly based on an idea by García Márquez, and it has elements that would lend credence to that. But the degree of his involvement has been called into question a number of times, not least by García Márquez himself.

Through *El grupo de Barranquilla*, García Márquez met other young writers, including the poet Meira Delmar, with whom

he would share a long-lasting friendship.[15] The center of gravity and inspirational figure around whom the group revolved
was Don Ramón Vinyes, immortalized in *One Hundred Years of
Solitude* as *el sabio catalán*, the Catalan wise man. Born in 1882
in Berga, a village in the Pyrenees, Catalonia, Vinyes later
became an icon to García Márquez, Cepeda Samudio, Germán
Vargas Cantillo, and Alfonso Fuenmayor.[16] A voracious reader,
he was a European expatriate who cut an elegant figure. He
had immigrated to the Americas in 1911, arriving in Puerto
Colombia on June 16. What brought him to Colombia? An
adventurous spirit, no doubt. He first worked as a bookkeeper
for Correa Hermanos, a cocoa exporting company. Vinyes
wrote an autobiography that includes the following segment:
"I arrived in Colombia fleeing from literature. The influence of
Catalonia over me may be seen in my verses, '*La ardiente cabal-
gata*' and '*Consejas a la luna.*' I tore up the last copies because
they were overwhelmed with pretentious symbolism during an
ocean crossing that took me from Barcelona to the Colombian
beaches. I had also written a play, *Al florecer de los manzanos*,
which was awarded a prize. I had believed naïvely in literature
with almost mystic candor. Thus, the disappointment I suffered
was violent. Violent enough to make me not want anything to
do with it. And believe me, I did need courage. Anyway, on
the ship an Italian woman lent me a copy of *The Divine Comedy*.
Due to the fact that I would never return the book to her, a
new lasting alliance with literature was established."[17]

Vinyes moved to Barranquilla in 1914, and, in partnership
with another Catalan immigrant, Xavier Auqué i Masdeu,
opened the bookstore Librería Ramón Vinyes y Cía. Known
as a superb *anfitrión*, a host and erudite entertainer, he was an
amicable, entertaining host to his clientele, always recommend-
ing new books.

In Europe, World War I was raging. At the time,
Barranquilla had a population of approximately one hundred

thousand. It was a thriving, if chaotic, city. Vinyes's bookstore became a watering hole for artists and intellectuals. Soon, with the backing of friends and supporters, Vinyes launched a literary magazine, *Voces*, which quickly made a name for itself both in Colombia and the rest of Latin America. In Barranquilla, people referred to the publication as *"la revista de Vinyes,"* Vinyes's magazine. Contributors included Julio Gómez de Castro, José Félix Fuenmayor (father of Alfonso Fuenmayor), Rafael Carbonell, and Enrique Restrepo. Its approach was liberal, cosmopolitan, and democratic: "We battle against the negative, against those that find darkness in the work of art when darkness resides in them; against those that don't accept any other manifestation of sensibility but their own, narrow and dark." The magazine folded in 1920.

It isn't known exactly when García Márquez met Vinyes, but the encounter probably took place between September 1948 and June 1949, while García Márquez was in Barranquilla. Vinyes wrote in his diary: "A good Colombian storyteller. Gabriel García Márquez. *'La otra orilla de la muerte'* is a good story. A brother whose twin has just died. Nightmare, end of story. He has died of a tumor. The putrid matter will reach the one alive. They complemented each other. The story is strong. A rainy night. A leak in the middle of the bedroom, with a drop that falls insistently. A scent of violets and formaldehyde. The persistent nightmare. Pus, night, philosophy."[18]

In the early twenties, Vinyes went back and forth between Barranquilla and Barcelona. He married a Colombian woman, María Salazar. His bookstore mysteriously burned down. Rather than rebuilding it, he took the opportunity to switch careers and began writing editorials and reviews for the newspaper *La Nación*. He continued writing for the theater. In September 1948, Vinyes met Alfonso Fuenmayor and Germán Vargas Cantillo, who idolized him. They enjoyed many conversations, mostly in La Cueva, which Vinyes recorded in his diaries.

Fuenmayor said, "Vinyes came from rejecting the dull Spanish poetry revolving around Rubén Darío's modernism. He could cite in their respective languages the Latin classics as well as Chaucer, Rabelais, Boccaccio, Villon, Auden or a buffoon from the Middle Ages. He knew where William Blake's madness began and why Picasso had not continued painting boxes for the raisins; he could distinguish fourteen thousand shades of green and he noticed when the mayonnaise had an extra drop of oil."[19] Vinyes was a relentless dissident who embraced the ideas of the enlightenment while questioning their ideological dogmas.

Vinyes is credited with reintroducing García Márquez to Joyce, among other writers. García Márquez once said that whatever *El sabio catalán* recommended to him, he would devour.[20] To the extent possible, Vinyes followed the careers of his friends. In 1950, García Márquez, Cepeda Samudio, Vargas Cantillo, and Alfonso Fuenmayor launched the magazine *Crónica*. In *Living to Tell the Tale*, García Márquez relates: "For me, *Crónica* had the later importance of allowing me to improvise emergency stories to fill unexpected spaces in the anguish of going to press. I would sit at the typewriter while linotypists and typesetters did their work, and out of nothing I would invent a tale the size of the space. This is how I wrote 'How Natanael Pays a Visit,' which solved an urgent problem for me at dawn, and 'Blue Dog's Eyes,' five weeks later."[21] Unfortunately, no copies of *Crónica* seem to have survived. The magazine was quite important in his growth as a writer. For eight months it featured a foreign short story, often translated from the French by García Márquez. And it was in *Crónica* where he wrote an early piece, published in 1950, called *"La casa de los Buendía"* (The Buendía House), in which he first presented some of the material he would later develop in *One Hundred Years of Solitude*.

In the article *"El cuento del cuento,"* García Márquez revealed that his friend Cepeda Samudio, just before dying, gave him the plot of *Chronicle of a Death Foretold.* Don Ramón Vinyes told him: *"Cuéntala mucho...Es la única manera de saber lo que una historia tiene por dentro"* (Tell it many times over...It's the only way to know what a story has in its insides).[22] Vinyes himself died on May 5, 1952. His influence and that of *El grupo de Barranquilla* on García Márquez is undeniable. Thirteen years later, when García Márquez sat down to write the expanded version of *La casa,* he included, in chapter nineteen, a humorous tribute to *El sabio catalán* and the folks of *El grupo de Barranquilla,* in which the last Aureliano meets the real-life characters: One afternoon Aureliano "went to the bookstore of the wise Catalan and found four ranting boys in a heated argument about the methods used to kill cockroaches in the Middle Ages. The old bookseller, knowing about Aureliano's love for books that had been read only by the Venerable Bede, urged him with a certain fatherly malice to get into the discussion." What follows is a disquisition on the cockroach's survival mechanism throughout history, a message that resonates in a novel concerned with the durability of a species: the Buendías.

The narrative then focuses on Aureliano's friendship with the group. "Aureliano continued getting together in the afternoon with the four arguers, whose names were Álvaro, Germán, Alfonso, and Gabriel, the first and last friends that he ever had in his life. For a man like him, holed up in written reality, those stormy sessions that began in the bookstore and ended at dawn in the brothels were a revelation. It had never occurred to him until then to think that literature was the best plaything that had ever been invented to make fun of people, as Álvaro demonstrated during one night of revelry. Some time would have to pass before Aureliano realized that such arbitrary attitudes had their origins in the example of the Catalan wise man, for whom wisdom was worth nothing if it could not be used to invent a new way of preparing chick peas."[23]

The use of the "plaything," (in the Spanish original, *"que la literatura fuera el mejor juguete que se había inventado para burlarse de la gente"*) appears to mirror Cervantes's narrative strategy in his satire of chivalry novels, in which few of his contemporaries emerge without a kick in the butt. Similarly, the tantalizing *mise en abysme* of García Márquez's scene (where he refers to himself), in which fictional characters interact with real people, echoes the recurrent metaliterary devices in *Don Quixote*. Among them, in Part II, are the moments in which the knight and his squire encounter people who have either read or heard about Part I and who compare the flesh-and-blood Don Quixote and Sancho with their literary counterparts. The essence of this playfulness is the art of being a *mamador de gallos:* not to take any aspect of life, no matter how serious, without cracking a joke.[24]

When García Márquez moved to Cartagena de Indias, he knew his own career as a student was at an impasse, maybe even at an end. His dream of becoming a writer occupied most of his attention, and journalism was intimately connected to it. "Journalism keeps you in contact with reality," García Márquez stated in 1982. "Literary people have a tendency to take all sorts of detours into unreality. Besides, if you stick to writing only books, you're always starting from scratch all over again."[25] To write and to do it well and under a deadline suited his aspirations. Plus, how else could he make ends meet?

In Cartagena, García Márquez had a fortuitous street encounter with the writer and doctor Manuel Zapata Olivella, who took him to the editorial offices of *El Universal,* a liberal newspaper founded just a few months earlier, in March 1948, by Domingo López Escauriaza. The offices were in the Plaza de San Pedro, on the corner of Calle San Juan. In May, García Márquez started writing a column called *"Punto y aparte."* These pieces were produced rapidly. They had a poetic quality to them, and they explored the enchanting, thought-provoking elements of daily life that would capture a reader's attention. In total, he wrote forty columns, the last one at the end of 1949.[26]

García Márquez led a bohemian life during his Cartagena years. He spent his evenings at the office, his nights in bars getting drunk with close friends, and his dawns in whorehouses. As a reporter, he needed to be able to move around, talk to people, and navigate Cartagena's treacherous neighborhoods, from the poorest to the most luxurious. He not only covered the city, he turned it into a larger home of sorts. With the exception of Aracataca and its tangible influence on the shaping of Macondo's mythical qualities, the Colombian place that is easiest to recognize—and to celebrate—in García Márquez's fiction is Cartagena. In his view, it was a place to experiment with the possibilities of love. For instance, at the Paseo de los Mártires he had spent the night sleeping on a bench while drunk when a biblical deluge soaked him to the bone. He caught a terrible case of pneumonia, spent a couple of weeks in the hospital, and was given a heavy dose of antibiotics, which, as he relates in *Living to Tell the Tale*, were said to have atrocious side-effects, such as early impotence. In his memoir, García Márquez recalls the Torre del Reloj, a bridge that in ancient times linked the Old City with a poor neighborhood known as Getsemaní, and the Plaza de los Coches, the site of a slave market in the colonial period, a reference that appears in *Of Love and Other Demons*. In his newspaper columns García Márquez often wrote about the Plaza de la Aduana, where there is a church that houses the remains of the Spanish priest Pedro Claver, who the people of Cartagena consider a saint.

In 1953, García Márquez worked as a book salesman. It allowed him to travel around the Magdalena River area and the Guajira peninsula. The following year, he returned to

Bogotá and became a staff writer at *El Espectador*, where he started writing *entre cachacos*, that is, for Bogotá readers. It appears that his job at the newspaper resulted from a visit García Márquez paid to Álvaro Mutis, then in charge of the publicity department at Esso, located on Avenida Jiménez. The offices of *El Espectador* were in the same building. His first surviving piece, dated February 1954, is a review of various movies, including *Testimonio de una amante*, starring Edward G. Robinson and Paulette Goddard. Whenever the newspaper was short on *redactores*, or news writers, his colleagues asked him to write a few words. He complied with pleasure. But García Márquez was planning to return to the Atlantic coast. Before he could do so, the newspaper editors offered him a full-time job for a monthly salary of 900 pesos. That was more money than he received at *El Heraldo*, so he decided to stay. He would be able to live better, and he wanted to send his parents some money.

In *El Espectador*, he helped with the daily section, *Día a día*. What distinguished García Márquez's work was the emphasis he placed on film criticism, a fledgling exercise in Colombia and Latin America. But the most exciting aspect, in terms of his literary development, was his interest in reportage. His desire to use his journalistic tools to produce expansive non-fiction pieces capable of looking objectively at a phenomenon in its entirety without sacrificing the stylistic component—in the fashion of New Journalists such as Tom Wolfe, Joan Didion, Truman Capote, Hunter S. Thompson, and Norman Mailer in the United States in the sixties and seventies—convinced García Márquez that newspaper serials would bring him more satisfaction than his regular dispatch.

In 1955 a terrific story—not without ideologically explosive elements—about the shipwreck of a Colombian vessel and the life at sea of the sole survivor, magically fell on his lap. García Márquez's story, serialized in fourteen consecutive issues, was a sensation. He had by far the most readers in his life, and he and the serial received a great deal of attention.

A decade and a half later, while living in Barcelona, García Márquez wrote: "February 28, 1955, brought the news that eight crew members of the destroyer *Caldas*, of the Colombian Navy, had fallen overboard and disappeared during a storm in the Caribbean Sea. The ship was sailing from Mobile, Alabama, in the United States, where it had docked for repairs, to the Colombian port of Cartagena, where it arrived two hours after the tragedy. A search for the seamen began immediately, with the cooperation of the U.S. Panama Canal Authority, which performs such functions as military control and other humanitarian deeds in the southern Caribbean."[27] The search went on for four days. Then it was abandoned. A week later, Luis Alejandro Velasco washed ashore on the beaches of northern Colombia. He had survived on a raft for ten days.

The sequence of events was established by the various sources involved. Velasco became a media darling. General Gustavo Rojas Pinilla's government used him as an emblem of courage. The nation was curious about and enchanted by this survivor, and Velasco began to profit financially from his story. He was hired by an agency to sell watches because his own watch didn't malfunction. And he was contracted to promote a line of shoes because, again, his own shoes held up during the ordeal.

Public curiosity about Velasco dwindled. At which point, the sailor showed up on his own accord at *El Espectador*, offering to sell his full story. Everyone was skeptical, mainly because it seemed that the fellow was so hungry for attention that he was capable of inventing anything in order to get it. The survivor's offer was declined. Velasco left and by sheer chance, he and Guillermo Cano were going down the newspaper building's staircase at the same time. They spoke and Cano changed his mind. He asked García Márquez to do an extensive interview with the shipwrecked sailor. Not only was the reporter available, he was known to have a sweet and patient way with interviewees.

As the dialogue between reporter and survivor unfolded, García Márquez realized that what he had was a treasure. He explained: "My first surprise was that this solidly built twenty-year-old, who looked more like a trumpet player than a national hero, had an exceptional instinct for the art of narrative, an astonishing memory and ability to synthesize, and enough uncultivated dignity to be able to laugh at his own story."[28]

He and Velasco met over twenty sessions of six hours each. García Márquez tried to poke holes in his story. He was fascinated by the complexity of the tale, which was "so detailed and so exciting that my only concern was finding readers who would believe it. Not only for that reason but because it seemed fitting, we agreed that the story would be written in the first person and signed by him."[29] Only when the reportage was published in book form was García Márquez's name attached to it.

There were more surprises in stock. At one point, García Márquez asked Velasco to talk about the storm, but the sailor replied that there had been no storm. Subsequently, García Márquez learned that it wasn't a storm that had caused the disaster but heavy winds that tossed the ship's cargo and its eight sailors into the sea. But the ship might have withstood the winds had it not been for the weight of its cargo. What was it carrying? García Márquez discovered that the ship was transporting black market goods: refrigerators, television sets, washing machines, etc. Army ships were not allowed to take such merchandise from the United States to Colombia.

When García Márquez's story was published in *El Espectador*, there was enormous interest. General Rojas Pinilla's government

was initially enthusiastic—until the revelations about the ille-
gal cargo and other embarrassing details began to appear.
The newspaper managed to find some of the other sailors
and asked for permission to print some of the photographs
the sailors had taken with their own cameras. The publication
of those images brought ridicule upon Rojas Pinilla's admin-
istration. The sailor's courage in the struggle against nature
had become, in the public imagination, about contraband and
government corruption. The initial exhilaration had given
place to deceit.

García Márquez was in a tight bind. His life was in jeop-
ardy. To protect him, the newspaper dispatched him to Europe
as a correspondent. In Latin America there is a long tradition
of sending persecuted intellectuals, artists, dissidents, and diplomats abroad. Sometimes these trips are organized hastily. This
one was meticulously planned. García Márquez was already in
Europe when he found out that the offices of *El Espectador* had
been shut down.

García Márquez's story about the shipwrecked sailor was
published as a book by Tusquets in 1970. He said that he
had not read the story in fifteen years and that the request
to bring it out between two covers came from an editor.
"I have never quite understood the usefulness of publishing
it," he stated in the preface, which was entitled "The Story
of This Story." "I find it depressing that the publishers are
not so much interested in the merit of the story as in the
name of the author, which, much to my sorrow, is also that
of a fashionable writer. If it is now published in the form of
a book, that is because I agreed without thinking about it
very much, and I am not a man to go back on his word."[30]
He added: "There's not a single invented detail in the whole
account. That's what's so astonishing. If I had invented that
story I would have said so, and been very proud of it, too. I
interviewed that boy from the Colombian navy—as I explain

in my introduction to the book—and he told me his story in minute detail. As his cultural level was only fair he didn't realize the extreme importance of many of the details he told me spontaneously, and was surprised at my being so struck by them. By carrying out a form of psychoanalysis I helped him remember things—for instance, a seagull he saw flying over his raft—and in that way we succeeded in reconstructing his whole adventure. It came out with a bang! The idea had been to publish the story in five or six installments in *El Espectador* but by about the third of the way there was so much enthusiasm among the readers, and the circulation of the paper had increased so enormously, that the editor said to me, 'I don't know how you're going to manage but you must get at least twenty installments out of this.' So then I set about enriching every detail."[31]

When the English translation by Randolph Hogan was published in 1986, the publisher used García Márquez's complete original title: *The story of a shipwrecked sailor who drifted on a life raft for ten days without food or water, was proclaimed a national hero, kissed by beauty queens, made rich through publicity, and then spurned by the government and forgotten for all time.* García Márquez felt somewhat detached from it, as if the volume had been composed by someone else. Still, it was greeted with enthusiasm. John Updike wrote in the *New Yorker:* "The starved, sun-baked, semi-delirious sailor, at last granted human contact, discovers within himself a primary aesthetic impulse: 'When I heard him [the first man Velasco meets] speak I realized that, more than thirst, hunger, and despair, what tormented me most was the need to tell someone what had happened to me.' Throughout Velasco's narrative we feel the thinness of the difference between life and death—a few feet of heaving ocean separate him from his less lucky shipmates in the confusion after they were swept overboard, and a fragile cork-and-rope raft keeps him afloat, through the black night and burning day, in 'a dense sea filled with strange creatures.' The closeness of the living and the dead is one of García Márquez's themes, but in this journalistic narrative it emerges without morbidity, as a fact among many. The factuality of the real sailor's direct and artless telling bracingly mingles with the beginnings of the writer's 'magic realism.' "[32]

Chapter 4

New Horizons

García Márquez continued writing fiction. In 1956, he published *"Un día después del sábado"* (One Day After Saturday).[1] Increasingly, motifs jumped from a story to a novel and vice versa. For instance, this story connects *Leaf Storm* and *One Hundred Years of Solitude* in its depiction of a plague of dying birds and in the appearance of the Wandering Jew. Alfonso Fuenmayor told critic Harley D. Oberhelman that "the plague of dying birds was suggested to García Márquez by a sentence in Virginia Woolf's *Orlando:* 'Birds froze in mid-air and fell like stones to the ground.'" García Márquez had marked that particular sentence in the margin of his copy of *Orlando,* which was in Fuenmayor's possession.[2]

When García Márquez accepted the *corresponsalía* in Europe in 1955, he was only twenty-eight; his knowledge of the world was extraordinarily limited. Leaving Colombia was a survival mechanism, but, perhaps more important, a stepping stone toward a broader, more cosmopolitan education as a writer.

Paris, in particular, was a magnet. Throughout the second half of the nineteenth century and the beginning of the twentieth, France had been the principal source of artistic and intellectual sustenance in Latin America. Having been under the oppressive influence of a stale Iberian culture until the so-called Age of Independence, which began around 1810, the newly independent republics looked to other foreign powers. In politics, the model was the United States, which, following its secession from England had institutionalized a democratic system of government based on separate but equally important branches of power—the executive, legislative, and judicial. But France was where ideas were discussed in earnest. Rubén Darío and other Modernistas spent time in Paris. The debt they owed to artistic movements such as Symbolism was substantial. Paris became a rite of passage for a long line of Latin American thinkers, poets, novelists, painters, and other artists, from César Vallejo and Vicente Huidobro to Alejo Carpentier and Octavio Paz.

Among them were members of what would become *El Boom:* Julio Cortázar, who escaped Peronism in Argentina; Carlos Fuentes, a much-traveled urban dandy, who saw the French capital as a place where he could start building an international reputation; and Mario Vargas Llosa, who left what he considered "the parochial mores" of Lima to travel, first to Spain, then to Paris. All three belonged to the middle class in their respective countries, and felt the angst of being a subaltern citizen of modernity. Their region of the globe was perceived as backward, exotic, and primitive. In Spanish the term popularized by figures like Franz Fanon, author of *The Wretched of the Earth,* was *subdesarrollado:* underdeveloped.

The ten years after the end of World War II were a period of reconstruction in Europe. A divided, bipolar Germany moved in opposite directions. In the West, the Nuremberg Trials were a public event that attempted to bring some closure to the Nazi atrocities. In 1955, West Germany became a sovereign state and joined the North Atlantic Treaty Organization, known as NATO, while England and France continued to rebuild their infrastructure. The East was rapidly adapting to the

Soviet-style model, implementing a communism that curtailed free speech and individual entrepreneurship. Other countries in the Soviet Bloc—Poland, Hungary, Bulgaria, Czechoslovakia, Lithuania, etc.—had economic systems that celebrated a universal view of "the age of proletariat," while they sought to preserve their distinct cultures. On May 14, 1955, eight communist countries, including the Soviet Union, signed a mutual defense treaty called the Warsaw Pact. It was meant as a counterpart to NATO.

The note published in *El Espectador* regarding García Márquez's departure announced that the first event he would cover as a European correspondent would be the July 18–23, 1955, meeting *"de los cuatro grandes,"* a summit of the four post–World War II powers to be held in Switzerland. The four were the United States, the U.S.S.R., England, and France.

García Márquez's itinerary in Europe has been the subject of debate. Although it appears to have been arranged in Colombia, it probably changed depending on where the news was. Jacques Gilard, who has scrutinized García Márquez's European sojourn, stated that it isn't clear exactly where the writer went and what he did. However, based on the historical records available, it is possible to make an objective approximation.

Before his departure, García Márquez returned to Barranquilla to say good-bye to his friends. From there he flew on El Colombiano, the airline, to Paris, where he traveled to Geneva and on to Rome. He said he wanted to be in Rome just in case "the Pope dies of the hiccups," so he could report on it. Although Pope Pius XII, also known as Hitler's Pope because of his anti-Semitic beliefs, was sick, he wasn't dying. In Italy, García Márquez attended the Venice Film Festival. Having reported for years on the film industry in Colombia, it was his dream to be there. From Venice he probably went to Paris, where he waited until the situation improved in Colombia. For García Márquez—who was still very much a country boy, in spite of his time spent in a number of metropolitan centers—the *aire urbaine* of Paris was alluring.

García Márquez also traveled to Vienna, seemingly en route to Czechoslovakia and Poland. One thing is clear: since his days in the *liceo* of Zipaquirá, García Márquez was obsessed with having a firsthand experience of the Marxist societies of the Soviet Bloc. His teachers at the *liceo* had sparked his curiosity about the utopian societies overseas. He wanted to use his time in Europe to understand those realities. When he was twenty, García Márquez had, for a short while, belonged to a cell of Colombia's Communist Party. He explained his participation in the following terms: "I was more of a sympathizer than a real militant."[3]

That sympathy is the subject of much debate. In 1983, García Márquez was asked by *Playboy* magazine if he was a communist. "Of course not," he replied. "I am not and have never been. Nor have I belonged to *any* political party. Sometimes I have the impression that, in the United States, there is a tendency to separate my writing from my political activities—as if they were opposites. I don't think they are. What happens is that, as an anticolonial Latin American, I take a position that annoys many interests in the United States. And so, simplistically, some people say I am an enemy of the United States. What I'd like to correct are the problems and errors in the Americas as a whole. I would think the same way if I were a U.S. citizen. Indeed, if I *were* a U.S. citizen, I would be even more of a radical, because it would be a matter of correcting the flaws in my own country."[4]

For García Márquez, spending time in Czechoslovakia, Poland, and other communist countries was a self-imposed requirement. Was equality a mere ideal or could it be fully realized as a way of life? And could such a model be applicable to Latin America?

He visited Prague and Warsaw. In the article *"Polonia: verdades que duelen"* (Poland: Painful Truths), García Márquez described his visit in the fall of 1955: "A dense, disheveled, depressed crowd wandered around disoriented through narrow streets...There were large groups of people who spent hours staring at shopping windows of state-owned department stores where new items were being displayed. The items looked old. At any rate, no one was able to afford them, since prices were sky-high." He saw decrepit trolleys making their way in ghostlike city landscapes. García Márquez was impressed by the unpopularity of the ruling class. He described this unease especially among the young. The university, he stated, was a barrel of dynamite that could explode at any minute with the tiniest spark. The critiques of the system were obvious and implacable. He was struck by the influence of the Catholic Church. People looked as if they were lost in a labyrinth of confusion. He heard that the country wasn't ruled by the dictatorship of the proletariat but by the Communist Party, who tried to impose the Soviet model on the country against all odds. His overall impression was that Poland was very far from the idealized socialism he had imagined while in school when he was twenty. Instead, it was a crude and sober reality, with an internal tension that would explode sooner or later. In other words, it wasn't a revolution suited to the country's internal conditions but one that followed a foreign model. *"Un callejón sin salida,"* a dead-end street.[5]

García Márquez moved to Paris in 1956. While there, he learned that General Rojas Pinilla's regime had shut down *El Espectador*. He decided to stay in France to work on his fiction. The decision was cathartic. His exposure to the European lifestyle was enormously rewarding. He needed to experiment, to learn, to test his talent. But he had no money. His newspaper salary, though small, provided for his basic sustenance. Without it, how would he survive? Through his contacts he could find freelance work, but the compensation would be minuscule. Plus, periodicals took a long time to send payment. García Márquez was prepared to be penniless. At least he was single. He didn't have any other mouths to feed. With a deep breath, he jumped into the world of freelancing. He earned some money by returning empty bottles he found in the garbage.

Being destitute sharpened his focus. He endorsed the model of the starving artist, the bohemian who, in order to achieve his dreams, needs first to hit bottom. Thanks to his friends, there was always someone to rely on. García Márquez began writing for *El Independiente,* a new newspaper, but it closed only two months after it was launched. Plinio Apuleyo Mendoza helped him from Venezuela, arranging for him to edit *Elite.* He wrote for *Momento* and other periodicals, often under several pseudonyms, some of which he would later forget. Jacques Gilard believes that García Márquez probably wrote under the pseudonym Gastón Galdós, although he wonders if the pseudonym was truly his. There is, of course, the coincidence of the first letter in both names matching his own. But García Márquez doesn't remember. He told Gilard that sometimes he would rewrite notes by Ramiro MacGregor and in such cases he would use a pseudonym.[6]

García Márquez's desire to understand communism as a possible panacea for Latin America compelled him to return to the Soviet Bloc—specifically, to East Germany—in 1957, this time with his friend Plinio Apuleyo Mendoza, whom he met in Paris that year. The trip lasted from June to September. He published "a series of chronicles" about his journey in the Colombian magazine *Cromos* and in the Venezuelan magazine *Momento.*

García Márquez was ambivalent about his trip. He discovered that the People's Democracies, as the countries in the

Soviet Block used to be described, were no such thing. "They were not authentically socialists nor would they ever be if they followed the path they were on, because the system did not recognize the specific conditions prevailing in each country." His strongest objection was that communism was an early form of globalism that pushed toward homogenization, which erased the differences and uniqueness on which each town, region, and country was built. "It was a system imposed from the outside by the Soviet Union through dogmatic, unimaginative local Communist parties whose sole thought was to enforce the Soviet model in a society where it did not fit."[7]

Unquestionably, the serial *De viaje por los países socialistas* (Journey through the Socialist Bloc) is García Márquez at his least impressive. The reportage is impressionistic but uninformative; it failed to give the reader a sense of the historical, social, political, and cultural aspects of each place. However, García Márquez was pushing the relationship between journalism and literature to new territories.

García Márquez said he was accompanied on his trip by Jacqueline, a French woman with roots in Indochina who was a designer for a French magazine, and Franco, an Italian freelance journalist who wrote for different periodicals in Milan. In truth, he was hiding the identity of two dear Colombian friends: Plinio Apuleyo Mendoza and Apuleyos Mendoza's sister Soledad. They were also accompanied by Luis Villar Bordo, whom García Márquez had met during his student years at the Universidad Nacional de Bogotá. In a Renault 14, they drove from one Germany to the other, passing through Checkpoint Charlie in Berlin. The trip lasted no more than a couple of weeks.

García Márquez and Apuleyo Mendoza then traveled with the dance troupe Delia Zapata to the Ukraine and Russia. García Márquez continued on to Hungary alone. The writer ranged wide and far afield, but his cumulative impressions were depressing.

There was substantial readers' interest in the chronicle of his travels but nothing close to the hoopla García Márquez had generated with his story about Luis Alejandro Velasco. However, twenty years later, in June 1978—as a sign of how his star was still on the ascendance more than a decade after *One Hundred Years of Solitude*—the series was published, albeit without his permission, as the book *De viaje por los países socialistas: 90 días en la "Cortina de Hierro"* by the Colombian publishing house Oveja Negra. As soon as García Márquez found out, he "made the book legal and included it in the volume of my complete works which are sold in popular editions on every street corner in Colombia. I haven't changed a single word." He added, the publication was "not, I imagine, out of any journalistic or political interest, but to show up the supposed contradictions in my personal political development."[8]

Oveja Negra did a first printing of a thousand copies, which sold out immediately in Colombia, the only territory where it was available. (The book still cannot be found elsewhere in the Spanish-speaking world.) In February 1979, there was a second printing of 9,500 copies. In December of the same year, a third printing of 10,500 was released. In May 1980, a fourth printing of 10,500 came out. By November, a fifth printing of 20,000 was issued, followed by a sixth printing of 10,000 in April 1982 and a seventh of 75,000 in December of the same year, when García Márquez received the Nobel Prize. In the parlance of the Spanish-language publishing industry, a printing is called either *una edición* or *una reimpresión.*

If nothing else the sojourn through the Soviet Bloc allowed García Márquez to solidify his commitment to fiction. He realized that the connection between journalism and fiction was mutually beneficial and that they fed one another. Years later, he said, "Fiction has helped my journalism because it has given it literary worth. Journalism has helped my fiction because it has kept me in a close relationship with reality." He added,

"I've always been convinced that my true profession is that of a journalist. What I didn't like about journalism before were the working conditions. Besides, I had to condition my thoughts and ideas to the interests of the newspaper."[9]

In November 1957, García Márquez went to London. One of his objectives was to learn English, which—as his European experience made clear—was crucial for a reporter and even for a novelist. García Márquez stayed in South Kensington, but he didn't get a chance to become fully acquainted with the city. The British capital was expensive. He didn't have much money, so he stayed in his hotel room most of the time. His only income came from his work for *Momento* and *El Independiente*.

Meanwhile, in Colombia, General Rojas Pinilla's regime was overthrown. The Liberal and Conservative parties agreed to alternate in power, in a system called the National Front. At the suggestion of Plinio Apuleyo Mendoza, *Momento* invited García Márquez to come to Caracas to work full-time for them. The magazine offered him a plane ticket, and he arrived in the Venezuelan capital the day before Christmas 1957.

Venezuela, an oil-rich country that borders Colombia, was under military rule. Dictator Marcos Pérez Jiménez had been in office since 1952. The nation's economy was stable but, as is often the case in Latin America, the abuse of power meant the reduction of civil liberties. García Márquez landed in Caracas just as the Pérez Jiménez chapter was coming to a close. In January an uprising took place that led to rioting. In response, Pérez Jiménez fled the country for the United States, which not only had backed his government but had awarded him the U.S. Legion of Merit.

García Márquez was excited to be back in South America. One of the reasons for his return was Mercedes Barcha Prado. He had pledged eternal love to Mercedes four years earlier and he was eager to marry her. She had waited for him all this time. Three months into his Venezuelan stay, he traveled to

Barranquilla, where, at the church of the Perpetuo Sepulcro, the wedding took place on March 21, 1958.

Married life was full of promise. He told Mercedes about his dream of writing a novel called *La casa,* and he swore to her that when he reached the age of forty he would write his masterpiece. He was committed to his dreams, but he needed to support his wife. Thankfully, he was on staff at *Momento*—but not for long. A couple of months later, he and Plinio Apuleyo Mendoza, who was *jefe de redacción,* roughly equilavent to managing editor, resigned from *Momento* in protest after the visit of Richard Nixon, then vice president of the United States, to Caracas, on May 13, 1958. There was rioting in the streets of Caracas, but the periodical wanted to distance itself from those events. *Momento* published an editorial note that claimed that the civil unrest didn't represent the feelings of most Caracas dwellers and that Venezuela and the United States were nations eager to explore their natural connections. Mendoza disagreed with the statement and published the text not as an editorial but as a news piece. This angered the editor in chief, Carlos Ramírez MacGregor, who reprimanded his *jefe de redacción.* Mendoza resigned abruptly and so did García Márquez.

His resignation was a fortuitous event. At the time, García Márquez was looking to concentrate on finishing a series of stories that would become part of the collection *Los funerales de la Mamá Grande* (Big Mama's Funeral); his departure from *Momento* gave him an unexpected six weeks off. He devoted them to *"La viuda de Montiel"* (Montiel's Widow), *"La maravillosa tarde de Baltazar"* (Balthazar's Marvelous Afternoon), and *"Rosas artificiales"* (Artificial Roses). According to Dasso Saldívar, the title story would be written by the middle of the following year in Bogotá.[10] But García Márquez couldn't afford to be unemployed for long.

Again with the support of his friend Plinio Apuleyo Mendoza, he was named *jefe de redacción* at the frivolous magazine *Venezuela Gráfica*. But at least he had a paycheck. He continued writing fiction. He devoted his energy to a novella about a military veteran whose pension was forgotten by the government. The only item of value the Colonel and his wife own is a rooster left behind by their son, whose fate isn't clear but whose memory the couple keeps alive through conversations and by preparing the rooster for an upcoming cockfight. The couple's destitution was a reflection of García Márquez's own financial situation. Entitled *El coronel no tiene quien le escriba* (No One Writes to the Colonel), the novella was first published in *Mito*.

Mercedes gave birth to the couple's first son, Rodrigo, on August 24, 1959. He was baptized by Father Camilo Torres, and Plinio Apuleyo Mendoza was the child's godfather. The couple enjoyed their newborn, who made them feel grounded. Around that time, García Márquez wrote a short story that, in its mythical ambition, opened the door to the Buendía saga: "Big Mama's Funeral," about a larger-than-life female political icon whose death generates much pomp and circumstance. Approximately 5,000 words (in the English translation by Gregory Rabassa), it has the feel of a lengthier narrative. Some critics have suggested that in its scope as well as in the way it conveys the violence at the heart of Colombia's life, the story is proof of the huge step, in terms of quality and maturity, García Márquez took at the end of the fifties. I beg to differ. Although "Big Mama's Funeral" is impressive in the daring manner in which it presents a broad picture of the intersection between the national and the popular realms, I've always felt that it is somewhat stale, even unfocused.

In 1958, a group of guerrilla fighters led by Fidel Castro staged an insurrection in Cuba. They landed secretly in the middle of the night and for the next few months, from the Sierra Maestra, they orchestrated a military campaign that concluded with the taking of Havana at the end of the year. The government of President Fulgencio Batista, which was backed by the United States, was overthrown. A few months later Fidel Castro arrived in the Cuban capital, an event that had enormous repercussions throughout Latin America. In a continent defined by extreme poverty and military dictatorships, hope suddenly materialized in the form of a bearded messianic figure who had previously tried to introduce socialism without success. In his exile in Mexico, Castro had met other revolutionary fighters, including the Argentine doctor Ernesto "Che" Guevara, who eventually joined the struggle for the liberation of Cuba.

According to Plinio Apuleyo Mendoza, he and García Márquez first heard about Fidel Castro in Paris, from Afro-Cuban poet and activist Nicolás Guillén, author of *Sóngoro Cosongo* and *West Indies, Ltd*: "There is a lawyer, *un muchacho medio loco...*" a half-crazy young man.

"Some mornings, from our respective rooms, we would hear the poet's sonorous voice screaming from the street: 'García Márquez! Plinio!' We would stick our heads outside the window (our hotels faced each other) and bellow, in the fog that covered the Rue Cujas, we would see a dark winter jacket and rowdy white hair. They were the poet's. 'The young men engaged in a shootout with Batista. In the very same Presidential Palace!'"[11]

News of Castro's triumph spread quickly throughout the world. Among Latin American intellectuals it was the equivalent of a seismic quake. Like other supporters, García Márquez dreamed of witnessing the transformation firsthand. His wish came true when he and Mendoza were invited to Cuba to witness "Operación Verdad," the public trial of Sosa Blanco, who had been in Batista's entourage and was accused of war crimes. The two Colombian journalists attended the proceedings in a sports arena. The Castro regime quickly established a new news agency, the brainchild of Argentine journalist

Jorge Ricardo Masetti. The hope was that it would break the monopoly on the news held by international agencies. It was called Prensa Latina.

Through his connections in the publishing world, Plinio Apuleyo Mendoza opened the Bogotá office of Prensa Latina. When a large sum of money arrived in his bank account for the new office, he asked García Márquez to join him there.

One of the primary initiatives of Prensa Latina was to set up branches in different parts of the world. García Márquez was offered the opportunity to open and run the Montreal office. He accepted. He traveled to New York City en route to Canada with Mercedes and Rodrigo, but upon arriving in New York (the office was located in Rockefeller Center), it became clear that the office was understaffed, so he stayed. The job description required some travel, and on one occasion he went on assignment to Washington, D.C., to report from the White House.[12]

He and his family lived in a hotel near Fifth Avenue. Those months were defined by his work on the novel *In Evil Hour* and by the Bay of Pigs invasion, ordered by President John F. Kennedy. Initially, García Márquez, who was close to the Cuban regime, was appalled. But the outcome of the invasion— the poor planning by U.S. troops and the Cuban defense of their own sovereignty—brought him tremendous satisfaction.

However, the internal situation in the New York office wasn't a hopeful one, and García Márquez resigned when his boss, Jorge Masetti, was pushed out by the old Stalinist guard. It was a difficult decision because it suggested a parting of ways with the Cuban regime but not a renunciation of its socialist ideals. Years later, he stressed that the decision to leave the agency was the right one: "If [Mendoza and I] had stayed on, with our views, we'd have ended up being slung out with one of those labels on our forehead—counter-revolutionary, imperialist lackey and so on—that the dogmatists of that day used to stick on you." He believed the best thing to do was to move to the sidelines and watch the evolution of the Cuban ideological debate from afar, which is what he did over the years.[13]

This break is important in light of García Márquez's future closeness not only with the Cuban Revolution as ideology and as a system of government but with Fidel Castro as a long-term friend. His view at the time was that Cuba was not a satellite of the Soviet Union. This is an important point. Castro didn't officially define his political relationship with the Kremlin in Moscow until a couple of years after he assumed power in Havana. During his first months in office his loyalties oscillated, even though it was clear that his position toward Washington was nothing if not antagonistic, a clear response to the hostilities initiated by the White House against the Caribbean island. On February 7, 1962, the United States imposed a trade embargo on Cuba. García Márquez perceived the Cuban Revolution of that period to be in a "constant state of emergency" because the United States would not tolerate "an alternative system of government ninety miles off the Florida coast."[14]

With the New York doors closing behind him, García Márquez pondered an invitation from Álvaro Mutis to join him in Mexico City. García Márquez's English was still poor, and he had few contacts in New York. Staying would be difficult. What made the invitation attractive was the growing Mexican movie industry. Mutis knew how passionate his friend was about *el séptimo arte:* filmmaking. But García Márquez didn't leave directly for Mexico City. With two hundred dollars in his pocket, he and his family took a Greyhound bus to the Deep South. He wanted to personally experience the landscape that defined the work of one of his literary idols: William Faulkner.

The landscape of Macondo was taking shape in his imagination. He had begun surveying it in different stories. Carlos

Fuentes once explained the impact of Faulkner on Latin American literature: "So I feel that Faulkner had and has a great lesson for us, and it is not only a formal lesson, of the modern use of the baroque, it is a profound historical lesson on how to face defeat, to admit the tragic possibility in history, it is a profoundly literary lesson, which is the discovery of the novel through the novel, the discovery of the story by telling the story, the discovery of the characters by letting the characters act, all these magnificent lessons which I think had a profound influence on the literature of Latin America."[15] García Márquez agreed, and he wanted to see the inspiration for Yoknapatawpha County.

The two-week trip took place in May 1961. They passed through Montgomery, Alabama, where they spent hours looking for a hotel for the night. The Civil Rights Movement was still in the future, and racism was rampant. Blacks were not its only targets; Mexicans were also persecuted. The family came across signs on windows that read: "No dogs or Mexicans allowed." No one offered to help them, thinking they were Mexicans. From Montgomery, they went to New Orleans and from there to Laredo, Texas. On June 2 they arrived in Mexico City. Ironically, his experience in the Deep South didn't affect the genuine affinity he felt for its people. But the Bay of Pigs invasion was something else entirely. Regarding this, García Márquez would say years later: "The people in the United States are one of the people I most admire in the world. The only thing I don't understand is why people that manage to do so many things so well cannot do better in choosing their presidents."[16]

Chapter 5

Lo real maravilloso

In the sixties, the Argentine journalist Rita Guibert illustrated a frustration with the way Latin Americans were perceived as second-rate citizens. "For example, when at a New York party [if] someone notices my accent I'm usually asked, 'Are you French?' 'No, I'm from Argentina,' I say, watching the charm of foreign glamour fade from their eyes as my social stock takes a plunge. Americans frequently ask me if Argentines speak Portuguese, or—as I was asked by the principal of one of the largest high schools in Westchester—'How big is Rio de Janeiro, the capital of your country?'"[1] From the perspective of Western civilization, the region existed in deep shadow. Octavio Paz said at the time that "the Latin American is a being who has lived in the suburbs of the West, in the outskirts of history." García Márquez raises a similar complaint in a scene in *No One Writes to the Colonel:* "To the Europeans, South America is a man with a mustache, a guitar, and a gun...They don't understand the problem."[2]

To a large extent, this frustration was the engine behind *El Boom*—a Hispanicization of the English term describing "a period of rapid economic expansion." The debate on the origins and proper definition of *El Boom* started in the early sixties. Only once before in the history of Latin American literature had something similar taken place, although the scope of that earlier phenomenon was dramatically narrower. The poet Rubén Darío, born in Metepa, Nicaragua, was barely twenty-two years of age in 1885, when he published his book *Blue . . .*, a collection of poems and prose, and launched the *Modernista* movement. The name is sometimes confused with its English-language equivalent, an aesthetic shared by Virginia Woolf, Ezra Pound, T. S. Eliot, and James Joyce. The Spanish-language *Modernistas* preceded them by about three decades. Led by Darío, their goal was not only to renew Spanish-language poetry but to do it in the Americas, a continent where literature was still the domain of a small elite influenced by European (i.e., Iberian) mores.

Their poetry was a response to French Parnassianism, a style in the nineteenth century, at a time when positivist phi-losophy, which was allergic to metaphysics, stressing instead the importance of factual information acquired through the senses, was in vogue. They were interested in gothic, gro-tesque imagery. Some were travelers and diplomats; others remained in their respective locales. The *Modernistas*—José Martí, Enrique González Martínez, José Asunción Silva, Delmira Agustini, and Leopoldo Lugones, among them—were read as "Latin Americans" for the first time, if only in the Iberian Peninsula, where a few intellectuals responded with appreciation and others with disdain. For many, though, the movement never quite coalesced; it remained a foggy enter-prise. What was the revolution about? What were its principal concerns? How did it achieve its objectives? In 1918, when the movement was way past its prime, Miguel de Unamuno com-plained: "I don't exactly know what this business of *Modernistas* and *Modernismo* is. Such diverse and opposing things are given these names that there is no way to reduce them to a common category."[3]

In spite of the *Modernistas*, the idea of the Americas as a unified cultural front remained a distant dream. It wasn't until the sixties that things began to change. It's essential to situate the shaping of *One Hundred Years of Solitude* and its author in the literary landscape of the time. After World War II, the novel as a literary genre was in a depressed state. The military campaigns that swept Europe, killing millions of people, and the machineries of death such as the one organized by Nazi Germany in labor, concentration, and annihilation camps had pushed the population of the continent to realize that the post-industrial society, armed with sophisticated technological devices, had reached a dead end. The proletarian regime in the Soviet Union and the bloc of countries in Central and Eastern Europe that had joined the Russians, mostly by coercion, in embracing a Marxist-Leninist philosophy, made fiction an instrument of politics. The style of so-called Social Realism forced writers to transform the novel into a means to educate people about the class struggle and the evils of a bourgeois society.

While Stalinism reigned unabated in the Soviet Union, the West read the works of Franz Kafka, Marcel Proust, James Joyce, and others. Kafka's novels *The Metamorphosis, The Trial,* and *The Castle* were cautionary tales about the evils of a pervasive government bureaucracy and the suffering of a middle class trapped by authoritarianism. On the other side of the spectrum, Proust's multivolume *À la recherche du temps perdu* (In Search of Lost Time), brilliant in its use of introspection, was an example of a self-serving, narcissistic genre. Proust didn't seem to care about plot. As the latest practitioner of an art that focused on the human experience, he appeared to have forgotten a crucial player in the literary equation: the reader. His novel was described as indulgent, hyperpsychological, and individualistic to a fault.

Joyce's novel *Ulysses* was not about reality but about language. A retelling of the *Odyssey* through a day in the life of

Dublin as seen through the eyes of a young Irishman, Stephen Dedalus; a Jewish antihero, Leopold Bloom; and Bloom's unsatisfied wife, Molly, Joyce's narrative was an extraordinary example of the novel pushed to its extremes. In *Finnegans Wake*, Joyce took the novel further. *Finnegans Wake* was about nothing; it was about itself. Successors like Samuel Beckett, who was Joyce's student, assistant, and friend, followed the same path.

By the time García Márquez began publishing books such as *No One Writes to the Colonel*, both Europe and the novel, which is a distinctly European literary genre, appeared to have run their course. As if forced to revitalize the novel, a fresh chorus of voices began to be heard from what was considered the periphery of Western civilization: Africa, Asia, the South Pacific, and Latin America. For centuries, these parts of the globe had been deemed secondary, reactors to rather than producers of culture. The renewal of the novel as a genre took place precisely in these regions because they were unencumbered by the guilt that resulted from the military destruction in the Old World. There was a sense of freedom and inventiveness that was conducive to a literary rebirth.

Participants of that renewal were Nadine Gordimer in South Africa, Chinua Achebe in Nigeria, Kenzaburō Ōe in Japan, Naguib Mahfouz in Egypt, Amos Oz in Israel, Jorge Luis Borges in Argentina, Juan Rulfo in Mexico, and the writers of *El Boom*, with García Márquez as the prime example. To some literary historians, this was "the return of the savage," a movement by subordinate artists in an effort to take control of their own destinies. Others describe this narrative effulgence as "the rise of the postcolonial mentality." What characterized the collective effort was the conviction that the concept of "Western civilization" was too narrow, too confining. The world was more open and elastic, its talent was no longer concentrated in a single geographic spot. It was democratic, egalitarian, and spread out across nations.

The emergence of new narrative voices forced readers to realize that the novel was a literary genre up for grabs. Writers from different countries could appropriate it and adapt it to their needs by employing a new language, a new style, a different way of telling stories.[4] The concept of originality was redefined. It now included the infusion of folklore from other traditions. Equally important was the emergence of a new reader, for the novel was no longer European property. Nations all over the world used the genre to explore local motifs. Those explorations were targeted to a local audience as much as they were destined for a global readership.

It would be foolish to suggest that novels had not been published anywhere else but Europe until then. The opposite is true. In Latin America, the genre had made some headway in the nineteenth century with works such as José Joaquín Fernández de Lizardi's *The Itching Parrot* and Domingo Faustino Sarmiento's *Facundo: or, Civilization and Barbarism*. Those novels were clearly designed as tools to meditate on individual and collective concerns, such as poverty in urban centers, the role of minorities, and gender relations. But these books were generally derivative in their approach, closely imitating European models. The new post-war literature was far less dependent on foreign ideas. Although it used universal archetypes, it had assimilated the European heritage in a way that allowed for freedom to create in accordance with the writer's own milieu.

Two major factors in the success of *El Boom,* and of García Márquez in particular, were the introduction of literary agents to Latin America, and, through them, the idea of a continental literature that could reach far and wide through translation. It would be impossible to imagine García Márquez's career without Carmen Balcells. A Catalan with offices in Barcelona, Balcells had worked as an unsuccessful theater administrator, among other jobs, before joining the exiled Hungarian novelist Vintilă Horia when he opened a literary agency. It was doing quite poorly until Carlos Barral, a flamboyant literary editor at the publishing house Seix Barral, asked Balcells—also known, because of her large size, as *Mamá Grande* (Big Mama), after García Márquez's character, and as Female Agent 007—to sell foreign rights for his authors. As Mario Vargas Llosa once put it in a tribute to Balcells in *El País*, it was a decisive moment not only for her but for the publishing industry in the Spanish-speaking world, and through negotiations, the industry on the international level. At various points, she represented Vargas Llosa, García Márquez, Camilo José Cela, Carlos Fuentes, and Alfredo Bryce Echenique.

According to Vargas Llosa, at the end of the sixties, when he was teaching at King's College, part of the University of London, Balcells showed up one day in his London apartment and told him: "Quit your teaching immediately. You have to devote yourself exclusively to writing." He replied that he had a wife and two children and didn't want them to starve. Balcells asked what his yearly salary was. He responded that it was around five hundred dollars. "I will give you that amount, starting at the end of this month. Leave London and install yourself in Barcelona, which is cheaper." Vargas Llosa followed her instructions to much success. He lived in Catalonia's capital for the next few years, describing those as the happiest of his life.[5]

It was through Carmen Balcells's agency that *El Boom* became a global phenomenon. Several authors (Vargas Llosa for *The Green House* and Guillermo Cabrera Infante for *Three Trapped Tigers*) won the Biblioteca Breve prize, which Barral managed. Through Balcells's efforts, this translated into a huge publicity campaign in the Spanish-speaking world. Bookselling in Latin America was, until then, defined by national boundaries. The major literary capitals were, in order of importance, Buenos Aires and Mexico City. Buenos Aires was the home of publishing houses Editorial Losada and

Editorial Sudamericana. Self-described as a European city in the Southern Cone, it prided itself on having a high-brow literary culture; its periodicals, such as *La Nación* and *Sur*—under the support and editorship of its founder, Victoria Ocampo—included literary supplements. It was in *Sur* where Borges published some of his most influential essays and stories and where national, continental, and foreign authors sought to have their work in print. Ocampo sponsored translations of Waldo Frank, Oscar Wilde, Ranbindranath Tagore, and Virginia Woolf. Exiles from the Spanish Civil War who had arrived in Buenos Aires contributed generously to maintaining a sophisticated literary discourse.

There was no transcontinental distribution strategy, so books published in Buenos Aires weren't readily available in other parts of Latin America. Books that enjoyed good word of mouth were passed on from one person to another; that was the only way devotees of a particular author could get a copy of a recently published novel or collection of stories. The same was true in Mexico City. There were publishing houses such as Fondo de Cultura Económica, created by historian Daniel Cosío Villegas in 1934 as an inexpensive venture to make the nation's classics available to the masses. There were elite houses such as Ediciones Era, founded by exiles of the Spanish Civil War. But Mexican books rarely traveled beyond the nation's borders.

As a publishing center, Cuba was a distant third. The island was an intellectual hotbed during the nineteenth and early parts of the twentieth century, and attracted exiles from the Spanish Civil War who were involved in publishing. The island's prime geographic location in the Caribbean Sea and its value as a commercial getaway for the Americas had earned it the nickname "the pearl of the Antilles." It may have been smaller than those of Mexico and Argentina, but in the sixties Cuba's publishing industry received the strong backing of

Castro's regime. It undertook a mammoth effort to make books available to everyone at cheap prices, a project that was burdened by heavy censorship; the Communist Party wanted only a certain type of material made available to the population. Cuban books didn't travel abroad.

All this to say that the Spanish-speaking world, from the Iberian peninsula to the Pampas, was a fragmented market. Readers in one city didn't have access to titles published in another. It was a reflection of the limited impact of books, and of the printed media, in the Spanish-speaking world. Balcells changed that. Through publicity and a trans-Atlantic marketing strategy, Balcells made the writers of *El Boom* a phenomenon throughout the Spanish-speaking world. This, in large part, was the result of her success in selling foreign rights to New York, Paris, Rome, and other cultural capitals.

In *No One Writes to the Colonel,* a curious dialogue about censorship takes place. The Colonel waits for the mail in front of his friend the doctor's office, and the two have a conversation about Europe, its wellbeing, and how easy it is to get there by boat. At one point the postman opens the mailbag but finds nothing for the Colonel, only a bunch of newspapers addressed to the doctor. Disappointed, the Colonel doesn't even bother to read the headlines. The passage reads: "He made an effort to control his stomach. 'Ever since there's been censorship, the newspapers talk only about Europe,' he said. 'The best thing would be for the Europeans to come over here and for us to go to Europe. That way everybody would know what's happening in their own countries.'"[6]

Balcells achieved something along the same lines. By selling world rights to works by Latin American writers, she generated, in their respective countries, the feeling that they needed to be read because in the major cultural capitals they were being applauded as talented representatives of their respective national idiosyncrasies. Balcells had been García Márquez's agent since November 1925. In 1965, Balcells and her husband, Luis Palomares, visited García Márquez in Mexico City. She had just come from a tour of the United States, where she had stopped in New York City to visit various publishers, including Cass Canfield Jr. at Harper & Row. Given the solid reviews García Márquez's work had received everywhere, Balcells managed to get a four-book contract with Harper & Row for a total of $1,000. She was eager to meet García Márquez for the first time and give him the wonderful news. García Márquez greeted her with enthusiasm but told her: *"Es un contrato de mierda."* He had worked intensively on those four books. Getting only $1,000 was ridiculous to him. However, he did sign a contract, dated July 7, 1965, with Luis Vincens as a witness, authorizing Balcells's agency to represent him in all foreign languages for 150 years.[7]

El Boom was greeted with an uproar in different corners of the Spanish-speaking world. Was it a legitimate showcase of talent? Or was it a publicity-driven campaign devised by a savvy Barcelona agent? Wherever they went, the writers became targets of debate. In his memoir, *The Boom in Spanish-American Literature: A Personal History,* first published in Spanish in 1972, José Donoso, the author of *Coronation* and *The Obscene Bird of Night* and himself a member of *El Boom,* describes how, in spite of the hoopla, no author that was part of the movement was able to make ends meet exclusively from the royalties. With the exception of *One Hundred Years of Solitude,* Donoso writes, "I do not believe that the author's rights of any Latin American writer can justifiably be called 'substantial.' On the contrary, the life of *El Boom* writers is and has been rather difficult and their greatest struggle is to steal a few hours for writing from the work that grants them a modest subsistence."[8]

El Boom attracted the most publicity not through García Márquez, who in spite of the critical accolades was a rather opaque author, but through Carlos Fuentes. It was thanks to

Fuentes that the "legend of luxury" was born. Fuentes "embodied for the devouring eyes of the writers of an entire continent
that triumph, that fame, that power, even that cosmopolitan 'luxury' which from the isolated Latin American capitals
seemed impossible to obtain," Donoso wrote. "He was the first
to handle his works through literary agents, the first to have
friendships with the important writers of Europe and North
America—James Jones loans him his apartment in a famous
hotel on the Ile-St. Louis; André Pieyre de Mandiargues and
William Styron receive him as a friend—the first to be considered a novelist of the first rank by North American critics,
the first to realize the magnitude of what was happening in
the Spanish American novel of his generation, and, generously
and chivalrously, the first to make it known. His flamboyant
character colored and gave shape to the phenomenon itself as
viewed by a growing public. But even for Fuentes, who, outside of having his own income, which he supplemented with
his work for publishing houses and movie studios, things have
not been as easy as it appears, not even in that first moment of
the Boom, when he embodied it and really could say: *'Le Boom
c'est moi.'* He had never had the fame, the true fame of a popular novelist beyond the range of the Spanish language, despite
Mademoiselle telling its readers: *Hâtez-vous, Mesdames, connaissez
Fuentes.* When he arrived for the first time at the offices of
Gallimard, his publisher in France, to ask to meet the director
who had just bought his first novel, the secretary asked him
for his name and he gave it to her. The secretary's look continued to be inquisitive and disconcerted as if she were waiting
for clarification which Fuentes hastened to provide: *'Je suis un
romancier mexicain.'* In the presence of something so incredible,
the secretary could not restrain a *'Sans blague...!'*"[9]

The emergence of *El Boom* was immediately linked to the
style of magic realism (also known as magic*al* realism), which
has since been in fashion globally. It wasn't just that Latin

American writers such as García Márquez were the new kids on the block, it was that their style appeared to be unique: a blend of exoticism, magical thinking, and sexual exuberance. They often set their plots in humid jungles.

The pressure on the writers of *El Boom* was enormous. The Yale critic Emir Rodríguez Monegal put it this way: "Jacques Vaché was right: 'Nothing kills a man more than having to represent a country.' With Latin American writers, the burden was even greater. It matters little in what part of the vast continent they were born. Their readers (foreign as well as national) expect them to represent Latin America. As they read their works they ask: Are they Latin American enough? Is it possible to detect in their works the pulse of the heart, the murmur of the plains, the creeping of ferocious tropical insects, or similar clichés? Why must they always talk about Paris, London, or New York (or Moscow or Peking) instead of talking about their quaint hamlets, their endemic dictators, their guerrillas?" Rodríguez Monegal added: "The Latin American writer has had to prove he is Latin American before proving he is a writer. Who would think of asking Pound to be more North American and less Provençal? Who would complain that Nabokov has left out the silence of the vast Russian steppes in his novels? Why doesn't anyone attack Lawrence for having dared to write a novel called *Kangaroo?* But Latin American writers are always invited to prove their origin before they are asked to show their skills. In dealing with them, criticism seems more preoccupied with geographical and historical than with literary matters."[10]

This argument developed by Rodríguez Monegal stresses the unevenness of global culture up until the sixties. Before the time, the sense was that only Europe, enamored with its own logocentrism, could produce literary works of high caliber. This resulted in a condescending approach to anything that came from other regions of the world. Art that came from anywhere else was seen as an anthropological artifact: an item reflecting the metabolism of a bizarre civilization. Rodríguez Monegal suggests "a new curiosity about forms of culture based on other assumptions and values; the awareness (rather late, to be sure) that even within the Western fold there had long existed minorities who did not share in whiteness of skin, the Christian faith, or capitalistic affluence; the related realization that from its very beginnings the West itself had survived and prospered through the assimilation of alien cultures; the re-emergence of China and the Arab world as powers to be reckoned with—all these factors have helped to abolish the rather naïve image of a unified Western culture, happily autonomous and self-sufficient."[11]

The term "magic realism" has attached itself to García Márquez like a parasite. The signature mix of exoticism, magic, and the grotesque that García Márquez employs doesn't come from the world of soap operas. The category has achieved such ubiquity and elasticity as to become meaningless. For a while, it denoted an attempt to blur the boundary between fact and fiction, between the natural and the supernatural. But its current use is chaotic: it is as useful in cataloging García Márquez's second-rate successors, such as Isabel Allende, Laura Esquivel, and others, as it is in understanding Franz Kafka's exposé of the middle class in *The Metamorphosis,* Lewis Carroll's perversely innocent *Alice in Wonderland,* Salman Rushdie's baroque hodgepodge of dreams and nationalism in *Midnight's Children,* Naguib Mahfouz's labyrinthine novels about Cairo, and Toni Morrison's phantasmagoric meditation on slavery in *Beloved.* They have all been linked to magic realism, with varying degrees of success.

The first to use the term "magic realism" was the German art critic Franz Roh in his book *Nach-Expressionismus, Magischer Realismus: Probleme der neuesten Europäischen Malerei.*[12] He used it to refer to the pictorial output of the Postexpressionist period, beginning around 1925. Roh described the way the artists' innovations pushed beyond the limits of Expressionism and showed "an exaggerated preference for fantastic, extraterrestrial, remote objects." Roh's essay was translated into Spanish and published in Madrid in 1927 in José Ortega y Gasset's magazine *Revista de Occidente*. The impact of the piece in the Spanish-speaking world is subject to debate. It was certainly read by the intellectual elite on the Iberian peninsula, but Ortega y Gasset's magazine had only a minuscule circulation across the Atlantic Ocean. To what extent it was read in cultural capitals like Mexico City and Buenos Aires is impossible to assess.

Alejo Carpentier, in the prologue to his novel *El reino de este mundo* (The Kingdom of This World, 1949), which he also included in his collection *Tientos y diferencias* (Insinuations and Differences, 1964), wrote: "Toward the end of 1943, I had the good fortune to be able to visit the kingdom of Henri Christophe—the poetic ruins of Sans-Souci, the massive citadel of La Ferrière, impressively intact despite lightning bolts and earthquakes—and to acquaint myself with the still Norman-style Cap-Haitien (the Cap Français of the former colony) where the street lined with long balconies leads to the cut-stone palace inhabited once upon a time by Pauline Bonaparte." Carpentier attacked European artists for being unable to understand the complexity of the New World. "We should note that when André Masson tried to draw the forest on the island of Martinique, with the incredible entangling of its plants and the obscene promiscuity of certain fruits, the marvelous truth of the subject devoured the painter, leaving him virtually impotent before the empty page. And it had to be a painter from America, the Cuban Wilfredo Lam, who showed us the magic of tropical vegetation and the uncontrolled Creation of Forms in our nature—with all its metamorphosis and symbiosis—in monumental paintings whose expression is unique in contemporary art."

Magic realism was perceived by critics to be a response to Europe's realist literary mores, where the distinction between what is real and what is imagined, between day-to-day consciousness and madness, was at the core of the intellectual revolution known as the Enlightenment. Works like *Don Quixote* tested the limits of this view but did not dismantle it. For some historians, the impulse was "to reestablish contact with traditions temporarily eclipsed by the mimetic constraints of nineteenth- and twentieth-century realism." For them, in a work of magic realism "the supernatural is not a simple or obvious matter, but it is an ordinary matter, an everyday occurrence— admitted, accepted, and integrated into the rationality and materiality of literary realism. Magic is no longer quixotic madness, but normative and normalizing. It is a simple matter of the most complicated sort."[13]

Carpentier described how, during his visit to Haiti, he stumbled upon something he called the *real marvelous—lo real maravilloso*. "But I also realized that the presence and authority of the real marvelous was not a privilege unique to Haiti but the patrimony of all the Americas, where, for example, a census of cosmogonies is still to be established. The real marvelous is found at each step in the lives of the men who inscribed dates on the history of the Continent and who left behind names still borne by the living: from the seekers after the Fountain of Youth or the golden city of Manoa to certain rebels of the early times or certain modern heroes of our wars of independence, those of such mythological stature as Colonel Juana Azurduy." For Carpentier the break brought by *lo real maravilloso* was with religion. He wrote: "the sensation of the marvelous presupposes a faith. Those who do not believe in saints cannot be cured by the miracles of saints, in the same way that those who are not Quixotes cannot enter, body and soul, the world of Amadis de Gaula or Tirant lo Blanc." Carpentier added: "Because of the virginity of its landscape, because of its formation, because of its ontology, because of the Faustian presence of the Indian and the Black, because of the Revelation its recent discovery constituted, because of the fertile racial mixtures it favored, the Americas are far from having used up their wealth of mythologies."[14]

Carpentier used the term again in his essay "The Baroque and the Marvelous Real," a lecture given at the Caracas Athenaeum on May 22, 1975, and included in his book *La novela hispanoamericana en vísperas de un nuevo siglo.* In it, Carpentier offered a more sustained literary analysis of the style in Latin American literature. Other intellectuals such as Arturo Uslar Pietri employed the term. In the United States, critics such as Ángel Flores debated it. Flores suggested that it derived from Kafka's vision. Some argue that the style originated with Borges and Rulfo but others disagree. The critic Luis Leal wrote: "Magical realism is, more than anything else, an attitude toward reality that can be expressed in popular or cultural forms, in elaborate or rustic styles, in close or open structures. What is the attitude of the magic realist toward reality? . . . the writer confronts reality and tries to untangle it, to discover what is mysterious in things, in life, in human acts."[15]

There's another, chronologically older component to magic realism that needs to be acknowledged: surrealism. André Breton, during a trip to Mexico in 1938 that was commissioned by the French government, became infatuated with the country's primitivism. He met the political activist and Russian exile Leon Trotsky, with whom he coauthored *Pour un art révolutionnaire indépendent,* and whose circle of friends included the muralist Diego Rivera and his wife, Frida Kahlo. Breton was amazed by the way, in festivities such as the Day of the Dead, the living and the deceased coexisted in the Mexican practice of religion. More than a decade before, in

1924, he had defined surrealism in a manifesto as pure psychic autonomism. He believed that autonomism, a way to let the subconscious free, was present in Mexican culture. Breton developed the concept of *le hazard objectif,* objective chance, juxtaposing coherence and chaos. What made the reality he encountered on his trip to Mexico so enchanting was precisely the role chaos played in it.

As Breton was making his statements, psychoanalysis was gaining professional ground in Europe. Sigmund Freud's theories—of sexual forces defining a person's life since childhood and of dreams as a window to the unconscious, a means by which the internal struggle emerges into the realm of awareness—had at first been rejected as unfounded. But after World War I, these theories became fashionable among members of the middle, upper-middle, and upper classes in Austria, England, France, and Germany. The surrealist revolution in art was an extension of this awareness. As Freud himself had pointed out, art itself was an expression of the hidden, irrational, sexual messages kept in check by reason. Breton, in his Surrealist manifesto, explored the idea of the marvelous along these lines, making it synonymous to that which is strange, unexpected, dreamlike, and even macabre. "All that is marvelous is beautiful," he stated, and, "only the marvelous is beautiful." He was infatuated with writers such as Jonathan Swift and Edgar Allan Poe, whose work, in his view, gave artistic expression to animalistic forces within the human mind. In Breton's opinion, these authors gave free rein to their inner child, revealing the impulsive, uncivilized components of human life.

Although Breton visited only Mexico on his trans-Atlantic journey (in his *L'Anthologie de l'humour noir,* published in 1940, he made references to his trip, direct and otherwise), his vision, metonymically, was taken to encompass Latin America as a whole.

García Márquez's international audience immediately acknowledged the surrealist component in his magic realism. Tales like *"La increíble y triste historia de la cándida Eréndira y de su abuela desalmada"* (The Incredible and Sad Tale of Innocent Erendira and Her Heartless Grandmother, also known in its abbreviated form as Innocent Eréndira), about a girl whose grandmother forces her to prostitute herself with hundreds of men in order to pay back a debt she owes her, were read as parables of a misconstrued, primitive sexuality that still existed in Latin American. Similar moral judgments were made about stories such as "A Very Old Man with Enormous Wings" and *"El ahogado más hermoso del mundo"* (The Handsomest Drowned Man in the World), both published in the same collection as "Innocent Eréndira." (In English, the former originally appeared in *New American Review*, edited by Harper & Row editor Ted Solotaroff, and the latter in *Playboy*.) These pieces, which could be read as either reverses or extensions of the other (unlike García Márquez's other stories, these two are subtitled: "A Tale for Children"), explore manhood and the male body. In the first, the local community reacts to the sudden appearance of an angel of advanced age who has fallen from the sky; in the second, a similar premise is explored as a giant washes up from the sea.

They were understood as meditations on religion in a landscape where Christianity had assimilated elements from the indigenous cultures, creating a hybrid in which monotheism and idolatry coexisted. García Márquez frequently inserts in his cast of characters a priest who acts as the official spokesman of the Church but is viewed by the townspeople as untrustworthy—as either more interested in his own advancement or representative of foreign powers whose influence is only symbolic. These stories were also seen as a commentary on political corruption in a region defined by violent civil wars and the inability to become fully democratic.

The publication of *One Hundred Years of Solitude* in 1967 almost single-handedly turned magic realism into a fashion. The prohibition against incest serves as the novel's leitmotif. The Buendías attempt to avoid it in a clan where cousins are physically attracted to one another, where the same prostitute satisfies the sexual needs of various generations of family men, where beauty defines certain women to such an extent as to make them celestial. *One Hundred Years of Solitude* was proof that Breton was right in his theory of Latin America as a region where the marvelous is synonymous with the bizarre and where unstoppable sexual impulses are allowed to run wild. García Márquez's saga also supported Franz Roh's assumption: Macondo on Colombia's Caribbean coast did not share the mores of the industrialized nations of Europe and the United States. Macondo was defined by exaggerated, fantastical features, such as the epidemic of insomnia that afflicts it at one point, with amnesia as a side effect, the furious rainstorms that sweep it, the unexpected descent of millions of butterflies, and so on. Even the daily noon arrival of a yellow train into town seems strange.

Just like the strange events in Lewis Carroll's *Alice in Wonderland* and Kafka's *The Metamorphosis*, these happenings are presented as nothing out of the ordinary. They may be abrupt, macabre, and magical to the unaccustomed reader, who may view them as childlike, primitive, ritualistic, and the stuff of myth, but to the people of Macondo they are perfectly normal. Therein lies García Márquez's true contribution. *One Hundred Years of Solitude* is written in a matter-of-fact way. The omniscient, third-person narrator isn't surprised by the plot. The plot unfolds like stories in the Bible: in a direct, noninterpretative, straightforward fashion. In Carpentier's words, magic realism was a different attitude toward reality: it portrayed its reality as normal.

Although it's clear that critics had known about the concept of magic realism for some time, setting the stage for the reception of García Márquez's masterpiece, it is important to point out that he did not write his novel with that in mind. There is no record of him having read any of the essays I've discussed in this chapter. He wasn't a member of the obsessed literati (and never would be), who anxiously followed intellectual debates in literary supplements. There's a strong anti-intellectual quality to García Márquez's way of thinking, and he certainly did not write to satisfy other people's aesthetic needs. The mythical world of Macondo is authentic precisely because it is representative of his vision of the world.

One can argue that García Márquez himself had trained his readers. An example is *In Evil Hour,* which served as a preview of his future capabilities, although its provocative plot isn't successfully executed. It reads like a failed attempt at building the infrastructure of the large, ambitious theater of possibilities—and impossibilities—that Macondo would become approximately a decade later. Set in a small Colombian town, the narrative explores the reaction, both private and public, to the sudden appearance of mysterious lampoons posted everywhere that articulate in images and words the rumors about the political authorities and important events. There's a Freudian undercurrent in the novel: the posters serve as an outlet for the collective thoughts, both secret and unconscious, of the population.

Like other pieces in García Márquez's *opera prima,* there are references in *In Evil Hour* to places and characters in the author's later magnum opus, such as a passing comment about Colonel Aureliano Buendía visiting the fictional town. It reads, "on his way to Macondo to draw up the terms of surrender in the last civil war, [Colonel Buendía] had slept on the balcony one night during a time when there weren't any towns for many leagues around."[16] Gregory Rabassa had an immediate, instinctual reaction to *In Evil Hour.* He thought it was a little gem, although he didn't see it as a foreshadowing of García

Márquez's masterpiece. "There are those who say that the town resembles Macondo," Rabassa later wrote, "but I doubt that García Márquez fostered any such feelings for his magical creation. It may be that he was showing us the dark side of paradise in more strident terms."[17]

Chapter 6

The Silver Screen

In early June 1961, García Márquez, Mercedes, and their almost-two-year-old Rodrigo arrived in Mexico City. He was in his mid-thirties, with just $100 in his pocket, the remnants of a sum Plinio Apuleyo Mendoza had wired to him. To support the family, García Márquez started working for a couple of advertising agencies, among them J. Walter Thompson. In the words of a journalist who met him at the time, he was "stocky, but light on his feet, with a bristling mustache, a cauliflower nose, and many fillings in his teeth. He wears an open sport shirt, faded blue jeans, and a bulky jacket flung over his shoulders."[1]

People were impressed by his unpretentiousness. In an interview, he was described thus: "he talks fast, snatching thoughts as they cross his mind, winding and unwinding them like paper streamers, following them in one end and out the other, only to lose them before he can pin them down. A casual tone with a deep undertow suggests he is making a strategy of negligence. He has a way of eavesdropping on himself, as if he were trying to overhear bits of a conversation in the next room. What matters is what is left unsaid."[2]

El De Efe, as the city was known (after its acronym for *Distrito Federal*), was an exciting cultural capital. With a population of approximately four million people, it was brewing with all types of business deals. Barely two decades after the end of the *campensino* revolution—the first of its kind in the twentieth century, prior even to its Bolshevik counterpart in Russia—the populist president Lázaro Cárdenas, who had promised to give Mexicans what "rightfully belonged to them," nationalized the oil industry and formed a state-run company called PEMEX.

That was in 1938, and the uproar that ensued pushed the nation's markets to an impasse. But Cárdenas's decision resulted in the so-called *el milagro mexicano,* the Mexican Miracle, a period of economic bonanza that lasted four decades, from 1940 to 1980. A single party was in power, the Partido Revolucionario Institucional, known as P.R.I. Although it ruled with an iron fist, a democratic atmosphere prevailed (freedom of expression, openness to foreign investment, a thriving print, radio, and television media, and a multi-party system). However, the presidential election, which came up every six years, was always won by the handpicked P.R.I. candidate.

The city was defined by its cosmopolitanism. In the thirties *El De Efe* was a safe haven for refugees and exiles from the Spanish Civil War, who flocked to Mexico in hordes. Their presence redefined education, media, and publishing. During the early years of World War II, Mexico, although it was neutral, deployed a small battalion to fight in the European front, the *Escuadrón 201* (201st Air Fighter Squadron). It was attached to the U.S. Army Air Forces, which was engaged in the liberation of the Philippine island of Luzon in 1945. Rivalries and disillusionment in Russia and elsewhere brought Leon Trotsky and photographers Henri Cartier-Bresson and Tina Modotti, to Mexico. Some joined the communist circle of artists including Diego Rivera and his wife, Frida Kahlo, José Clemente Orozco, and David Alfaro Siqueiros. Their relationships highlighted the intersection of politics and culture, which defined the age. In 1945 the city welcomed other types of émigrés, from Jews who had survived the concentration camps to Russian, French, Italian, and German activists and intellectuals seeking a better environment.

Some time after García Márquez arrived in the Mexican capital, he received the news that one of his literary role models, Ernest Hemingway, had committed suicide, in Ketchum, Idaho, by shooting himself in the head with a shotgun. It was July 2, 1961, and Hemingway had been about to turn sixty-two.

What García Márquez most admired in Hemingway was his succinct, almost telegraphic narrative style, which had been inspired by popular crime fiction dime novels. He appreciated the way the American writer explored the crossroads of literature and history, his passion for reporting (Hemingway had started his career as a journalist), his readiness to use his war experience in his fiction, and his exploration of violence, overt and tacit, in human relationships. García Márquez had not only imitated Hemingway's style, he had closely followed his career. Upon hearing the news of his death, he wrote the essay "A Man Has Died a Natural Death," published in *México en la Cultura,* the literary supplement of the newspaper *Novedades,* in which he argued that those who perceived Hemingway as a pulp author of the type linked to B-movies would be proven wrong by time, for Hemingway would eclipse so-called "major" writers.

García Márquez's reference to B-movies wasn't arbitrary. The cinema was one of his favorite pastimes and an artistic form that became an essential outlet for his talent. What had attracted him to *El De Efe* was an opportunity to fulfill his dream of writing for the screen. García Márquez had seen numerous Mexican comedies as well as high-brow art house releases. The city was the epicenter of a magnificent movie industry whose productions were enthusiastically received in Spain, Latin America, the Caribbean, and even the United States. Hollywood stars, directors, and cameramen came to visit. The city was a magnet for European exiles, particularly from Spain.

Época de oro, the golden age of Mexican cinema, spanned from 1935 to 1960. World War II had crippled the film industries in Europe and the United States. Looking to take advantage of a market hungry for entertainment but incapable of satisfying the demand, the Mexican cinematic boom embarked on an effort to produce quality dramas that would not only attract audiences in the Spanish-speaking world but around the globe. Production costs were relatively inexpensive. The country had stellar actors and directors, as well as entrepreneurial producers eager to invest their money while exploring different horizons. Plus, modernity was fundamentally changing the way Mexican society behaved, a transformation that resulted in a plethora of stories about the struggle to accommodate to the new mores.

One of the oldest movie studios, Estudios Churubusco, which opened in 1945, was located in *El De Efe.* Its black-and-white films were produced at astonishing speed but with artistic integrity. The subject matter ranged from ranchero life, the cruelty and confusion of urban life, Catholic fervor in the countryside (During the *Cristero* uprising, a war was fought at the end of the twenties as a side effect of the *campesino* revolution. For some it was an anti-revolution, a response to the anticlerical articles of the Constitution of 1917.), to military recruitment during the Mexican Revolution and immigration to the United States. Fernando de Fuentes directed *Allá en el rancho grande* and *Vámonos con Pancho Villa.* Actors such as Pedro Infante, Jorge Negrete, Dolores del Río, and María Félix were courted by numerous production companies.

The *Época de oro* established a new aesthetic. Mexico was portrayed as a land of contrasts, a nation where modernity coexisted with poverty, pre-Columbian traditions, and raw emotions. Actors depicted the poor in an unapologetic, even melodramatic fashion, exploring the labyrinthine paths of the nation's collective identity. Gorgeous mestizo faces and an exuberant natural environment were showcased on the silver screen, mesmerizing audiences. This aesthetic was created, to a large extent, by cinematographers such as Gabriel Figueroa, who used the camera to depict the country in unique ways.

Equally significant was the emergence of *carperos* and other street comedians of astonishing magnetic power, such as Mario Moreno, better known as Cantinflas, and Germán Valdés, the *Pachuco* clown Tin Tan, whose blockbuster comedies used humor to explore political, social, ethnic, and religious tensions. (*Pachuco* is a term used to refer to Mexican American youths from the thirties to the fifties, known for their idiosyncratic attire, use of slang—which would later evolve into Spanglish—and rebellious spirit against the oppressive white establishment in the United States.) These actors ridiculed urban characters like *el peladito,* the charming hoodlum who entertains everyone with his verbal pyrotechnics but is incapable of holding a steady job, or the urban dweller who decides to cross the border and live in Los Angeles, where there was a growing population of Mexicans.

The growth of the film industry led to the opening of new, state-of-the-art theaters in middle- and upper-class neighborhoods in *El De Efe* and in major provincial cities, such as Monterrey, Guadalajara, and Puebla. But ticket prices were affordable for the lower class, beneficiaries of *el milagro mexicano.* There was a voracious audience who closely followed the industry and bought tickets on a weekly basis.

This movie fever was far from being an exclusively local affair. Mexican movies were distributed all over the Spanish-speaking world—from Montevideo, Uruguay, to San José, Costa Rica—and pleased these audiences more than Hollywood could. But Hollywood wasn't far away. There were constant collaborations: Dolores del Río, the star of *María Candelaria,* traveled to Los Angeles to do some projects, and Emilio

"El Indio" Fernández directed *La perla,* an adaptation of John Steinbeck's novella.

The idea of making a career in the movies was tempting to García Márquez. He was ready to settle down and have more children. Until then he hadn't received a single royalty check for his books. The film industry allowed him to nurture dreams of stability.

Perhaps García Márquez's love of film is rooted in his childhood passion for comics and drawing. In Colombia he had been involved, however peripherally, with the making of *El grupo de Barranquilla*'s short, *La langosta azul.* During his European sojourn, he stayed briefly in Italy and enrolled in some film classes at Cinecità.

García Márquez went to the movies "almost every day." His newspaper columns were regularly devoted to film reviews. His favorite filmmakers were Orson Welles (he especially admired *The Immortal Story*) and Akira Kurosawa (whom he met in 1990 in Tokyo). He followed French New Wave and Italian Neorealism and was an enthusiast of François Truffaut's *Jules et Jim* and Roberto Rossellini's *Il generale della Rovere.* If one wished to collect everything García Márquez ever wrote about *el séptimo arte,* as filmmaking is known in Spanish, it would easily fill a couple of three-hundred-page volumes.*

---

* For instance, in *El Universal* in Cartagena, García Márquez wrote mostly about Hollywood and European cinema in September 1948. In his column *"La Jirafa"* in *El Heraldo* in Barranquilla, which he wrote under the pseudonym Septimus, he discussed an adaptation of William Faulkner's *Intruder in the Dust,* among other notes on film. In *El Espectador* in Bogotá he had a regular weekly section on film, including reviews of Mervy LeRoy's *Quo Vadis?*, Edward Dmytryk's *The Caine Mutiny,* Billy Wilder's *Sabrina,* and Francois Truffaut's *The 400 Blows.*

García Márquez's life-long passion for film is in sharp contrast to his ambivalence to sports. Colombia, Venezuela, and Cuba are known as fertile baseball cradles, yet none of his columns—or his novels—contain a single reference to the sport, although *Living to Tell the Tale* does mention, in passing, some games of soccer he played when he was a child.[3] Soccer is the most popular sport in Europe, as well as Mexico and other parts of Latin America. Again, there is absolute silence about it in his work. The sole exception is a serial in *El Espectador* of Bogotá entitled "The Triple Champion Reveals His Secrets," about Ramón Hoyos, a Colombian bicycle champion. The story was based on one-on-one interviews with the athlete, but was written by García Márquez in the first person as though the installments were part of Hoyos's autobiography.

Álvaro Mutis had arrived in Mexico City in 1956. He had worked in public relations for Esso, Standard Oil, Panamerican, and Columbia Pictures, but Esso accused him of misappropriating the company's money. Apparently, Mutis had at his disposal a fund for charitable endeavors, but he spent the money rather capriciously on other projects, most of which were cultural endeavors. Esso judged the behavior to be unacceptable and sued Mutis. Before any action could be taken, he flew to *El De Efe* on an emergency trip arranged by one of his brothers and some acquaintances. He settled there, thriving in the city's intellectual atmosphere.

At the age of thirty-three, Mutis had moved from Bogotá. He had brought with him a couple of letters of recommendation, one of which was addressed to Luis Buñuel, the Spanish filmmaker who lived in exile in Mexico. Like most young intellectuals in Latin America, Mutis had been hypnotized by Buñuel's surrealist style. *Un chien andalou*, released in 1929, was an epoch-making experiment in which dreamlike images allowed audiences to see *el séptimo arte* as a conduit to the unconscious. Buñuel's *Los olvidados* (*The Young and the Damned*), which won the Palme d'Or at the Cannes Film Festival in 1950, dissected the Mexico City slums with astonishing power. Intellectuals such as Octavio Paz and Carlos Fuentes were effusive about the daring way in which Buñuel used the camera to create a documentary-like fictional account of neglected street children, the failure of schools and government institutions to help them, and the resulting violence from this social problem. Mutis applauded the connection between cinema and politics that Buñuel achieved in his movie.

Eventually, his problem with Esso caught up with him and in 1959, Mutis was arrested for having misappropriated company funds while he was an employee in Colombia. The process was rather quick. In spite of the support of his friends Juan Rulfo, Octavio Paz, poet and editor Ali Chumacero, scholar José Luis Martínez, Colombian painter Fernando Botero, and García Márquez, Mutis's legal fortunes worsened. Faced with extradition, he was instead sent to the Mexican prison of Lecumberri, known as *"El Penal," el palacio negro,* the black palace. He was in prison for fifteen months, a time he wrote about in an extraordinary document entitled *Diary of the Lecumberri.*[4]

By the time the García Márquezes arrived in *El De Efe,* Mutis had been out of prison for months. He had kept his friend aware of his dramatic incarceration and the efforts to free him. Once released, he continued to keep him abreast of the latest on various intellectuals and artists. The Lecumberri episode had not diminished Mutis's gratitude toward his host country. The love for Mexico he expressed to García Márquez no doubt served to lure the writer and his family.

At this point, Mutis was working for Producciones Barbachano Ponce, a film company at the heart of the Mexican movie boom. He first housed the García Márquezes in one of the Apartamentos Bonampak on Calle Mérida, then at Renán #21, in the Anzures neighborhood. Eventually, the family moved to the well-to-do neighborhood of San Ángel Inn, in the southern part of the city, not too far from the Universidad Nacional Autónoma de México, the oldest and largest institution of higher learning in Latin America. Their first child, Rodrigo, was still a baby. They had a mattress, a crib, a table and two chairs. Still, Mutis did everything possible to make them feel comfortable.

For García Márquez, Mutis served as a key to the Mexican intelligentsia. He was acquainted with important figures of the time, including the crème de la crème of the Mexican cultural scene: novelist Carlos Fuentes; poet, essayist, and diplomat Octavio Paz; fiction writer Juan Rulfo; editor and anthropologist Fernando Benítez; short-story writer and public intellectual Juan José Arreola, and journalist and novelist Elena Poniatowska, as well as expatriate filmmaker Jomí García Ascot and his wife, María Luisa Elio.

García Márquez's friendship with Carlos Fuentes dates to this period. One year García Márquez's junior, Fuentes was born in Panama City in 1928. His father was a Mexican diplomat, and the family lived in Montevideo, Rio de Janeiro, Washington D.C., Santiago, and Buenos Aires. This diasporic existence contributed not only to Fuentes's universalist view of Hispanic civilization, which he perceived as a sponge that absorbed elements from every other important culture, but to his pitch-perfect command of both English and Spanish. In 1959, Fuentes published his magnum opus, the Balzakian saga *La region más transparente* (Where the Air Is Clear) and *Las buenas conciencias* (The Good Conscience). *Aura,* a Henry James-inspired novella about the young biographer of a caudillo, a military figure active during the Mexican Revolution of 1910, is arguably his most popular, perhaps his most successful, work. Published by the Spanish refugee-sponsored Ediciones Era in 1962, the narrative uses the second-person singular ("You wake up...") as an experimental device. Fuentes's fascination with the revolution is at the heart of his masterpiece, *The Death of Artemio Cruz,* also released in 1962. These works are set in Mexico City, where Fuentes returned as an adolescent and lived until 1965. Although he spent many years abroad, he always considered the metropolis his center of gravity.

Mutis gave Carlos Fuentes some of García Márquez's work which had been published in Bogotá's periodical *Mito.* Fuentes was then co-editor, along with Emanuel Carballo, of the prestigious *Revista Mexicana de Literatura.* He reprinted some of the stories in his magazine, including *"Monólogo de Isabel viendo llover en Macondo"* (Monologue of Isabel Watching It Rain in Macondo). When the second edition of *No One Writes to the Colonel* was published, Fuentes wrote a review in *La Cultura en México,* the supplement of the magazine *Siempre!*

Referred to by the Mexican press as *el duo dinámico,* Fuentes and García Márquez remained friends into their eighties, long after other members of *El Boom* had died and the few remaining ones had become distant, largely as a result of ideological differences. In 2007, the Royal Spanish Academy published a commemorative edition of *One Hundred Years of Solitude* to celebrate García Márquez's eightieth birthday and the book's fortieth anniversary, for which Carlos Fuentes wrote an affectionate piece praising their friendship and ratifying the novel's standing among the classics. And he was next to García Márquez when, in April of that year, the volume was presented to the public during the IV Congreso Internacional de la Lengua Española, in Cartagena. Likewise, in 2009, when the Royal Spanish Academy published a commemorative edition of *Where the Air Is Clear* to coincide with its fiftieth anniversary, García Márquez joined Fuentes in Mexico City to present it to the public.

The empathy they shared went beyond an emotional bond. The left-wing ideological persuasion that defined Fuentes and

García Márquez when they were young remained strong as they matured while other Latin American writers shifted in different political directions. They remained supportive of Fidel Castro's regime, sympathized with the Sandinista revolution in Nicaragua, and sharply criticized neoliberalism as a veiled marketing strategy in the eighties. It is important to remember that upon meeting Fuentes in *El De Efe*, García Márquez was the less accomplished of the two. Fuentes was a polyglot (his English and French were impeccable) and an extraordinarily dynamic intellectual. Known for his looks, he was also intimately connected to the film world. His first wife was actress Rita Macedo, whom he married in 1957. He claimed to have had an affair with actress Jean Seberg, iconic for, among other reasons, her role in Jean-Luc Goddard's 1959 film *À bout de souffle*, known to American audiences as *Breathless*. The relationship appears to have been imagined by Fuentes. In part to refute accusations that it never took place, he wrote the 1994 novella, *Diana, The Goddess Who Hunts Alone*, in which the lead female character is modeled after Seberg.

García Márquez's sojourn in Mexico was a period of fresh encounters. In addition to Fuentes—with whom he spent part of his Sundays having tea—he and Mercedes became close with Jomí García Ascot and María Luisa Elío, to whom the Spanish edition of *One Hundred Years of Solitude* is dedicated. (The French edition has a different dedication: "Pour Carmen et Álvaro Mutis.") García Márquez also befriended the Catalan filmmaker García Ascot, who was born in Tunis, Morocco, in 1927. The son of a diplomat who spent his childhood in Portugal, France, Belgium, and Morocco, García Ascot arrived in Mexico City in 1939 as a refugee from the Spanish Civil War. He studied at Universidad Nacional Autónoma de México and was a founder of the institution's film club. He directed the movies *Un día de trabajo* (A Day of Work, 1960) and *El viaje*

(The Journey, 1976), and a short documentary on surrealist painter Remedios Varo.

María Luisa Elío and her husband were the García Márquezes' neighbors in the San Ángel Inn section of Mexico City. The Colombians lived in Loma #19 and the Spaniards in Cárpatos #14. The connection was fruitful. Not only would the couples go to the movies together but Elío later recalled how García Márquez would regale them with extraordinary stories he would tell, even an entire plot, which he improvised in front of them. *One Hundred Years of Solitude* was taking shape.[5] In the essay *"La odisea literaria de un manuscrito"* (The Literary Odyssey of a Manuscript), published in the Spanish newspaper *El País* in 2001, García Márquez wrote: "María Luisa Elío, with her clairvoyant drive, and Jomí García Ascot, her husband, paralyzed with poetic stupor, listened to my improvised stories as if they were ciphered signals from the Divine Providence. Thus, I didn't doubt for a second, from their early visits onward, that I would dedicate the book to them."[6]

On April 16, 1962, García Márquez's second son, Gonzalo, was born.[7] The family moved to a larger apartment at Calle de Ixtaccíhuatl #88, in Colonia Florida. At the time, García Márquez's principal source of income was screenplays. Mutis had introduced him to Miguel Barbachano Ponce, and, through him, García Márquez met other screenwriters, directors, and actors. His reputation as an exemplary fabulist began to earn him commissions. Writing for the screen was exciting but frustrating. He would spend weeks drafting a script only to find out, after a long process, that it would be shelved, sometimes forever. García Márquez worked on various scripts simultaneously, if only to make ends meet for his growing family.

A few of them did see the light of day, albeit not immediately. He made the adaptation, along with Barbachano Ponce, for *Lola de mi vida* (Lola of My Life, 1965), but the screenplay was credited to Juan de la Cabada and Carlos A. Figueroa. *En este pueblo no hay ladrones* (No Thieves in This Town, 1965) was based on one of his stories and adapted by Emilio García Riera, who would become one of Mexico's most distinguished film critics, together with Alberto Isaac. Isaac's brother, Jorge, directed the film. There were others, too, such as the two-part *Juegos peligrosos* (Dangerous Games, 1966), based on another of his stories—directed by Arturo Ripstein, Buñuel's one-time assistant (who would adapt other García Márquez material for the screen, including the 1999 coproduction among Mexico, Spain, and France, *No One Writes to the Colonel*), and Luis Alcoriza—and *Patsy mi amor* (Patsy My Love, 1969), directed by Manuel Michel.

Although it was a cornerstone of his career, García Márquez's work for film never produced first-rate movies, neither did the ones for which he wrote an original screenplay, nor those for which he adapted his own or others' fiction. It wasn't for lack of trying. His filmography (always in connection with the screenplay; he never acted or directed) is long. The reason for this handicap may be intrinsic: García Márquez is a visual writer who fills the page with vivid, baroque images that resist adaptation. No screenwriter, no film director, no matter how dexterous, has been able to match the Colombian's fertile imagination. It may be argued that the best screen adaptations of his work are those in which the director uses a subtle, naturalistic style, and gives up any attempt at competing with literature. In an interview with Rita Guibert, García Márquez said that the starting point of his novels is "a completely visual image. I suppose that some writers begin with a phrase, an idea, or a concept. I always begin with an image."[8] In another interview years later, he was asked if cinema had treated him badly. García Márquez responded: "No, cinema hasn't treated me badly as far as what has been screened, but for other reasons. Things have gone badly because although I've worked more for cinema than for literature, I don't manage to do all I would like to. I would like cinema as a form of artistic expression to have the same value in Latin America that literature has at the moment."[9]

In 1965, Carlos Fuentes and García Márquez embarked on what is arguably the most inspiring and fruitful cinematic endeavor of the period. Together, they developed the plot for a story for which García Márquez wrote his first original screenplay, *Tiempo de morir* (A Time to Die). Shot in Pátzcuaro, in the state of Michoacán, from June 7 to July 10, 1965, it was the first feature film directed by Arturo Ripstein. García Márquez was present on location, and assisted with the production. The cast included Marga López, Jorge Martínez de Hoyos, Enrique Rocha, Alfredo Leal, and Blanca Sánchez. Inspired by the Western, it is the story of a man who returns to town after eighteen years in prison for murder. He intends to get on with his life, but the victim's son won't allow it.

It was through García Márquez's friendship with Fuentes and his involvement in the film industry that one of the most significant moments in his Mexican period took place: his discovery of Juan Rulfo's oeuvre. By the time García Márquez arrived in *El De Efe*, Rulfo was already a popular writer and a cult figure. Later, García Márquez would say that during his first six months in the city, everyone frantically spoke to him about Rulfo. It isn't difficult to guess why he reacted positively to the buzz.

Juan Rulfo was born in 1917 (although the exact date is under dispute, because he might have given the wrong year in order to avoid the military draft), in the small town of Sayula, Jalisco, Mexico. His father was killed when he was little, and his mother died when he was around ten. Rulfo came from a family of landowners ruined by the Mexican Revolution and the *Cristero* war. He was strongly attached to the countryside, especially to the indigenous population. He moved to Mexico

City, where he audited classes at the Universidad Nacional Autónoma de México but never enrolled as a full-time student. Largely self-taught, he read voraciously (though he was never bookish) and began to put pen to paper. In the end, he published only two, equally slim, books: the collection of stories *El llano en llamas* (The Burning Plain, 1953) and the novel *Pedro Páramo* (1955). They were enough to turn him into one of the most influential figures in Latin American literature.

Rulfo's language is sparse, Hemingwayesque. Although brief, his stories are powerful explorations of the human response to despair. They focus on the ordeal of *campesinos* deprived of a means to survive. "Do You Hear the Dogs Bark?" for instance, is structured as a monologue by a father carrying on his back his wounded son as he tries to find a doctor for the boy. In "Luvina," a visitor plans to go to a ghost town inhabited only by women, children, and the elderly. All the men had left long ago. Many of García Márquez's famous stories were being crafted in those years, between the time just prior to his arrival in *El De Efe* and the late sixties. Among them, "There Are No Thieves in This Town," "Tuesday Siesta," and "One of These Days" have a genuine Rulfo feel: a similar concern for the indigent, an emphasis on the little disturbances that comprise life, and an attraction to the countryside.

Anyone who reads *Pedro Páramo* will recognize the extent to which it inspired García Márquez's masterpiece. Rulfo created a fictional town, Comala, where the novel's protagonist goes in search of his father. The Homeric echoes of the short volume are stronger than any you will find in *One Hundred Years of Solitude,* and there is more psychologizing in it as well. The Faulknerian recreation of an alternative reality in the Latin American heartland mesmerized García Márquez. (Uruguayan author Juan Carlos Onetti created the fictional town of Santa María, which features in *The Brief Life* [1950], among other books.) But Rulfo wasn't a full-fledged endorser of magic realism. He was a slender, somewhat wooden, rather shy person who spoke little and socialized less. Discovering him, though, was a coup de grace for García Márquez: here was a writer of tantalizing talent who didn't court public applause. Reading Rulfo made him aware of his own potential.

In 1964, García Márquez collaborated with Fuentes on a screenplay adaptation of Rulfo's short story *"El gallo de oro"* (The Golden Cock), an experience that surely triggered his renewed enthusiasm for literature. Roberto Gavaldón was the director, and Gabriel Figueroa was the cinematographer. Set in rural Mexico, the plot contains similar motifs to those in García Márquez's *No One Writes to the Colonel:* Dionisio is a humble *campesino* who is given a dying rooster. Dionisio feeds the rooster and brings it back to health in order to enter it in a cockfight at the feria of San Juan del Río. The rooster beats an opponent from an important farm owned by Lorenzo Benavides, whose lover, Bernarda Cutiño, aka "La Caponera," is impressed. Lorenzo tries to buy Dionisio's rooster, but Dionisio refuses until La Caponera seduces him. The film's cast included the famous Mexican actors Ignacio López Tarso, Lucha Villa, and Narciso Busquets.

García Márquez's sojourn in the Rulfian universe had another chapter. Fuentes had written the screenplay of *Pedro Páramo*, but the movie's director, Carlos Velo, didn't quite like it and asked García Márquez to doctor it. A good number of people got involved, and García Márquez was never listed in the credits, which turned out for the best. Produced by Barbachano Ponce, the film *Pedro Páramo* was a flop. Subsequent adaptations were equally unsatisfying.

Adapting such a demanding work of literature for the silver screen is a daunting task. The novel is full of ambiguities. It is hard to tell, for example, who of the characters is alive and who isn't, and whether incest is at the heart of the novel.

García Márquez was always conscious of his debt to Rulfo, whose work, in his view, he became well acquainted with as a result of his activities in the Mexican film industry. In an interview with Miguel Fernández-Braso, he openly admitted that he had lifted—i.e., plagiarized as a form of tribute—a sentence from Rulfo's *Pedro Páramo*. Since then, there has been enormous speculation about which sentence it was. Perhaps it is in chapter ten, where Remedios the Beautiful is described as *"no era un ser de este mundo,"* not a being of this world. In Rulfo's novel, Susana San Juan is described as *"una mujer que no era de este mundo."*[10] In a speech entitled *"Asombro por Juan Rulfo"* (Astonishment for Juan Rulfo), delivered on September 18, 2002, to commemorate the fiftieth anniversary of the publication of *The Burning Plain*, García Márquez described the writer's block he suffered after finishing his first four books, and how his discovery of *Pedro Páramo* in 1961 opened his way to the composition of *One Hundred Years of Solitude*. He noted that, altogether, Rulfo's published works "add up to no more than three hundred pages; but that is almost as many, and I believe they are as durable, as the pages that have come down to us from Sophocles."

One should take the diagnosis of writer's block, as presented by García Márquez, with a grain of salt. The block was more conceptual than real. García Márquez felt that he had reached a certain limit with his stories and novellas and was ready for something larger and more ambitious. He might not have considered these highlights a true sign of productivity, but in those years García Márquez saw the publication of new editions of three of his books. He had kept the manuscript of *In Evil Hour* with him, from its inception in Paris, through his trips to Bogotá, Caracas, New York, and now Mexico City. He hoped his work in an advertising agency and in the movie industry would open the door of the publishing world to him, but nothing materialized and he was disappointed. So when Mutis and another friend, Guillermo Angulo, suggested that he submit the novel to the 1961 Premio Esso de Novela in Colombia, sponsored by the transnational oil company, he did.

The judges were surprised by the untitled anonymous manuscript. The Academia Colombiana de la Lengua, which administered the prize, awarded it to the book, thinking it had been authored by Mutis, who had worked for the oil company in Bogotá. Germán Vargas collected the $500 prize. But the experience turned traumatic. A pernicious editor in charge of overseeing the book through the production process had taken the liberty of changing its style, replacing the stylized Colombian rhythms with a Madrileño's voice. When García Márquez received a copy, printed in the Madrid-based Imprenta Luis Pérez, he was furious. He wrote a letter to *El Espectador* declaring that edition, now titled *In Evil Hour*, an orphan. Only when the novel was reprinted (simultaneously with new editions of a couple of his other novellas), six years later, in Mexico City, by the elegant Ediciones Era, with its original voice reestablished, did he acknowledge its paternity. By then, he was already deep into the crafting of *One Hundred Years of Solitude*.

García Márquez had a better experience with the publication of *No One Writes to the Colonel*, which was released in August 1961 in Medellín under the editorship of Alberto Aguirre. Thanks to Aguirre's enthusiasm and to the support of some of his friends in *El grupo de Barranquilla*, the novel, in my mind a stunning masterpiece, received critical accolades and was embraced by the public. The third item by García Márquez to appear at the time (published in English in *Esquire* magazine) was the novella *The Incredible and Sad Story of Innocent Eréndira and Her Heartless Grandmother*.

In these three volumes García Márquez began to build a counterpart to Faulkner's Yoknapatawpha County. Elements continue reappearing as the reader goes from one narrative to another and beyond. For instance, as a motif (or better, as an obsession), the young woman pushed into prostitution by her grandmother was already present in his early work. In the short story *"El mar del tiempo perdido"* (The Sea of Lost Time, 1961), the character Herbert comes across an anonymous prostitute who, in order to pay a large debt, has to go to bed with hundreds of men. The story of Eréndira has precisely that theme. And in *One Hundred Years of Solitude,* a similar scene takes place.

In the *New Republic,* Martin Kaplan praised *Innocent Eréndira:* "García Márquez's fictional universe has the same staggeringly gratifying density and texture as Proust's Faubourg Saint-Germain and Joyce's Dublin. As his friend Mario Vargas Llosa said of *One Hundred Years of Solitude,* García Márquez's is 'in the tradition of those insanely ambitious creations which aspire to compete with reality on an equal basis, confronting it with an image and qualitatively matching it in vitality, vastness, and complexity.'" Kaplan added that since the death of Neruda in 1973, García Márquez was arguably "the best of the Latin Americans; as testimony from both the United States and Europe accumulates, his early reception as a great regional writer is giving way to a climate in which Proust and Joyce can be invoked by enthusiasts without worried sidelong glances at the critrical pack." But Kaplan saw *Innocent Eréndira* as a minor work. "'For me, literature is a very simple game, all the rules of which have to be accepted,' [García Márquez] has said, and for the twenty years that he's stuck to that conviction he has beggared Houdini. The early stories, with their O. Henry punch lines, purple atmosphere, and 'experimental' ambitions, are simply less fun—and less haunting—than the later work."[11]

Luis Harss and Barbara Dohmann, two interviewers who visited him (the former would be instrumental in helping García Márquez find a publisher for *One Hundred Years of*

Solitude), asked him how a story took shape. He writes, they stated, "without a set plan, in a sort of total alert, registering imponderables. He has no cut-and-dried recipe by which to perform." "I have firm political ideas," he told them. "But my literary ideas change according to my digestion." Harss and Dohmann added that García Márquez tells a story "less to develop a subject than to discover it. Theme is less important than wavelength. His facts are provisional, valid not as statements but as assumptions, what he feels today he may discard tomorrow. If in the end not everything adds up to a net result, it is perhaps because we must subtract, not add, to reach a final balance. His world has no beginning or end, no outer rim. It is centripetal. What holds it together is inner tension. It is always on the verge of taking concrete shape, but remains intangible. He wants it that way. Its relation to objective reality is that of an eternally fluctuating mental portrait where resemblances at any given moment are striking but tenuous."[12]

Chapter 7

Sleepless in Macondo

In the *Dictionary of Imaginary Places,* first published in 1980, Alberto Manguel and Giovanni Guadalupi catalog the non-existent geographies invented by literati, such as Lewis Carroll's Jabberwocky Wood, Daniel Defoe's Crusoe Island, Jonathan Swift's Brobdingnag, J. R. R. Tolkien's Middle-Earth, and Jules Verne's Saknussemm's Corridor. Each of these places is surveyed in a succinct, provocative entry. The following describes Macondo in *One Hundred Years of Solitude:*

> **Macondo**, a Colombian village founded in ancient times by José Arcadio Buendía, whose boundless imagination always stretched farther than the inventiveness of nature. The founder had placed the houses in such a way that the inhabitant of each could reach the river and then fetch water with exactly the same degree of effort as his neighbor; and the streets had been planned in such a manner that all houses received the same amount of sunshine throughout the day. For the benefit of the population he built small traps to catch canaries, robins, and nightingales and in very little time the village was so full of their singing that the gypsy tribe

which every year visited Macondo to show the inhabitants the newest eighth marvel of the world would let
themselves be guided by the music.

Toward the east Macondo is protected by a high
and forbidding range of hills; toward the south by
marshes covered with a kind of vegetable soup. The
marshes rise toward the west and become a large body
of water in which cetaceans of delicate skin, with the
face and torso of a woman, lure sailors with their firm
and tempting breasts. To the north, many days' march
away through a dangerous jungle, lies the sea.

From a small village of some twenty mud and
bamboo huts, Macondo became a town with shops
and a marketplace. The prosperity made José Arcadio
Buendía free all the birds he had carefully trapped and
replace them with musical clocks which he had obtained
from merchants in exchange for parrots. These clocks
were so synchronized that every half-hour the town
would shake with a sound of ringing bells and every
midday a musical explosion of cuckoos and waltzes
would glorify the beginning of the siesta. Buendía also
replaced the acacias lining the streets with almond
trees and found a system of giving them eternal life.
Many years later, when Macondo became a city of
wooden houses and zinc roofs, ancient almond trees
still bloomed in the older streets, though there was no
one in the town who could remember having witnessed
their planting.

Among the most notable events which form the
history of Macondo is the unusual insomnia epidemic
that struck the town. The most terrible thing about it
was not the impossibility of sleep—because the body
would not tire itself either—but the gradual loss of
memory. When the sick person became accustomed

to staying awake, memories of his childhood would start to vanish, followed by the names and concepts of things; finally he would lose his own identity and consciousness of his own being, sinking into a calm lunacy without a past. Bells were set up around the village and whoever passed them would give them a tug to prove that he was still sane. Visitors would be advised not to eat or drink in Macondo, because the illness was supposed to be contagious. The inhabitants soon became accustomed to this state of affairs and dispensed with the useless activity of sleep. In order not to forget what the different objects around them were, they labeled each thing with its proper name: "pail," "table," "cow," "flower." However, the inhabitants realized that even though the names of things could be remembered in this fashion, their utility could nevertheless be forgotten and a more extensive explanation was added on the labels. For instance, a large placard on the cow informed the onlooker: "This is a cow; it is necessary to milk her every morning to produce milk and the milk must be boiled and then added to coffee to produce coffee with milk." At the entrance to the village the inhabitants erected a sign that said "Macondo" and, a little farther on, another saying "God exists."

The inhabitants of Macondo also invented an ingenious system to counteract the effects of their strange illness and learned to read the past in the cards, as before the gypsies used to read the future. Buendía also created a memory machine into which every morning he would record the past events of his life. In this way, at any point, he would make the machine work and recall his whole past day by day. The epidemic reached an end when the gypsy Melquíades—who had been dead but had returned because he could not stand the loneliness of death—brought to Macondo an insomnia antidote in the form of a sweet liquid in little bottles. The inhabitants drank the potion and immediately were able to sleep.

Another important event in the history of Macondo was the proposed building of a huge temple organized by Father Nicanor Reyna, who was traveling throughout the world with the intention of establishing a sanctuary in the center of impiety and envisioned a temple full of life-sized saints and stained-glass windows. However, the people of Macondo, who had lived for so many years without a priest, had established a personal contact with God and were free of the stain of the original sin. They could levitate some twelve centimeters off the ground after drinking a full cup of chocolate. Seeing that Macondo was not the center of impiety he was searching for, Father Reyna continued on his travels.

In more recent years Macondo saw the creation of an American banana plantation on its land, and the town was linked to the rest of the world by a railway. But due to a strike, heavy rains and then drought, the plantation was abandoned and it is said that Macondo's prosperity was wiped off the surface of the earth by a violent cyclone.

Its inclusion in the *Dictionary of Imaginary Places* affirms that Macondo is not quite a parallel reality that imitates our own world in appearance and sophistication but is an extension of that world, with its own flora and fauna, its continents and nations, its record of social, political, and economic upheaval— in other words, its own metabolism. In their foreword, Manguel and Guadalupi described how they came upon the idea of putting together their encyclopedic volume: "We agreed that our approach would have to be carefully balanced between the practical and the fantastic. We would take for granted that fiction was fact, and treat the chosen texts as seriously as one treats the reports of an explorer or chronicler." They were interested in places that, while imaginary, actually exist, "that they can indeed be visited and are mapped in the real world, that the authors looked upon real landscapes and installed on these landscapes their visions."[1]

García Márquez's Macondo possesses that immediacy. After reading the novel, one feels that the town isn't an escapist's dream but is within reach. And its metabolism, in my view, carries in it the DNA of Latin America.[2] Or, as critic Edna Van der Walde put it, its imprint on the region's psyche has turned "el macondismo como latinoamericanismo."[3] Mario Vargas Llosa, in his doctoral dissertation *García Márquez: Historia de un deicidio,* defended at the Universidad Complutense de Madrid and published in 1971, called *One Hundred Years of Solitude* a "total" novel. "The process of edification of the fictitious reality achieved is a culmination: this novel integrates in a superior synthesis the previous fictions [created by the author], builds a world of extraordinary richness, exhausts that world and is exhausted by it."[4]

In the mid-sixties, García Márquez reached the conclusion that an author and a book are matched at birth. Work for the cinema helped him support his family, but it wasn't altogether rewarding. He felt empty, in debt to his own talent. For years, he had been dreaming of writing a novel that could sum up not only his childhood experiences but his overall vision of the world. The more he let his imagination free, the faster he realized that no matter how many short and long stories he produced, they were all part of a single book, what Mallarmé had visualized as an all-encompassing volume that mirrored, even competed, with reality in all its complexity.

He told Plinio Apuleyo Mendoza that in general, he thought "a writer writes only one book, although the same book may appear in several volumes under different titles." García Márquez considered Balzac, Conrad, Melville, Kafka, and Faulkner as models of the one-book author. One of their books often stands out above the rest, giving the impression that the author is connected to a primordial work. He asked: "Who remembers Cervantes's short stories? Who remembers *The Graduate Who Thought He Was Made of Glass*, for instance? But that can still be read with as much pleasure as any of his major works. In Latin America, the Venezuelan writer Rómulo Gallegos is famous for *Doña Barbara* which is not his best work, and the Guatemalan Miguel Ángel Asturias is known for *El Señor Presidente*, a terrible novel, not nearly as good as *Legends of Guatemala*."[5]

In his mind, his magnum opus wasn't a summing up. He perceived himself as "a slave to a perfectionist's exactitude," as he put it, decades later, in *Living to Tell the Tale*. He polished every sentence, ensured the arc of a plotline in any given piece was well-rounded, looked at each character as if he or she were an autonomous entity, and reduced dialogue to the bare essentials; these were all representative of what he conceived to be his supercilious dedication as a writer. His book of books needed to be at once sumptuous, abundant, baroque, but straightforward, distilled, and self-sufficient.

There is much debate about exactly when García Márquez started writing *One Hundred Years of Solitude*. It's unquestionable that its essence had been with him for a long time. In June 1950, he had published "*La casa de los Buendía: Apuntes para una novela*" (The Buendía House: Notes for a Novel) in *Crónica*.[6] But no copies of the magazine exist, so until one manifests itself, what the piece contained is the subject of mere speculation. This is the period when García Márquez got sick in Barranquilla; he was writing his newspaper column, "La Jirafa," for *El Heraldo*.

He asked to take a leave of several weeks to return to Sucre, where he convalesced with his family. His illness was described as pneumonia. But his friends knew he used the time to work on a novel.

"It was supposed to be a drama about the Thousand-Day War in the Colombian Caribbean," García Márquez said later, "about which I had talked to Manuel Zapata Olivella on an earlier visit to Cartagena. On that occasion, and with no relation at all to my project, he gave me a pamphlet written by his father about a veteran of the war whose portrait was printed on the cover, and who, with his *liquiliqui* shirt and his mustache singed by gunpowder, reminded me somehow of my grandfather. I have forgotten his name, but his surname would stay with me forever after: Buendía. That was why I thought I would write a novel with the title *La casa*, the epic tale of a family that could have in it a good deal of our own history during the sterile wars of Colonel Nicolás Márquez."[7]

Judging by the description of its content, if not by its prophetic title, it is clear that, seventeen years before *One Hundred Years of Solitude* was published, García Márquez was already defining its parameters. *La casa* was his working title, which he used any time he referred to the project. It is important to note that the house is a ubiquitous symbol in Latin American fiction, appearing in a number of novels by or related to *El Boom*, such as Vargas Llosa's *The Green House*, Isabel Allende's *The House of the Spirits*, and Álvaro Cepeda Samudio's *La casa grande*.[8] Yet for years García Márquez has said that the true beginning was a trip he took with his mother on a yellow train back to Aracataca in 1950 or 1951; this journey serves as the opening of his memoir *Living to Tell the Tale*. It was then, he says, looking at the place where he had grown up, invaded by the ghosts of the past, that the idea of writing a book about the house, the family, and the town came to him. In an interview, he stated: "When I got there it was at first quite shocking because I was now twenty-two and hadn't been there since the age of eight. Nothing had really changed, but I felt that I wasn't really looking at the village, but I was *experiencing* it as if I were reading it. It was as if everything I saw had already been written, and all I had to do was to sit down and copy what was already there and what I was just reading. For all practical purposes everything had evolved into literature: the house, the people, and the memories."[9]

Dasso Saldívar, author of the biography *El viaje a la semilla,* believes that the novel's inception took place when the movie producer Antonio Matouk proposed that García Márquez and Luis Alcoriza, who had worked as a screenwriter with Luis Buñuel, write a series of screenplays for a regular salary. Ten years García Márquez's senior, Alcoriza was originally from Badajoz, in Extremadura, Spain. He lived in exile in Mexico, where he wrote the screenplays for Buñuel's *The Brute, The Exterminating Angel,* and what became the defining movie about Buñuel's political engagement, *Los olvidados.* They both collaborated with other filmmakers and went into seclusion in order to work. They wrote at least three screenplays and came up with a number of other ideas, but the producer kept on rejecting their output. This, Saldívar argues, was the excuse García Márquez needed to focus his concentration away from the uncertain profession of screenwriting and on his magnum opus, which had been taking shape in his imagination for quite some time.[10]

All in all, the composition of *One Hundred Years of Solitude* took eighteen months, from 1965 to 1967. García Márquez has told friends, acquaintances, and reporters that it was while driving from Mexico City to Acapulco in his Opel with Mercedes for a family vacation that he had an epiphany. (In some versions of the story, the automobile is a Volkswagen.) In any case, the legend behind the work isn't unlike that behind Samuel Taylor Coleridge's poem "Kubla Khan: or, A Vision of a Dream," an example of how the muse of inspiration takes over an artist at a particular time. Coleridge, an English Romantic, claimed to have "received" the poem about the Mongol and Chinese emperor Kubla Khan during an opium-induced dream in the fall of 1787, at a farm house in Exmoor, England. When he awoke, he proceeded to write down the lines, which have since become famous: "In Xanadu did Kubla Khan/ A stately pleasure-dome decree;/ Where Alph, the sacred river, ran/ Through caverns measureless to man/ Down to a sunless sea."

The key point is that Coleridge didn't struggle to compose the poem; it simply came to him from a higher power. The idea is fitting to the nineteenth-century Romantic movement, which perceived the poet as a conduit with inspiration coming from the celestial sphere. As Coleridge wrote, he was interrupted by a knock on the door by "a person from Porlock." He attended to it, but when he returned to his task, the remainder of the poem had vanished from his mind. He couldn't remember the rest. "Kubla Khan" was left unfinished, with only fifty-four lines.

It may appear farfetched to link Coleridge to García Márquez. Their historical contexts couldn't be more different. The Romantic vision of the poet in communion with the sublime belongs to another period in Latin American culture: the *Modernista* movement. One of its leaders, the Nicaraguan *homme des lettres* Rubén Darío, described poets as "towers of God." Darío's legacy lived on among intellectuals in the early part of the twentieth century. But by the time García Márquez came along, *Modernismo* emitted only a distant murmur. By then the *autor*, in a land marked by the wound of colonialism, was a belligerent, an agent of change, committed to giving voice to the voiceless. His inspiration didn't come from a divine source but from the injustice that surrounded him. His profile was of a committed, nonspiritual, down-to-earth man of the people, a foe of the status quo.

That was certainly García Márquez's profile, but the legend that surrounds the writing of *One Hundred Years of Solitude*, one fanned by the author himself—of the artist as an instrument of the muses—is surely Romantic in tone. García Márquez has described the process as less like writing and closer to taking dictation. While he struggled to find the right narrative tone, there is an element of alchemy to his creation. When he was ready to put pen to paper, García Márquez secluded himself from the world for months until the product was ready to be seen.

The García Márquezes lived at Calle Lomas #19 in the neighborhood San Angel Inn. The writer called his study *La Cueva de la Mafia*. It was a smoked-filled place where he battled his demons.

During those eighteen months, the García Márquezes were overwhelmed with debt. He tapped into savings from his journalism and screenplays. Mercedes was in charge of the family finances and used the scant resources to buy food and clothes for the boys. But when the money ran out, she needed to look for alternatives. Álvaro Mutis, as usual, came to the rescue and lent her some money, as did other friends. Later, García Márquez would recall that he didn't even have enough to photocopy and post the manuscript. They were $10,000 in debt (roughly 120,000 Mexican pesos) when he finished the manuscript. Mercedes, always a source of strength for her husband, persuaded their landlord to let them fall behind with the rent for seven months. "She has helped construct walls around him that protect his privacy, ensure his creative comforts, and allow him to write,"[11] suggested Pete Hamill in a profile.

Even though legend has it that García Márquez remained in *La Cueva de la Mafia* for the duration of the writing, he ventured far out, to Cartagena, in March 1966, to attend the premiere of *Tiempo de morir* at the Cartagena Film Festival. He boarded a ship in Veracruz and sailed to his old Caribbean town, where he had found his voice as a reporter. It was an

opportunity to visit family and friends, to take a respite from
the project. Although García Márquez wasn't fully satisfied
with Arturo Ripstein's direction of the movie, it nonetheless
received first prize at the festival. He traveled to Bogotá
and Barranquilla. Plinio Apuleyo Mendoza received a phone
call at his office in Barranquilla from García Márquez, who
surprised him by telling him he was having a whisky in
Mendoza's own home.[12] He spoke with him and with Álvaro
Cepeda Samudio about the novel, suggesting it was a departure. "Either I'm going to succeed big time or fall miserably
on my face."[13]

The manuscript was 1,300 pages long. He had written in
eight-hour stretches every day. García Márquez calculated that
he had destroyed maybe twice or three times that amount of
paper.[14] In twenty symmetrical chapters, each approximately
twenty dense pages, a third-person narrator—is it Melquíades
the gypsy?—chronicles, with frightening precision, the rise and
fall of Macondo, exploring its geographical, temporal, ideological, and cultural dimensions. In spite of the title, the narrative time spans more than a century. The Buendía genealogy
consists of dozens of archetypical figures surrounded by a cast
of thousands.

The need to belong shapes each of the Buendías and their
entourage, from Colonel Aureliano Buendía, modeled after
the real-life military hero General Rafael Uribe Uribe, who
fought in Colombia's Thousand-Day War, to Remedios the
Beautiful, whose beauty is so overwhelming she ascends to
heaven. There's a rainstorm of small yellow flowers, a woman
who eats soil, a clairvoyant, and a character obsessed with
photographing God. The novel's matrix is Úrsula Iguarán, a
patient, down-to-earth woman, the closest one gets in Macondo
to Mother Nature, who keeps the family afloat for almost a
century. Afloat but not together: Úrsula's progeny don't know
how to love healthily.

The word *Macondo* is the name of a finca, a piece of land in the countryside that García Márquez saw when he returned with his mother to Aracataca on the yellow train. The word was written prominently on a gate. He talks about it in *Living to Tell the Tale:* "This word had attracted my attention ever since the first trips I had taken with my grandfather, but I discovered only as an adult that I liked its poetic resonance. I never heard anyone say it and did not even ask myself what it meant." Later, he discovered in the pages of the *Encyclopedia Britannica* that in Tanganyika, Africa, there are a nomadic people called Makonde. He believed this was likely the origin of the word.[15] To what extent did these inspirations define the setting of *One Hundred Years of Solitude?* Arguably at the most unconscious level. At the beginning of the novel, Macondo is a small, nondescript town on the Caribbean coast of Colombia, comprised of twenty houses built on the edge of a river with clear water running over large stones that resemble prehistoric eggs. The word—*Ma-con-do*—rings stridently in that opening paragraph: the name and the place it refers seem intimately connected. It suggests a primitive, Edenic quality, as if the place was located at the edge of the world and remained untouched by Western civilization.

Ours is the age of mediated kitsch. A single episode of a Mexican *telenovela* is watched by far more people on a single evening than all the readers of García Márquez's novel, maybe of his entire oeuvre. A soap opera perishes almost the second it stirs up its audience's passion. *One Hundred Years of Solitude* is imperishable. Yet, when read closely it's clear that first and foremost the novel is a melodrama, albeit a glorious one, with syrupy scenes of unrequited love, sibling animosity, and domestic backstabbing. García Márquez's original title could have been *Blood & Passion*. But isn't that what all good novels are about, a rollercoaster of emotions that request from the reader a suspension of disbelief?

The novel's central motif is incest: the Buendías don't seem capable of targeting their sexual desire at anyone but each other. This Hieronymus Bosch—like Garden of Earthly delights—is narrated in a flamboyant style but with equanimity, as if nothing were out of the ordinary. There are references to buccaneers and adventurers such as Francis Drake and Walter Raleigh, as well as accounts of Spanish explorers and missionaries to the Americas in the sixteenth and seventeenth centuries. *One Hundred Years of Solitude* is full of tricks. García Márquez himself shows up toward the end, and he makes coded references to his friends and colleagues, including Carpentier, Julio Cortázar, and Carlos Fuentes. The novel may all be a joke, the reader finds himself thinking as the novel reaches its climatic conclusion.

For Spanish-speaking readers, one of the most astonishing aspects of the book is its lavish, baroque language. There is not a word out place; everything is exactly where it should be. This is all the more impressive when one realizes that in the Spanish-speaking world at the time—and to a large extent, still today—there were no such things as developmental editors and copyeditors. Instead, there are *correctores de estilo,* style editors, in charge of correcting slight grammatical lapses. Their work is unintrusive as compared to what editors do—asking an author to flesh out ideas, rewrite sections, and reconfigure chunks of the plot—or copyeditors, for that matter, who standardize a manuscript by ensuring its orthography and factual components are in place. There were no such professionals in Buenos Aires when the manuscript arrived at the offices of Editorial Sudamericana. What García Márquez wrote is what the reader got—minus a few corrected typos.

In the last chapter of *One Hundred Years of Solitude,* there is a plethora of inside jokes. "I was having fun," said García

Márquez about the chapter. "It was the end of my eighteen-month siege, and the book was advancing nicely at that point; I had the feeling nobody could stop it, that I could do anything I wanted with it, that the book was in the bag. In that state, I was so happy, especially after the early agonies, that I started to make those private jokes. There are many more jokes in that section that are apparent to the casual reader. Friends see them and they die laughing, because they know what each one refers to. That was a book that *had* to be finished with great joy—because, otherwise, it is a very sad book."[16]

In spite of the Romantic idea of inspiration, finding the right tone for the narrative was a challenge. Iberian interviewer Miguel Fernández-Bermejo observed to García Márquez that "some grunt work" must have taken place "as far as enriching your language was concerned, because in *One Hundred Years of Solitude* there's a luxuriant handling of the prose." García Márquez responded that the novel was written that way "because that's how my grandmother talked. I tried to find the language that was most suitable for the book, and I remembered that my grandmother used to tell me the most atrocious things without getting all worked up, as if she'd just seen them."

He realized that that imperturbability and that richness of imagery with which his grandmother told stories was what gave verisimilitude to his. He added: "And my big problem with *One Hundred Years of Solitude* was credibility, because I believed it. But how was I going to make my readers believe it? By using my grandmother's same methods. You'll notice that in *One Hundred Years of Solitude,* especially in the beginning, there are a huge amount of deliberate archaisms. Later, halfway through the book, I was swimming like a fish in water and in the last parts there aren't only archaisms, there are neologisms and invented words and whatever. 'Cause I believe the final parts reflect the joy I felt at having found the book."[17]

Since its original publication, there have been innumerable discussions about García Márquez's writing technique. For instance, rumors circulated early on that *One Hundred Years of Solitude* was longer and that García Márquez had burned a thousand pages of it. "False," he stated, "...but it's strange how in all legends there are elements of truth. After I finished [it], I threw out all the notes and documentation so there wouldn't be any trace of them left. That way, the critics would have to take the book on its own merits and not go looking in the original papers. Whenever I write a book, I accumulate a lot of documentation. That background material is the most intimate part of my private life. It's a little embarrassing—like being seen in your underwear."[18]

Unsurprisingly, on a continent where success is a source of unveiled envy and resentment, García Márquez was accused of plagiarism. At a writer's conference in Bonn in 1970, Günther Lorenz leveled the accusation that *One Hundred Years of Solitude* was a veiled rewriting of Balzac's *La recherche de l'absolu*. In Paris, Marcelle Bargas compared the two novels and suggested that some elements of one appeared in the other. And in Honduras, the magazine *Ariel* ran an article by Luis Cova García entitled "Coincidence or Plagiarism?" García Márquez recalled that someone who had heard about the allegations sent Balzac's book to him. "I had never read [it]," he said. "Balzac doesn't interest me now, although he's sensational enough that I read what I could of him at one time—however, I glanced through it. It struck me that to say that one book derives from the other is pretty light and superficial. Also, even if I were prepared to accept that I had read it before and decided to plagiarize it, only some five pages of my book could possibly have come from *La Recherche*, and in the final analysis, just a single character, the alchemist."

He added: "I think the critics ought to have gone on and searched two hundred other books to see where the rest of the characters come from. Besides which, I'm not at all afraid of the idea of plagiarism. If I had to write *Romeo and Juliet* tomorrow I would do it, and would feel it was marvelous to have the chance to write it again. I've talked a lot about the *Oedipus Rex* of Sophocles, and I believe it has been the most important book of my life; ever since I first read it I've been astonished by its absolute perfection. Once, when I was at a place on the Colombian coast, I came across a very similar situation to that of the drama of *Oedipus Rex,* and I thought of writing something to be called *Oedipus the Mayor.* In this case I wouldn't have been charged with plagiarism because I should have begun by calling him Oedipus. I think the idea of plagiarism is already finished. I can myself say where I find Cervantes or Rabelais in *One Hundred Years of Solitude*—not as to quality but because of things I've taken from them and put there. But I can also take the book line by line—and this is a point the critics will never be able to reach—and say what event or memory from real life each comes from. It's a very curious experience to talk to my mother about such things; she remembers the origins of many of the episodes, and naturally describes them more faithfully than I do because she hasn't elaborated them as literature."[19]

The accusation of plagiarism ought to be read in context. García Márquez belongs to the generation of *El Boom,* which was defined by Borges's "Pierre Menard, Author of the *Quixote,"* a short story structured as an essay that was first published in May 1939 in the Buenos Aires magazine *Sur.* In it, the protagonist, a nineteenth-century French symbolist, seeks to rewrite—not to copy word for word, but to rewrite without having access to the primary text—Cervantes's masterpiece, *Don Quixote of La Mancha,* written four centuries prior and published in two parts, the first in 1605 and the second in 1615. The idea is ingenious: Borges offers a meditation on the art of reading and on the concept of plagiarism. Can an author "write" a book that belongs to someone else? In Borges's story, that is the deliberate intention. In the end, although the versions by Cervantes and Menard are identical, their meaning varies because of the context in which the respective pieces were drafted.

Borges's implicit statement is that anything produced by Latin American authors is, in some way, a recreation, a rewriting of a European model. García Márquez isn't an exception. *One Hundred Years of Solitude*, while utterly original, fits within the Latin American literary tradition, which is heavily indebted to Europe. Without the European literary models, the Colombian author would never have been able to craft his Macondo saga. His contribution lies in his capacity to upset and expand that foreign tradition, that is, to renovate the novel as a literary genre, infusing it with ingredients indigenous to the Americas. In that sense, its embrace by writers of the so-called Third World is a form of appropriation, a theft. García Márquez's rejection of the charge of plagiarism is a comment on the novel's postcolonial nature.

During those eighteen months of writing, Mutis, Jomí García Ascot, and María Luisa Elío visited the García Márquez family frequently. When the three first chapters of the novel were ready, they began to circulate them among friends. García Márquez sent them to Fuentes, who was in Europe at the time and who wrote an ecstatic notice in the cultural supplement of *Siempre!*: "I have just read the first seventy-five pages of *One Hundred Years of Solitude*. They are absolutely magnificent... The entire 'fictitious' history coexists with the 'real' history, what has been dreamed with what has been documented, and thanks to the legends, the lies, the exaggerations, the myths... Macondo becomes a universal landscape, an almost biblical story about foundations and about generations and degenerations, in a story about origins and the fate of human time and dreams and desires with which men survive and destroy themselves."[20]

Some sections of García Márquez's novel were published as advance serials in periodicals such as *Mundo Nuevo* in Paris, edited by Emir Rodríguez Monegal; *Amaru* in Lima, edited by Adolfo Westphalen; and *Eco* in Bogotá, edited by Hernando Valencia Goekel. There were early pieces discussing the material in *El Espectador*. The buzz was intense. Mutis stated, *"One Hundred Years of Solitude* is everything except a novel according to the nineteenth-century literary canon, as established by the principal novelist of that time…it's a masterful book, a book without limits, impossible to fit—happily! fortunately!—any preconceived classification."[21] After reading a section, Mario Vargas Llosa remarked, "If everything is like this fragment, the novel must be a marvel."[22]

According to Tomás Eloy Martínez, García Márquez's friend and a prominent Argentine journalist known for his novel *Santa Evita,* García Márquez had to sell a food processor "that was his most cherished wedding gift in order to be able to pay the postal charge to send the five hundred pages of the book from Mexico to Buenos Aires." Yet the claim that García Márquez had barely enough money to send one copy is contradicted by the fact that, according to Germán Vargas Cantillo and Alfonso Fuenmayor, after he finished the manuscript, he sent a copy to his friends from *El grupo de Barranquilla.* It first went to Vargas Cantillo, along with a request from García Márquez: "I want you to tell me how you find the fact that I have involved people from real life inside the novel. After you both read it, talk to Alfonso and tell me about your discussion." According to Heriberto Fiorillo, "both responded that they were very happy to be the friends of the last of the Buendías."[23]

How many copies of *One Hundred Years of Solitude* existed? Apparently, there were four. In his article *"La odisea literaria de un manuscrito,"* García Márquez said that the manuscript he and Mercedes placed in the mail had 590 double-spaced typewritten pages. The paper he used was "ordinary." He specifically stated that they put *los originales* [the originals] in the mail. The postage was eighty-two pesos, but the couple only had forty-three. The opened the package they had just prepared, divided the manuscript in two, and sent the first half by mail. Subsequently, they went to *El monte de piedad*, a pawn shop. They thought of pawning García Márquez's typewriter but decided against it because it still could earn them money. So they sold some home appliances, returned to the post office, and mailed the second half to Buenos Aires.

Of the four copies, Mutis read the original, the same one the García Márquezes divided in two and sent to Argentina. Mutis had another copy, which he took with him to Buenos Aires on a trip not long after. The third copy circulated among García Márquez's Mexican friends, and the fourth was sent to Barranquilla, to Alfonso Fuenmayor, Germán Vargas, and Álvaro Cepeda Samudio, whose daughter Patricia, according to García Márquez, cherished it like a treasure.[24] That fourth copy, by all accounts, is the only surviving manuscript.

The other three have vanished. And there are no galley proofs in existence. Amazingly, García Márquez told Rita Guibert that "I only changed one word [in them], although Paco Porrúa, editor of [Editorial] Sudamericana, told me to change as many as I liked." He added: "I believe the ideal thing would be to write a book, have it printed, and correct it afterwards. When one sends something to the printers and then reads it in print one seems to have taken a step, whether forward or backward, of extreme importance."[25]

The connection to Editorial Sudamericana was established at the beginning of 1966. Luis Harss and Barbara Dohmann, who had interviewed him for their book *Into the Mainstream*, recommended García Márquez to Francisco (Paco) Porrúa.[26] García Márquez received a letter from Porrúa requesting permission to reprint his earlier books. He replied that he had already made arrangements with another house, Ediciones Era, for reprints, but he offered Porrúa the novel he was currently working on.

In any event, for the short time the manuscript was in transit, he and Mercedes felt at once a sense of freedom as well as a growing uncertainty. She wondered if the novel was good enough, if all the time he had invested those solitary months would pay off. For about two weeks the couple didn't receive any news. Could the book have been lost in the mail?

The book's publication was inauspicious. Editorial Losada had rejected it. Carlos Barral, the *padrino*, the godfather of *El Boom*, had brushed it aside. Barral had discovered Mario Vargas Llosa and Guillermo Cabrera Infante, which in turn made his connection with García Márquez easy. Barral felt guilty about failing to recognize the quality of *One Hundred Years of Solitude.* Eventually, he explained that he had been on vacation when the manuscript arrived and the novel was dismissed by a member of his staff. He didn't have enough time to get to it; Editorial Sudamericana had already sent it to the printer.

Gerald Martin had access to a letter García Márquez wrote to Apuleyo Mendoza during this period. In it, García Márquez says that after years of "working like an animal I feel overwhelmed with tiredness, without clear prospects, except in the only thing that I like but which doesn't feed me: the novel." He dreamed of spending quality time writing. He speaks of the early response to *One Hundred Years of Solitude* with excitement, but also feels that—as he said to Mendoza when he last saw him in Barranquilla—he "embarked on an adventure that could as easily be catastrophic as successful." But he didn't have much choice other than to embrace his dream. "My conclusion from all of this is that when you have a topic that pursues you it starts growing in your head for a long time and the day it explodes you have to sit down at the typewriter or run the risk of murdering your wife."[27]

Chapter 8

Convergences

Just as García Márquez was writing *One Hundred Years of Solitude*, the Latin American literary "Boom" was coalescing as a global phenomenon. Mario Vargas Llosa, the youngest of the group (born in 1936) but one of the most energetic, had published his collection of stories *Los jefes* in 1959. He followed that with two novels that established him as a major voice in the Spanish-speaking world: *La ciudad y los perros* (1963), known in English as *The Time of the Hero*, and *The Green House* (1966). Vargas Llosa had exchanged some correspondence with García Márquez prior to 1967. At this time, they still had not met.

In 1967, Carlos Fuentes published an important novel as well: *A Change of Skin*, an experimental exercise à la the French *nouveau roman*, in which a group of friends travel from Mexico City to Veracruz during Holy Week in a Volkswagen. The novel stirred interest among readers in Spain. It was Fuentes who served as a bridge between García Márquez and a number of other Latin American authors who would be the principal players of *El Boom*.

Its leading voice, who had heard about García Márquez from numerous sources but had not met him personally, was the exiled Argentine writer Julio Cortázar. Born in Brussels in 1914, Cortázar wrote some of the best short stories of the twentieth century, including those in the collections *Blow Up*, *End of the Game*, and *We Loved Glenda So Much*. His experimental essays in *Around the Day in Eighty Worlds* and his translations (he rendered an enormous amount of Edgar Allan Poe's oeuvre into Spanish) made him highly influential. His novels, especially *Hopscotch*, published in 1963—four years before *One Hundred Years of Solitude*—was an early cornerstone of *El Boom* and is said to have helped pave the way for the consolidation of Latin American literature worldwide as tradition of its own. Cortázar died in Paris in 1984 and is buried in Montparnasse.

Vargas Llosa, Fuentes, and Cortázar, along with a loose cadre of others, including Juan Carlos Onetti (Uruguay, 1909–1994), João Guimarães Rosa (Brazil, 1908–1967), José Lezama Lima (Cuba, 1910–1976), Adolfo Bioy Casares (Argentina, 1914–1999), Augusto Roa Bastos (Paraguay, 1917–2005), José Donoso (Chile, 1924–1996), Guillermo Cabrera Infante (Cuba, 1929–2005), Manuel Puig (Argentina, 1932–1990), and, later, women such as Luisa Valenzuela (Argentina, born in 1938) and Isabel Allende (Chile, born in 1942), produced avant-garde work about Latin America that awakened readers beyond their national borders to the political, social, economic, and religious reality of a continent defined by the ghosts of colonialism centuries after it had entered modernity.[1] *El Boom* was as much an aesthetic phenomenon as it was a commercial endeavor. From Barcelona—which considered itself the literary capital of the Spanish-speaking world, especially when it came to the acquisition, production, and distribution of commercial books—came an infusion of refreshing, provocative ideas that were ingrained on a heterogeneous yet hungry readership in the vast Hispanic world.

Bursting with references to García Márquez's early literary influences, *One Hundred Years of Solitude* is filled with echoes of other Latin American writers and their fiction. In chapter ten, there is an outburst of rabbits, a clear homage to Julio Cortázar's story "Letters to Mother." Elsewhere, there are characters in Macondo who perform in front of a passing train, just as Cortázar's protagonists had done in "End of Game." The important Latin American figure, baroque Cuban novelist Alejo Carpentier, is mentioned, as are Carlos Fuentes and Mario Vargas Llosa.

In and of itself, the *rezeptiongeschichte* of García Márquez's book is intriguing. Toward the middle of April 1967, Francisco Porrúa of Editorial Sudamericana phoned Tomás Eloy Martínez "in an exalted voice," asking him to come immediately to his house and read an extraordinary book. Porrúa said: "It's so exhilarant—in Spanish, *delirante*—that I don't know if the author is a genius or is crazy."[2] Years later, Martínez recollected that it was raining heavily that day. "On the sidewalk of the street where Porrúa lived there were some loose pavers. Trying not to stumble, I got soaked. The long hallway that went from the apartment entrance to the studio was carpeted with rows of papers that appeared to be inviting the guest to clean his shoes. That's what I did: I stepped on them. They were the originals of *One Hundred Years of Solitude* that Porrúa, excited with his reading, had left on the floor. Fortunately, the shoe prints didn't erase any of those sentences that readers of García Márquez continue to repeat devotedly, as if they were prayers."[3]

Martínez recalled that the following day he and Porrúa invited García Márquez to Buenos Aires to be part of a three-member committee that Editorial Sudamericana and the weekly *Primera Plana*, of which Martínez was in charge, organized annually to judge a literary prize. In the June issue, the cover of *Primera Plana* was dedicated to *One Hundred Years of Solitude*, which it described, interestingly, as "*la gran novela de América*," the great American novel—not as the great Latin American novel but as the great novel of the Americas, regardless of language. The cover story was written by Martínez himself and is arguably the very first, or one of the first, enthusiastic reviews of the novel ever to appear.

The colophon of the Editorial Sudamericana edition, on page 352, contained the following information: the *edición prínc- ipe*, first edition, was printed on May 30, 1967, by Talleres Gráficos de la Compañía Impresora Argentina, at Calle Alsina No. 2049, in Buenos Aires. A few days later, the novel appeared in bookstores and on newspaper stands throughout the city. It was placed alongside other titles published by Emecé and Minotauro, with whom Sundamericana shared distribution. The publishing house didn't do any publicity, which makes its instant success all the more astonishing.

The publication day was set for May 30, but the original cover, which García Márquez had asked his friend the pain- ter Vicente Rojo to design, was late. Rojo had not received the manuscript in time, so the first edition was printed with another cover. Ultimately, Rojo's cover, which was used for a subsequent edition and became an icon in Latin America when the novel sold millions, would be as recognizable as the novel itself. It is a simple geometrical design that includes what appear to be lottery motifs (four bells, four moons, three stars within squarish octagons); according to some, the design approximates a children's game played in the banana region of Colombia's coast, where the novel takes place.[4]

Rojo's design is in sharp contrast to the covers of the first edition and subsequent foreign editions, including the American translation published in 1970. These covers, awash in greens and yellows, showcase sunken boats in a jungle landscape or an assortment of parrots, prostitutes, and gener- als. The imagery showcases the erotic, mythical nature of the plot as perceived outside Latin America. This type of design successfully marketed the novel and—especially for audiences in Europe—became synonymous with the literary themes of *El Boom.*

Rojo's cover was somewhat controversial. Just like other prepublication readers, the artist fell in love with *One Hundred Years of Solitude.* Amazed by its baroque style, he had purposely taken the opposite approach in his design, which, in essence, was uncomplicated. He preferred for the reader to encounter the novel's labyrinthine quality directly. The font he used for the author's name, title (in a slightly larger point size), and publisher was in all capitals and appeared slightly distressed. At the last minute, Rojo opted to invert the E of SOLEDAD, for no apparent reason. That inversion generated much debate. The E looked as if perceived through a mirror. Did the design contain a hidden meaning through which one could unravel the mysteries in the storyline? According to one biographer, Editorial Sudamericana received a number of letters from booksellers complaining that it looked like a typographical error that needed to be corrected in a future edition. Some actually made the correction themselves.[5]

After much delay, the novel's publication was rescheduled to Monday, June 5. The date didn't carry the weight that it did in New York publishing: for publicity departments, it's the target date for reviews and other media to come out. In Buenos Aires, it was simply the moment the book was made available to readers. On June 5, Argentine newspapers (including the principal ones, *La Nación, Clarín,* and *La Razón*) devoted their headlines to the conflict in the Middle East. The Israeli army, led by Minister of Defense Moshe Dayan, had invaded the Sinai desert, which is Egyptian territory, through the Gaza Strip. There was enormous tension in the air. Jordan and Syria were ready to join other Arab countries in opposition to the Zionist attack.[6]

The book sold about 800 copies in the first week, which, according to Martínez, was unusual for a novel by an unknown author. The following week that number tripled, largely due to the *Primera Plana* cover story. The first two printings— approximately 11,000 copies—sold out in a month. By the time García Márquez arrived in Buenos Aires, his novel had been on the best-seller list for a month and a half.[7] Martínez remembers that García Márquez's plane landed at 2:30 A.M. He and Porrúa "were the only people in the airport, tormented by the inclement cold of that end of winter. We saw him descend with his indescribable plaid jacket, in which sparkling reds were intertwined with electrifying blues. He was accompanied by a gorgeous woman, of big oriental eyes, that looked like a Colombian-coast version of Queen Nefertiti. It was his wife, Mercedes Barcha." According to Martínez, the two were ravenously hungry. "They pretended to look at the rising sun coming out against the infinite Pampa, near a bonfire where beef was cooking. And that's how it was. Dawn surprised us in a restaurant on the banks of the River Plate in which García Márquez entertained waiters with endless stories. Neither he nor I have forgotten the name of that *fonda*, which no longer exists. It was called *Angelito el insólito*, the astounding little angel. García Márquez left us hypnotized and exhausted that sunrise. It was the first time Porrúa and I saw the tropic in the act of exploding."

Martínez's recollection of those days is an invaluable source that allows us to determine the moment in which García Márquez's life changed forever. His description of the Colombians' stay in Buenos Aires ranges from equanimity to exhilaration. "García Márquez and Mercedes spent two or three days in an unfair state of anonymity," he recalled. Argentine readers devoured the novel by the millions but "had forgotten the photograph on the cover of *Primera Plana* and, thus, didn't recognize him on the street." That soon changed. On the third morning, the García Márquezes were having breakfast on Avenida Santa Fe when they saw a housewife, coming back from the market with shopping bags of lettuce and fresh tomatoes, pass by with a copy of *One Hundred Years of Solitude*. According to Martínez,

> That same night we went to the theater. At the Di Tella cultural center the play *Los siameses*, one of the best plays by the Argentine playwright Griselda Gambaro, had its debut. We went into the theater a few minutes before the curtain went up, with the room lights still on. García Márquez and Mercedes appeared to be disoriented by the parade of needless leather and shining feathers. I was following closely only three steps away. They were about to sit down when an unknown person screamed "Bravo! Bravo!" and started applauding. A woman added, "For your novel, García Márquez!" Once his name was uttered, the entire theater stood up and ignited in a long ovation. In that precise moment, I felt as if fame was descending from heaven, as if a living creature.
>
> Three days later I lost track of them. Secretaries were needed for the phone calls trying to reach them to be screened and to move him to another hotel so that readers would allow him to rest. The one before last time I crossed paths with him in Buenos Aires was in order to point to him on a map a secret corner in the park of Palermo were he could finally kiss Mercedes without being interrupted. The last time was at the airport, when the two were returning to their home in Mexico City, overwhelmed with flowers. He was covered with the kind of glory that since then has become his second skin.[8]

García Márquez's experience in Buenos Aires in June 1967 was the beginning of a new chapter in his life. It was there where he acquired his newfound fame, but the shock of becoming a public figure overnight didn't sit well with him. His natural shyness, his sense that privacy was something to be protected, had been challenged by the insatiable hunger of readers eager to learn as much as possible about his life: his family, his past, his craft as a writer, and the inception of *One Hundred Years of Solitude.*

The García Márquezes returned to Mexico, but they did not stay for long. They moved to Barcelona, where the writer hoped to find a suitable, quiet environment in which to write another novel he already had in mind, about a Latin American dictator. It would be called *The Autumn of the Patriarch.* Its plot would fit into what has come to be known in *El Boom* as "*la novela del dictador,*" long narratives with tyrants as the protagonist. Aside from García Márquez's novel, which would be published in 1975, there are Miguel Ángel Asturias's *El Señor Presidente* (Guatemala, 1946), Augusto Roa Bastos's *I, the Supreme* (Paraguay, 1974), Alejo Carpentier's *Reason of State* (Cuba, 1974), Luisa Valenzuela's *The Lizard's Tale* (Argentina, 1983), Tomás Eloy Martínez's *The Perón Novel* (Argentina, 1985), and Mario Vargas Llosa's *The Feast of the Goat* (Peru, 2000).[9]

In 1967, Pablo Neruda met García Márquez during the poet's brief stay in Barcelona.[10] In *Fin del mundo,* a collection of Neruda's poetry from 1968 and 1969, he includes, in section X, a bouquet of five pieces that functions as a personal chronicle of the enormous interest *El Boom* writers were generating worldwide. Neruda praises Julio Cortázar, César Vallejo, Mario Vargas Llosa, Juan Rulfo, Miguel Otero, Augusto Roa Bastos, Carlos Fuentes, and others. But García Márquez is the only one about whom Neruda writes an entire poem, a section within the series, never rendered into English. In the thirteen-line poem, Neruda sings to the author of *One Hundred Years of Solitude.* The poem is simply called "García Márquez."

The poem, although simple, records the epoch-making events of his age. Although it includes some imagery that may evoke the Buendía saga, it isn't concrete enough to allow the reader to understand Neruda's vision of the novel itself—beyond that he celebrates it as being extraordinarily vivid in its depictions of the life of the indigent in Colombia.

There are photographs of Neruda and García Márquez in Barcelona, accompanied by, among others, Carlos Fuentes and Emir Rodríguez Monegal, the latter responsible for the 1966 biography of Pablo Neruda, *El viajero inmóvil* [The Unitinerant Traveler]. It isn't difficult to understand the empathy between Neruda and García Márquez. The latter sometimes said unflattering things about the former—for instance, that Neruda was loyal to his wife Matilde, rather than faithful—but he admired the Nobel laureate and nurtured affection for him as a person. In 1992, García Márquez said:

> Pablo Neruda...devoted a morning with us to major book hunting in second-hand bookshops. He walked among the crowds like an invalid elephant, with a childish interest in the internal mechanisms of every single thing. The world, to him, seemed like an immense wind-up toy...I have never met anyone closer to the idea we have of a refined gluttonous Renaissance Pope...Matilde, his wife, put a bib on him which looked more like something out of a barber's shop than a dining-room. But it was the only way to stop him from bathing himself in sauces. That day...was a typical example. He ate three whole lobsters, pulling them apart with a surgeon's mastery, and at the same time devoured everyone else's wishes with his eyes, and picked at a bit of everyone's, with a delight in eating that was contagious: Galician clams, Cantabrian barnacles, Alicante prawns...And all the while, just like

the French, all he talked about was other exquisite dishes, especially the prehistoric seafood of Chile which he carried with him in his heart.[11]

With the publication of *One Hundred Years of Solitude* having established him as the commanding leader of *El Boom*, García Márquez spent the next three years trying to satisfy the growing interest of his international public. This entailed responding to interviewers, participating in public dialogues, and taking care of his literary affairs.

In August 1967, he met Vargas Llosa for the first time in Caracas, Venezuela, specifically in Maiquetía, where Simón Bolívar International Airport is located, a few miles from La Guajira. Caracas had recently suffered an earthquake. Vargas Llosa was coming from London, where he had been teaching, to receive the Premio Rómulo Gallegos for his novel *La casa verde*. García Márquez was arriving from Mexico, to participate in the XIII Congreso Internacional de Literatura Iberoamericana. In his book *García Márquez: Historia de un deicidio*, published by Barral in Barcelona four years later, Vargas Llosa wrote that their airplanes landed almost at the same time. "That's the first time we saw each other's faces. I remember his very well that night: distraught as a result of the fear of flying—of which he is viscerally scared—uncomfortable with the photographers and journalists that were cornering him. We became friends and spent the next two weeks together, which was the time the conference lasted, in that Caracas which, with dignity, buried its dead and swept the debris from the earthquake. The very recent success of *One Hundred Years of Solitude* had turned him into a popular character; and he enjoyed the role: his colorful shirts blinded the brainy professor during the plenary sessions; he told journalists, with a stone face like his Tía Petra's, that his novels were written by his wife but he signed them because they were very bad and Mercedes didn't want to shoulder the responsibility; asked by television if Rómulo Gallegos was a great novelist, he meditated and responded: 'In Canaima there is a description of a rooster that is quite good.' But behind all those games there is a personality increasingly fed up with his role as a star. There is a shy person for whom it is torture to speak in front of a microphone or in public. On August 7, he was unable to refuse participating in a seminar at the Ateneo in Caracas, titled 'The Novelists and the Critics,' in which he was scheduled to deliver a fifteen-minute talk about his own work. We are sitting together, and before his time came, he infected me with his infinite terror: he was ashen, his hands were sweaty, he smoked like a chimney. He spoke while seated, at a speed during the first few seconds that made us all be at the edge of our seat, and finally pulled off a story that brought down the house."[12]

From Caracas, García Márquez traveled to Bogotá and continued to Lima, where he'd been invited by the Universidad de Ingeniería to talk about his life and work. He then visited Buenos Aires for the Premio Primera Plana, went to Colombia, and returned with his family to Barcelona, where they lived. He told Daniel Samper: "There is no day in which I don't get calls from two or three editors or the same amount of journalists. Since my wife is the one who answers the phone, she has to say that I'm not in. If this is glory, it's a piece of crap. (No, you better don't state that because that line in printed form will look ridiculous.) But it's true. One doesn't even know who one's friends are. So I'll start by saying that I won't give any more interviews because I'm up to my eyeballs. I came to Barcelona because I thought that here no one would know me but the problem is the same. At first I said: no more radio or television but I'll say yes to the printed media because they are my colleagues. But no more printed media either. The journalists come, we end up getting drunk together until two o'clock in the morning and they end up leaving what I said out in their reportage. Also, I never go over what they write. In the last two years, every published statement of mine is nonsense."[13]

Elsewhere, García Márquez said, "I was once asked, I can't remember where, how my life differed before and after that book, and I said that after it 'there are four hundred more people.' That's to say before the book I had my friends, but now there are enormous numbers of people who want to see me and talk to me—journalists, academics, readers. It's strange...most of my readers aren't interested in asking questions, they only want to talk about the book. That's very flattering if you consider case by case, but added up they begin to be a problem in one's life. I would like to please them all, but as that's impossible I have to act meanly...you see? For instance, by saying I'm leaving town when all I'm really doing is changing hotels. That's how vedettes behave, something I always hated, and I don't want to play the vedette. There is, besides, a problem of conscience when deceiving people and dodging them. All the same I have to lead my own life, so the moment comes when I tell lies. Well, that can be boiled down to a cruder phrase...I say, 'I've had it to the balls with García Márquez!'"[14]

His *El Boom* colleagues were simultaneously in awe and envious of his ascent to stardom. In his personal history of the period, José Donoso argued that from 1967 on, things had obviously changed for the region. It was no longer a backwater forgotten by the rest of the world. Donoso stated that "the triumph at the level of commotion and scandal of García Márquez's novel—and I must clarify that the 'scandal' is a product, above all, of how unbearable it is to some people that a book of such literary quality can be an unprecedented public success—has made it the *only* novel whose sales may justifiably be called 'substantial.' And only as of 1969 could the Colombian novelist enjoy the 'luxury' of living where and how he wants and of writing when he wants, besides taking pleasure in imposing his own conditions on the publishers and the movie producers who surround him."[15]

By 1969, García Márquez managed to keep the hoopla at bay, at least to some degree. Finally able to give up screenwriting and freelancing to become a professional writer, his biggest challenge was to establish a routine. He told Rita Guibert, an Argentine journalist compiling a book of conversations with seven Latin American writers, that he always woke up very early, "at about six in the morning. I read the paper in bed, drink my coffee while I listen to music on the radio, and about nine—after the boys have gone to school—I sit down to write." He wrote without any interruption "until half past two, which is when the boys come home and noise begins in the house. I haven't answered the telephone all morning...my wife has been filtering calls. We have lunch between half past two and three."

"If I've been to bed late the night before," García Márquez added, "I take a siesta until four in the afternoon. From that time until six I read and listen to music—I always listen to music, except when I'm writing because I pay more attention to it than to what I'm writing. Then I go out and have coffee with someone I have a date with and in the evening friends always come to the house. That seems to be an ideal state of things for a professional writer, the culmination of all he's been aiming at. But, as you find out once you get there, it's sterile. I realized that I'd become involved in a completely sterile existence—absolutely the opposite of the life I led when I was a reporter... Yes, there's a natural tendency—when you have solved a series of material problems—to become bourgeois and shut yourself in an ivory tower, but I have an urge, and also an instinct, to escape from that situation—a sort of tug-of-war is going on inside me."[16]

One Hundred Years of Solitude was translated into dozens of languages, but García Márquez was unhappy with the Russian edition. The translation by Valeri Stolbov was censored by the Soviet regime and a number of supposedly erotic episodes were eliminated. Stolbov defended the deletions as "unimportant," stressing that the structural bulk of the narrative remained intact and that Soviet readers were able to access García Márquez's novel just like anybody else in the world. When asked in 1979 by a journalist how an essential ingredient in the Colombian writer's universe could be eliminated, the Russian translator answered: "Yes, it's true, we cannot divorce the erotic element, something profoundly human, of García Márquez's oeuvre. But I want to be clear that we didn't have a censoring spirit; had we had one, we wouldn't have published the book altogether. One must take into consideration that the novel had the largest printing ever in the history of the world. In the Socialist world itself, three and a half million copies represent something altogether inconceivable, such as the 'black market.'" Stolbov added that the novel was being sold on the Moscow streets for far more than its retail price in bookstores.[17]

Arguably, the most prominent translation is that of Gregory Rabassa into English. But it is crucial to understand the cultural climate in which it arrived. In the October 1968 issue of *Atlantic Monthly*, Lionel Trilling—the famed professor of English at Columbia University, whose work on Matthew Arnold, Sigmund Freud, and Henry James made him one of the most influential literary critics of his time (he was the first Jew to get tenure in the English Department at Columbia)—responded to a question from student David Shapiro about teaching old and new literary works from Latin America and Africa. "Well, Mr. Shapiro, I've read this Latin American literature. It has, I think one might say, an anthropological interest."[18] This type of condescension was typical among educated readers, despite the fact that a number of influential books from Latin America were already available in English. To the old boys' club, the region was synonymous with primitivism and backwardness.

The end of the sixties marked the apogee of the Beat Revolution. There was a sense that the rigid educational system that had defined the United States for generations needed to change. But the period was first and foremost about racial equality. The struggle for civil rights for blacks manifested in marches, boycotts, strikes, and building takeovers. Leading literary voices, such as Jack Kerouac and Allan Ginsberg, called for a new way of looking at things. Their interest in pre-Columbian and Oriental religions was tangible in their work. For many, the discovery of Latin American literature was a door to another reality, one ignored by the intellectual and political establishment. The magic realism of García Márquez allowed American readers to appreciate how the Spanish-speaking countries to the south evolved in parallel to the United States.

The late sixties also saw the rise of the Chicano Movement— led by Cesar Chavez, Dolores Huerta, Reies López Tijerina, Rodolfo "Corky" Gonzales, and others—which brought to the nation's attention the plight of itinerant farm workers in the Southwestern states, especially Arizona, Colorado, Texas, and California. The image of the *mexicano* in the media at the time was of an illiterate mestizo picking lettuce, strawberries, and oranges in the fields. Hence Lionel Trilling's suggestion that the culture was lacking in sophistication. As a professor, he supported a literary canon defined by the European masters, from the ancient Greeks such as Sophocles to early twentieth-century greats such as Kafka, Proust, and—among Trilling's favorites—Isaac Babel, the Russian author of short stories in the mode of Maupassant. To him, Latin American novels didn't belong in the classroom as serious literature capable of exploring universal themes and motifs.

García Márquez's first work to appear in English was *No One Writes to the Colonel* in 1968, which included "Big Mama's Funeral." For the translation of *One Hundred Years of Solitude*,

Julio Cortázar recommended Gregory Rabassa to García Márquez. But Rabassa was busy working on Guatemalan Nobel Prize laureate Miguel Ángel Asturias's "banana trilogy" for Delacorte: *Mulata* (in Spanish *Mulata de tal,* written in 1963, translated in 1967), *Strong Wind* (*Viento fuerte,* 1950, English 1969) and *The Green Pope* (*El papa verde,* 1954, English 1971). Cortázar, whose novel *Hopscotch* had been translated by Rabassa in 1966 for Pantheon and for which Rabassa received the National Book Award, advised García Márquez to wait. As a general rule, Rabassa did not read a novel before he translated it, to allow the thrill of discovery to inspire his work. *One Hundred Years of Solitude* was an exception. "People who had read the novel in Spanish were talking about it intelligently, sometimes not so intelligently, but always with a kind of awe. I suppose that this should have scared me off, but in manners of translation and a few other things I don't frighten easily and I was ready to take it on."[19]

In the article *"Los pobres traductores buenos"* (Poor Good Translators) syndicated in 1982, García Márquez discussed the art of translation. He began by invoking the Italian maxim: *Traduttore, traditore.* He explained that when one reads an author one likes in a language that isn't the reader's native tongue, one experiences the urge to translate. "It's explainable," he argues, "because one of the pleasures of reading—as is the case of music—is the need to share it with friends." García Márquez said he understood Marcel Proust's desire to translate into French a writer who was very different from him: English–speaking John Ruskin. He claimed he would have liked to translate two French writers, André Malraux and Antoine de Saint-Exupéry, "both of whom, by the way, don't enjoy a high estimation by their contemporaries in France." But he never went beyond the sheer desire.

García Márquez confessed to translating, slowly, the *Cantos* by Giacomo Leopardi, "but I do it in hiding, away from others and in my very few free hours, with complete awareness that this will not be a road to glory for either me or Leopardi. I do it as one of those bathroom pastimes Jesuit priests describe as solitary pleasures. For now the attempt has been sufficient to make me realize how difficult, and how consuming, it is to fight for the same bread with professional translators." Toward the end of the article, García Márquez discussed the various translations of *One Hundred Years of Solitude* in the languages he was able to understand. "I don't recognize myself in any of them, only in Spanish."

But he celebrated Gregory Rabassa. He once called him "the best Latin American writer in the English language." Of Rabassa, García Márquez said: "I've read some of the books translated into English [by him] and I must recognize that I found some passages that I liked more than in the original. The impression one gets of Rabassa's translations is that he memorized the book in Spanish and then writes it in its entirety in English: his fidelity is more complex than simple literality. He never includes a footnoted explanation, which is the less valid and most frequented strategy of bad translators. In this sense, the most notable example is of the Brazilian translator of one of my books, who gave a footnoted explanation to the word *astromelia:* imaginary flower invented by García Márquez. The worse thing is that later on I forget that astromelias not only exist, as everyone knows in the Caribbean, but that their name is Portuguese."[20]

The story of Rabassa's masterful rendition begins with Cass Canfield Jr. at Harper & Row in New York, the son of Cass Canfield, one of the company's founders. As a young acquisition editor, Canfield Jr. was interested in Latin American writers. There was buzz in the American publishing industry about the new crop from Latin America. A long-time professor at the City University of New York, Rabassa made the mistake of accepting from Cass Canfield Jr. a work for hire agreement for his translation of *One Hundred Years of Solitude.*[21] It's "quite heartening for me as a lover of good literature" to see the success of the novel, which has gone through endless reprints, but it's "saddening to me as a translator."

Rabassa's contract wasn't unique. It was common for translators to be paid a flat fee and not receive royalties, unless it was for a translation of the Greek classics. Nowadays, many translators have royalties written into their contracts. In retrospect, Rabassa considered it akin to "spreading manure on a suburban lawn."[22] Canfield fought to get Rabassa royalties for the first paperback, but that dried up rather quickly for concrete reasons: Harper & Row had a long-standing contract with Carmen Barcells Literary Agency to publish García Márquez on a regular basis. But after García Márquez won the Nobel Prize for Literature in 1982, the agency, according to Canfield, wanted to amend the old contracts, which is not an accepted practice in the industry.

Although García Márquez was a best-selling author, Canfield and others at Harper & Row were adamant against the change. They offered a higher bid for García Márquez's most recent novel, *The General in His Labyrinth,* translated not by Rabassa but by Edith Grossman. The page proofs had already been produced when Carmen Balcells decided to move her author to another New York publisher, Alfred A. Knopf. García Márquez's previous books remained with Harper & Row, but the complication prevented royalties from being paid.[23] "There is something on occasion from the Book-of-the-Month Club," Rabassa has said, "but in general, as far as I'm concerned, the book might just as well be in the public domain...Let me stop whining, though. It's too prevalent among translators as, like so many famished locusts, they pounce hungrily on the hors d'oeuvres at literary affairs. We must take what small comfort we can doing something honorable in a world of imposters, pretenders, and bourgeois tradesmen, as old Prince François so aptly put it in *The Fallen Sparrow*."

Rabassa's first challenge was the title. "A simple declarative title *Cien años de soledad* should offer no trouble whatever," he argued later in his book *If This Be Treason*.[24] "Think again. We can pass *de* and *años*, they stand up fine, even though *años* would have to go if we opted for *century*, because that's what a hundred years comprise. I turned that option down rather quickly. *Cien* is our first problem because in Spanish it bears no article so that the word can waver between *one* hundred and *a* hundred. There is no hint in the title as to which it should be in English...I viewed the extent of time involved as something quite specific, as in a prophecy, something definite, a countdown, not just any old hundred years. What is troublesome, of course, is that both interpretations are conjoined subconsciously for the reader of the Spanish...But an English speaker reading the Spanish will have to decide subconsciously which meaning is there. They cannot be melded in his mind. I was convinced and I still am that Gabo meant in the sense of *one* as this meaning is closer to the feel of the novel. Also, there was no cavil on his part over the title in English."[25]

Rabassa took great care with the names in the novel. "In order to avoid confusion between father and son (although confusion is subtly encouraged throughout the book) I had to make sure that the old patriarch was always José Arcadio Buendía, never any truncated version, much the way that Charlie Brown is never called anything but Charlie Brown in *Peanuts*. There is some kind of personal essence that must be preserved as we handle names and as the novel progresses this essence becomes clear and the names go on unchanged and exude this essence while taking on new accretion. When I was growing up the president was Franklin Delano Roosevelt, as he always put it, or Franklin D. Roosevelt, not to mention FDR. It rubs against a nerve today when I hear him called simply Franklin Roosevelt. Part of his essence has been left out, making him akin to Franklin Pierce, God save us! What if we went about speaking of John Whittier, Henry Longfellow, Oliver Holmes? Gabo had wise reasons for keeping the name José Arcadio Buendía intact, singling him out in distinction from his son, who was simply José Arcadio, with no surname ever mentioned, and from his great-grandson José Arcadio Segundo. In this last case I chose to keep the Spanish word for second, it being understood as a cognate, thinking that José Arcadio II or José Arcadio the Second sounded too royal or too highfalutin."[26]

The question of how to translate the first line of the novel made Rabassa think. *"Muchos años después, frente al pelotón de fusilamiento, el coronel Aureliano Buendía había de recordar aquella tarde remota en que su padre lo llevó a conocer el hielo."* Rabassa claimed, "People go on repeating this all the time (in English) and I can only hope that I have got them saying what it means. I wrote: 'many years later, as he faced the firing squad, Colonel Aureliano Buendía was to remember that distant afternoon when his father took him to discover ice.' There are variant possibilities. In the British army it would have been a 'firing party,' which I rather like, but I was writing for American readers. *Había de* could have been *would* (How much wood can a woodchuck chuck?), but I think *was to* has a better feel to it. I chose *remember* over *recall* because I feel that it conveys a deeper memory. *Remote* might have aroused thoughts of such inappropriate things as remote control and robots. Also, I liked *distant* when used with time. I think Dr. Einstein would have approved. The real problem for choice was with *conocer* and I have come to know that my selection has set a great many Professor Horrendo all aflutter. It got to the point that my wife Clem had to defend my choice (hers too) against one such worthy in a seminar in which she was participating. The word *seen* straight means to know a person or thing for the first time, to meet someone, to be familiar with something. What is happening here is a first-time meeting, or learning. It can also mean to know something more deeply than *saber*, to know from experience. García Márquez has used the Spanish word here with all its connotations. But *to know ice* just won't do in English. It implies, 'How do you do, ice?' It could be 'to experience ice.' The first is foolish, the second is silly. When you get to know something for the first time, you've discovered it. Only after that can you come to know it in the full sense. I could have said 'to make the acquaintance with ice,' but that, too, sounds nutty, with its implication of tipping one's hat or giving a handshake. I stand by what I put down in this important opening sentence."[27]

García Márquez wasn't fluent enough in English to be of useful help to Rabassa when choosing variants. Rabassa communicated with him a number of times, by mail, to ask about the flora and fauna of the Caribbean and of Colombia in particular, and for other precise matters.[28] The first edition published by Editorial Sudamericana didn't contain a family tree. It was García Márquez's intention to allow the reader to experience some confusion about the characters, as well as time and place. Rabassa claims that the editors at Harper & Row asked him to create a family tree for the English translation. "At the time I thought it was a good idea, something to help readers keep all the characters straight and to let them see the complex interrelationships. Later on, after the book had come out, I had second thoughts. If García Márquez had wanted such a table he would have put one in the first Spanish edition."

Rabassa speculated that the fusion and confusion were meant to be part of the novel, revealing how all members of our species must look to apes or horses, which may have trouble distinguishing among us. "This idea also ties in with the repetition of Christian names in the family, so that distinction is of little import after six or seven generations and a hundred years, when memory dissolves and all who went before become what Turgenev called 'gray people.' It's puzzling, or is it, since it was put together by academics, that the fine footnoted Spanish edition in the Cátedra series also carries a genealogical table at the beginning."[29]

There was enormous buzz in New York about García Márquez's novel. Arguably the most important review of *One Hundred Years of Solitude* in English was by John Leonard in the March 3, 1970, issue of the *New York Times* daily. Leonard started by saying that the reader emerges "from this marvelous novel as if from a dream, the mind on fire." He continued: "A dark, ageless figure at the hearth, part historian, part haruspex, in a voice by turn angelic and maniacal, first lulls to sleep your grip on a manageable reality, then locks you into legend and myth. *One Hundred Years of Solitude* is not only the story of the Buendía family and the Colombian town of Macondo. It is a recapitulation of our evolutionary and intellectual experience. Macondo is Latin America in microcosm: local autonomy yielding to state authority; anticlericalism; party politics; the coming of the United Fruit Company; aborted revolutions; the rape of innocence by history. And the Buendías (inventors, artisans, soldiers, lovers, mystics) seem doomed to ride a biological tricycle in circles from solitude to magic to poetry to science to politics to violence back again to solitude."

Leonard placed García Márquez's achievement in the context of world literature. "Family chronicle, then, and political tour de force, and metaphysical speculation, and, intentionally, a cathedral of words, perceptions and legends that amounts to the declaration of a state of mind: solitude being one's admission of one's own mortality and one's discovery that that terrible apprehension is itself mortal, dies with you, must be rediscovered and forgotten again, endlessly. With a single bound Gabriel García Márquez leaps onto the stage with Günter Grass and Vladimir Nabokov, his appetite as enormous as his imagination, his fatalism greater than either." Leonard concluded with a single word: "Dazzling."[30]

On March 8, 1970, in the *New York Times Book Review,* Michael Kiely wrote a flat, unintelligent appraisal. Kiely seemed trapped in an understanding of fantasia based on Tolkien's *The Lord of the Rings:* "To speak of a land of enchantment, even in reference to a contemporary novel, is to conjure up images of elves, moonbeams and slippery mountains. Along with the midgets and fairies, one can expect marvelous feats and moral portents, but not much humor and almost certainly no sex. The idea, it would seem, is to forget the earth. At least that is one idea of enchantment." But Kiely suggested that this approach is not shared by García Márquez, "who has created in *One Hundred Years of Solitude* an enchanted place that does everything but coy...Macondo oozes, reeks and burns even when it is most tantalizing and entertaining. It is a place flooded with lies and liars and yet it spills over with reality. Lovers in this novel can idealize each other into bodiless spirits, howl with pleasure in their hammocks or, as in one case, smear themselves with peach jam and roll naked on the front porch. The hero can lead a Quixotic expedition across the jungle, but although his goal is never reached, the language describing his quest is pungent with life...This is the language of a poet who knows the earth and does not fear it as the enemy of the dreamer." Kiely concluded, "Stew is too modest an image with which to describe the wit and power of this lusty fantasia, but if the strong savor banishes visions of twinkle toes, it has served a purpose."[31]

V. S. Pritchett, in the *New Yorker,* let his admiration spill forth: "the history of the Buendía family and their women in three or four generations is written as a hearsay report on the growth of the little Colombian town; it comes to life because it is continuously leaping out of fact into the mythical and the myth is comic. One obvious analogy is to Rabelais.

It is suggested, for example, that Aureliano Segundo's sexual orgies with his concubine are so enjoyable that his own livestock catch the fever. Animals and birds are unable to stand by and do nothing." For Pritchett the story was a social history "but not as it is found in books but as it muddles its way forward and backward among the sins of family life and the accidents of trade." He thought that *One Hundred Years of Solitude* denied interpretation. "One could say that a little Arcady was created but was ruined by the 'Promethean ideas' that came into the head of its daring founder. Or that little lost towns have their moment—as civilizations do—and are then obliterated."[32]

By mid-month, *Time* magazine ran an anonymous piece that sang the novel's praises. "Gabriel García Márquez spent the first eight years of his life in Aracataca, a steamy banana town not far from the Colombian coast. 'Nothing interesting has happened to me since,' he has said. His experiences there were eventually transformed into a tenderly comic novel, just published in the U.S. after three years of enormous success in Latin America. It has survived export triumphantly. In a beautiful translation, surrealism and innocence blend to form a whole individual style. Like rum *calentano*, the story goes down easily, leaving a rich, sweet burning flavor behind...Reduced to essence, the exotic Buendías become immediate—yet mythically compelling like Tolstoy's Rostov family, or the doomed scions of Faulkner's *Sartoris*. But *One Hundred Years of Solitude* is more than a family chronicle. The author is really at work on an imaginative spiritual history of any and all Latin American communities. In the process, he fondly reveals more about the Latin soul than all Oscar Lewis's selective eavesdroppings does."[33]

García Márquez's reaction to these reviews, according to Cass Canfield Jr., was ecstatic. In time, he learned to temper his response to readers. About criticism, García Márquez stated: "Critics for me are the biggest example of what intellectualism is. First of all, they have a theory of what a writer should be. The try to get the writer to fit their model, and if he doesn't fit, they still try to get him in by force...I really have no interest in what critics think of me; nor have I read criticism in many years. They have claimed for themselves the task of being intermediaries between the author and the reader. I've always tried to be a very clear and precise writer, trying to reach the reader directly without having to go through the critic."[34] García Márquez's dismissal of what critics said about him and his books runs deeper. Not only did he mistrust their instincts but he resented their pretentious philosophizing. Yet his own statements, then and later, distill a sense of false modesty, even pomposity, making him seem arrogant and aloof. It could be, of course, that his success fosters undiminished envy, for which he is penalized.

An example of this attitude is clear in an interview he gave years later to Raymond Leslie Williams. "There's no doubt that the author's vision of his or her books is very different from the vision of the critic or of the reader..." he stated. "Readers don't tell you why they liked the books, nor do they know why, but you feel that they really liked them. Of course, there are also people who say they don't like the books, but in general my readers seem to be swept away. And my books are sold in enormous quantities, which interests me, because that means that they are read by a broad public. They are read by elevator operators, nurses, doctors, presidents. This gives me a tremendous security, while the critics always leave the writers with a spark of insecurity. Even the most serious and praiseful critics can go off on a track you hadn't suspected, leaving you wondering if perhaps you made a mistake. Besides, I understand the critics very little. I'm not exactly sure what they are saying or what they think." He wanted to go back to the source, to be truthful to the art of story-telling. In the same interview, García Márquez added: "Everything comes from inside or is in my subconscious or is the natural result of an ideological position or comes from raw experience that I haven't analyzed, which I try to use in all innocence. I think I'm quite innocent in writing."³⁵

Hollywood quickly became interested in a screen adaptation. In a newspaper column many years later, García Márquez wrote about all the invitations he had received throughout the years to turn the novel into a movie. He described a request by Anthony Quinn, offered during a dinner party around 1977, to adapt *One Hundred Years of Solitude* into a fifty-hour TV series. He quotes Quinn as saying, "I offered him a million dollars and he didn't want them, because García Márquez is a Communist, and he doesn't want anyone to know he has received a million dollars. Because afterwards, once the dinner was over, he came and told me: How could you offer me that money in public? Some other time you can offer it to me without any witnesses nearby." The story is more complicated. Quinn had arrived in Mexico City with the offer, which he announced to the media before he presented it to García Márquez. The Colombian told the media that he would do it not for one but for two million, one for him "and the other for the Latin American revolution." To which Quinn responded, "I'll give him one million. The second million he can get it from someone else." Anthony Quinn's offer wasn't the first, nor would it be the last. Some years before, a consortium of North American and European producers had offered García Márquez two million dollars. There were rumors, apparently unfounded, that Francis Ford Coppola, who directed *The Godfather* series, was also interested in an adaptation.³⁶

Still in his forties, García Márquez was at his apex. He was considered a living treasure, and he occupied a place on the shelf of world literature.

Afterword

A man's life is filled with unexpected twists and turns which shape his destiny. What would have happened if, by chance, García Márquez had not completed *One Hundred Years of Solitude?* Or if, in a burst of terrible luck, all four copies of the manuscript had been lost? Less farfetched is the possibility that a single mishap in García Márquez's life could have kept him one morning from returning to *La Cueva de la Mafia* to finalize his all-consuming literary endeavor. What then?

The idea is atrocious. It is easier for me to understand the world without a Greek island than without this essential novel.

Cyril Connolly, in his 1938 book *Enemies of Promise,* states that a writer's purpose is to create a single masterpiece. Everything must be geared in that direction. García Márquez was forty when he reached his audience. His age is crucial: it is roughly the time when, after much struggle distilling one's own style, the writer either shows the extent of his talent by stamping his vision in a single oeuvre whose value will outlast him—or he doesn't. This middle-class Colombian journalist from *"un moridero de pobres,"* a God-forsaken Caribbean town, accomplished this task. Everything he did before the Buendía saga is mere preparation. Macondo had been gestating in his imagination since childhood, ever since his grandmother filled his head with bizarre, entertaining stories. Its traces began to appear in fictional narratives he composed during his tenure as a newspaper reporter.

Today the reader recognizes those early references to Macondo, Colonel Aureliano Buendía, the banana workers' massacre, and other details in stories such as "One Day After Saturday" or "Big Mama's Funeral," or in the novellas *No One Writes the Colonel* and *The Incredible and Sad Tale of Innocent Erendira and Her Heartless Grandmother*.

The literary sleuth looking for earlier drafts of Macondian history is intrigued.

For instance, "Monologue of Isabel Watching It Rain in Macondo" is a first-person account of a deluge in the mythical town. That rainstorm plays a prominent role in *One Hundred Years of Solitude*. But the piece is written in an existential mode. Although it doesn't quite foretell any specific action to come in the Buendía chronicle, it served as a trigger: it enabled García Márquez to start visualizing the map of his imaginary habitat.

García Márquez's accomplishment is obvious from the response to his novel, one of universal adoration. What is mind-blowing is his reaction thereafter. Having reached his apex in 1967, what then? This isn't an academic question. As it turned out, he had not yet reached his midpoint, what Dante, in the first canto of "Hell," the opening third of the *Divine Comedy*, described as *"nel mezzo del cammin di nostra vita."* What should a writer do with the rest of his allotted time? How should he maximize it without repeating himself?

For years I thought that—paraphrasing Hamlet, whose famous last words were "The rest is silence"—the best García Márquez, the eponymous *Libertador* of Latin American culture, could do after that climax was disappear. I believed that, perhaps, for him the rest was silence, too. What else could an avid readership expect after such a bold, masterful act of invention?

I was wrong, of course.

Notes

Preface

1. The quote is from Ana María Ochoa's essay "García Márquez, Macondismo, and the Soundscapes of Vallenato," *Popular Music*, vol. 24, num. 2 (May 2005): 207–208. A number of scholars have explored the topic of Macondismo, among them José Joaquín Brunner in "Traditionalism and Modernity in Latin American Culture," in *Latin America Writes Back: Postmodernity in the Periphery, Hispanic Issues* vol. 28, edited by Emil Volek. New York and London: Routledge, 2002: 3–31.
2. This ambivalence is explored by Kelly Hargrave and Georgina Smith Seminet in "De Macondo a *McOndo*: Nuevas voces en la literatura latinoamericana," *Chasqui*, vol. 2 (November 1998): 14–26.

1   Aracataca

1. *Los diez mandamientos*. Buenos Aires: Editorial Jorge Álvarez, 1966. The translation is mine. García Márquez's piece was also published as *"Desventuras de un escritor de libros,"* in the *Magazín Dominical* of the Bogotá newspaper *El Espectador* (August 7, 1966).
2. For instance, Raymond L. Williams, in *Gabriel García Márquez*. Boston: Twayne, 1984, offers 1928 as the birth year. Among others, Mario Vargas Llosa, in *García Márquez: Historia de un*

deicidio. Barcelona: Barral Editores, 1971, makes the same mistake.

3. "Ni yo soy diablo ni Gabito es santo: Luis Enrique," in Silvia Galvis, Los García Márquez. Bogotá: Océano and Arango Editores, 1997: 133.

4. See Dasso Saldívar, García Márquez: El viaje a la semilla. Madrid: Alfaguara, 1997: 86, and Gerald Martin, Gabriel García Márquez: A Life. New York: Alfred A. Knopf, 2009: 29. Saldívar gives the exact time of the writer's birth a half hour earlier: 8:30 A.M.

5. Gerald Martin, Gabriel García Márquez: A Life: 40.

6. Plinio Apuleyo Mendoza, The Fragrance of Guava, translated by Ann Wright. London: Verso, 1983: 52.

7. García Márquez, "Caribe mágico," in Notas de prensa: 1980–1984. Bogotá: Grupo Editorial Norma, 1991: 59–62.

8. The sentence serves as the epigraph to Herbert Braun, The Assassination of Gaitán: Public Life and Urban Violence in Colombia. Madison: University of Wisconsin Press, 1985.

9. Mario Vargas Llosa, García Márquez: Historia de un deicidio. Barcelona: Barral Editores, 1971: 14.

10. Gabriel García Márquez, Living to Tell the Tale, translated by Edith Grossman. New York: Alfred A. Knopf, 2003: 14–15.

11. Peter H. Stone, "Gabriel García Márquez: The Art of Fiction," Paris Review, no. 82 (1981), reprinted in The Paris Review Interviews, vol. II, edited by Philip Gourevich, prologue by Orhan Pamuk. New York: Picador, 2007: 190–191.

12. Gabriel García Márquez, foreword to La Casa Grande by Álvaro Cepeda Samudio, translated by Seymour Menton. Austin: University of Texas Press, 1991: xi.

13. Silvia Galvis, Los García Márquez. Bogotá: Océano Arango Editores, 1997: 259.

14. Plinio Apuleyo Mendoza, The Fragrance of Guava: 19.

15. Peter H. Stone, "Gabriel García Márquez": 188.

16. Peter H. Stone, "Gabriel García Márquez": 189.

17. Plinio Apuleyo Mendoza, The Fragrance of Guava: 18.

18. Gabriel García Márquez, Living to Tell the Tale: 68.

19. Pete Hamill, "Love and Solitude," Vanity Fair (March 1988): 131. See also Dasso Saldívar, El viaje a la semilla: 89–90.

20. Gabriel García Márquez, *Living to Tell the Tale*: 70.
21. Dasso Saldívar, *El viaje a la semilla*: 79–90.
22. Plinio Apuleyo Mendoza, *The Fragrance of Guava*: 19–20.
23. Plinio Apuleyo Mendoza, *The Fragrance of Guava*: 20.
24. García Márquez, "Vuelta a la semilla," published on December 21, 1983, in *Notas de prensa: 1980–1984*. Bogotá: Grupo Editorial Norma, 1991: 643–646. See also Gerald Martin, *Gabriel García Márquez: A Life*: 103.
25. Plinio Apuleyo Mendoza, *The Fragrance of Guava*: 17.
26. See Ilan Stavans, "Sangre y origen," *El Diario* (New York), April 14, 2009.
27. Gabriel García Márquez, *One Hundred Years of Solitude*, translated by Gregory Rabassa. New York: Harper & Row, 1970: 135.
28. Mario Vargas Llosa, *García Márquez: Historia de una deicidio*: 28.

2   *Apprenticeship*

1. Gabriel García Márquez, *Living to Tell the Tale*: 136.
2. When I wrote my essay "The First Book" (included in *Art and Anger*. Albuquerque: University of New Mexico Press, 1996) for *The Washington Post Book World* in 1995, I had a long debate with the newspaper's fact checker who pointed out that Emilio Salgari didn't exist because his name doesn't appear in the Library of Congress catalog. To my dismay, I realized he was right once I checked the source. How come such an influential young-adult author had no footing in the English-speaking world? It's a mystery...
3. Gabriel García Márquez, *Living to Tell the Tale*: 137.
4. Plinio Apuleyo Mendoza, *The Fragrance of Guava*: 96.
5. Registered at the Ministerio de Educación, in Folio 345, Libro 18.
6. Pete Hamill, "Love and Solitude": 130.
7. Pete Hamill, "Love and Solitude": 130.
8. Gabriel García Márquez, *One Hundred Years of Solitude*: 379.
9. Plinio Apuleyo Mendoza, *The Fragrance of Guava*: 39.

10. For instance, Silvia Galvis, *The García Márquez*: 73–106 and 133–156. Also, Dasso Saldívar, *El viaje a la semilla*: 75–128.

11. Jacques Gilard, *Gabriel García Márquez: Obra periodística*, vol. 1 *Textos costeños*. Barcelona: Editorial Bruguera, 1982: 7–8.

12. Plinio Apuleyo Mendoza, *The Fragrance of Guava*: 48.

13. Plinio Apuleyo Mendoza, *The Fragrance of Guava*: 48.

14. Plinio Apuleyo Mendoza, *The Fragrance of Guava*: 41.

15. Plinio Apuleyo Mendoza, *The Fragrance of Guava*: 30, 49. "Bloody Hell" is the same type of expression used by Úrsula Iguarán in *One Hundred Years of Solitude*, for instance, upon discovering the corpse of her son José Arcadio Buendía in the house he shared with Rebeca.

16. Efraín Kristal, *Invisible Work: Borges and Translation*. Nashville: Vanderbilt University Press, 2002: 186.

17. Cristina Pestaña Castro, "*¿Quién tradujo por primera vez 'La metamorfosis' de Franz Kafka al castellano?*," *Espéculo: Revista de estudios literarios*, Universidad Complutense de Madrid, 1999.

18. Gabriel García Márquez, "The Third Resignation," *Collected Stories*, translated by Gregory Rabassa. New York: Harper & Row, 1984: 5.

19. Eligio García Márquez, *Tras las claves de Melquíades: Historia de "Cien años de soledad."* Bogotá: Editorial Norma, 2001: 96.

20. See Ilan Stavans, "Buffoonery of the Mundane," *The Nation* (October 7, 2002). Reprinted as "Felisberto is an Imbecile," *A Critic's Journey*. Ann Arbor: University of Michigan Press, 2009.

21. Plinio Apuleyo Mendoza, *The Fragrance of Guava*: 32.

22. See Ilan Stavans, "Beyond Translation: Faulkner and Borges," in *Look Away!: The U.S. South in New World Studies*, edited with an introduction by Jon Smith and Deborah Cohn. Durham, NC: Duke University Press, 2004.

23. Juan Carlos Onetti, *Confesiones de un lector*. Madrid: Alfaguara, 1995: 20–21.

24. Gabriel García Márquez, "*El amargo encanto de la máquina de escribir*," in *Notas de prensa: 1980–1984*. Bogotá: Grupo Editorial Norma, 1991: 362–365.

25. See Raymond Leslie Williams, *Ideology and the Novel in Nineteenth- and Twentieth-Century Colombia: The Colombian Novel, 1844–1987.* Austin: University of Texas Press, 1991: 20–51.

26. Herbert Braun, *The Assassination of Gaitán*: 135.
27. Herbert Braun, *The Assassination of Gaitán*: 149.
28. Herbert Braun, *The Assassination of Gaitán*: 203.
29. Gabriel García Márquez, "Bogotá 1947," published on October 21, 1981, in *Notas de prensa: 1980–1984*. Bogotá: Grupo Editorial Norma, 1991: 218–220.
30. Peter H. Stone, "Gabriel García Márquez": 185.

3   *Mamador de gallos*

1. Peter H. Stone, "Gabriel García Márquez": 185.
2. Plinio Apuleyo Mendoza, *The Fragrance of Guava*: 55.
3. Germán Vargas Cantillo, "García Márquez y el Grupo de Barranquilla," *El arte de leer a García Márquez*, edited by Juan Gustavo Cobo Borda. Bogotá: Grupo Editorial Norma, 2007: 46.
4. Plinio Apuleyo Mendoza, *The Fragrance of Guava*: 55.
5. Gabriel García Márquez, "El amargo encanto de la máquina de escribir," in *Notas de prensa: 1980–1984*. Bogotá: Grupo Editorial Norma, 1991: 362–365. See Dasso Saldívar, *El viaje a la semilla*: 498.
6. Plinio Apuleyo Mendoza, *The Fragrance of Guava*: 55.
7. Peter S. Stone, "Gabriel García Márquez": 189–190.
8. Interview with Susana Cato, "Soap Operas Are Wonderful, I've Always Wanted to Write One," *Gramma* (January 17, 1988). Reprinted in Gene H. Bell-Villada, *Conversations with Gabriel García Márquez*. Jackson: University Press of Mississippi, 2006: 148–153. Tracing the possible inspirations of *One Hundred Years of Solitude* has become a sport of sorts among academics. As I state elsewhere in this volume, the usual suspects are, aside from *Diary of the Year of the Plague*, Virginia Woolf's *Orlando*, William Faulkner novels about the Deep South, and Honoré de Balzac's La Comédie humaine. I place at the top of the list the source of sources: the Bible. Intriguingly, David T. Haberly, in his essay "Bags of Bones: A Source for *One Hundred Years of Solitude*," *MLN*, vol. 105, num. 2 (March 1990): 392–3, suggests an unlikely option: Chateaubriand's

Atala, which is mentioned prominently in a predecessor of García Márquez's novel in Colombia, Jorge Isaac's *María*.

9. Plinio Apuleyo Mendoza, *The Fragrance of Guava*: 59.
10. Plinio Apuleyo Mendoza, *The Fragrance of Guava*: 59.
11. Alfred Kazin: "Review of *Leaf Storm and Other Stories*," *New York Times Book Review*, February 20, 1972: 14.
12. Alfred Kazin, "Review of *Leaf Storm and Other Stories*": 14.
13. Plinio Apuleyo Mendoza, *The Fragrance of Guava*: 33.
14. Heriberto Fiorillo, *La Cueva: Crónica del grupo de Barranquilla*. Barranquilla: Ediciones La Cueva, 2006: 354.
15. Meira Delmar, interview with the author, Barranquilla, November 2007.
16. Miguel Fernández-Braso, *La soledad de Gabriel García Márquez*. Barcelona: Planeta, 1972: 58–59.
17. Heriberto Fiorillo, *La Cueva*: 310.
18. Heriberto Fiorillo, *La Cueva*: 313.
19. Heriberto Fiorillo, *La Cueva*: 313.
20. Miguel Fernández-Braso: *La soledad de Gabriel García Márquez*: 59.
21. Gabriel García Márquez, *Living to Tell the Tale*: 373.
22. García Márquez: "*El cuento del cuento*," published on August 26, 1981 in *Notas de prensa: 1980–1984*. Bogotá: Grupo Editorial Norma, 1991: 188–190.
23. Gabriel García Márquez, *One Hundred Years of Solitude*: 393–394.
24. Regarding the metaliterary devices, another point of coincidence—another tacit tribute?—between *Don Quixote* and *One Hundred Years of Solitude* is the recurrence of the palimpsest (etymologically, from the Latin *palimpsestum*, meaning *scraped again*, and defined as "a manuscript, typically of papyrus or parchment, that has been written on more than once, with the earlier writing incompletely erased and often legible"). The narrator of Cervantes's novel finds in Toledo, a town known for its academy devoted to translation, a scroll written originally in Arabic by the historian Cide Hamete Benengeli and asks a Moor he comes across on the street to translate it for him. In the last pages of García Márquez's novel, the last

Aureliano finds a series of parchments written by the Gypsy Melquíades that chronicles the Buendía saga and includes an italicized epigraph that reads: *"The first of the line is tied to a tree and the last is being eaten by the ants"* (*One Hundred Years of Solitude*: 420). In other words, the two texts have murky origins. Or, to go even further with the cultural connotations, both narratives aren't only presented as spurious; furthermore, they have been composed by chroniclers (an Arab, a Gypsy) whose standing in Hispanic civilization is defined by rejection.

25. Gene H. Bell-Villada, "A Conversation with Gabriel García Márquez," *Gabriel García Márquez's One Hundred Years of Solitude: A Casebook*, edited by Gene H. Bell-Villada. New York: Oxford University Press, 2002: 22.

26. Gustavo Arango, *Un ramo de nomeolvides: García Márquez en "El Universal."* Cartagena: El Universal, 1995.

27. Gabriel García Márquez, *The Story of a Shipwrecked Sailor*, translated by Randolph Hogan. New York: Alfred A. Knopf, 1986: v.

28. Gabriel García Márquez, *The Story of a Shipwrecked Sailor*: vii.

29. Gabriel García Márquez, *The Story of a Shipwrecked Sailor*: vii.

30. Gabriel García Márquez, *The Story of a Shipwrecked Sailor*: ix. The reportage belongs to what has come to be known as the "Robinsonade" genre, i.e., narratives about shipwrecks and/or island survivors. It's a reference, obviously, to Daniel Defoe's *Robinson Crusoe* (1719), but the shelf is ample enough to include a predecessor: Thomas More's *Utopia* (1516), as well as Jonathan Swift's *Gulliver's Travels* (1726) and *Candide, ou l'Optimisme* (1759). The genre is a favorite of contemporary authors such as William Golding (*Lord of the Flies*, 1954), J. M. Coetzee (*Foe*, 1986), José Saramago (*The Stone Raft*, 1986), Umberto Eco (*The Island of the Day Before*, 1994), and Yan Martel's *Life of Pi* (2001).

31. Rita Guibert, *Seven Voices: Seven Latin American Writers Talk to Rita Guibert*. New York: Alfred A. Knopf, 1973: 317.

32. John Updike, *Odd Jobs: Essays and Criticism*. New York: Alfred A. Knopf, 1991: 493–494.

4 *New Horizons*

1. Gabriel García Márquez, *"La desgracia de ser escritor joven,"* published on September 9, 1981, in *Notas de prensa: 1980–1984.* Bogotá: Grupo Editorial Norma, 1991: 195–198.
2. Harley D. Oberhelman, "William Faulkner and Gabriel García Márquez: Two Nobel Laureates," in *Critical Essays on Gabriel García Márquez,* edited by George R. McMurray. Boston: G. K. Hall & Co., 1987: 78–79.
3. Plinio Apuleyo Mendoza, *The Fragrance of Guava*: 97.
4. Claudia Dreifus, "Interview; Gabriel García Márquez," *Playboy* (February 1983). Reprinted in *Conversations with Gabriel García Márquez,* edited by Gene H. Bell-Villada. Jackson, Mississippi: University Press of Mississippi, 2006: 97.
5. Gabriel García Márquez: *"Polonia: verdades que duelen,"* published on December 30, 1981, in *Notas de prensa: 1980–1984.* Bogotá: Grupo Editorial Norma, 1991: 255–258.
6. Jacques Gilard, *Obra periodística,* vol. 4: *De Europa y América*: 53.
7. Plinio Apuleyo Mendoza, *The Fragrance of Guava*: 97.
8. Plinio Apuleyo Mendoza, *The Fragrance of Guava*: 97.
9. Peter H. Stone, "Gabriel García Márquez": 181, 187.
10. Dasso Saldívar, *El viaje a la semilla*: 375.
11. Plinio Apuleyo Mendoza, *Aquellos tiempos con Gabo.* Barcelona: Plaza & Janés, 2000: 79.
12. Dasso Saldívar, *El viaje a la semilla*: 397.
13. Plinio Apuleyo Mendoza, *The Fragrance of Guava*: 99.
14. Plinio Apuleyo Mendoza, *The Fragrance of Guava*: 99.
15. Carlos Fuentes: "An Interview with John King," in *On Modern Latin American Fiction,* edited by John King. New York: Hill and Wang, 1987: 136–154.
16. Claudia Dreifus, "Interview; Gabriel García Márquez": 97.

5 *Lo real maravilloso*

1. Rita Guibert, *Seven Voices*: xv.
2. García Márquez, *No One Writes the Colonel,* translated by Gregory Rabassa, included in *Collected Novellas.* New York: Harper & Row, 1990: 127.

3. Quoted from the Introduction to *Rubén Darío: Selected Writings*, edited by Ilan Stavans. New York: Penguin Classics, 2005: xxx.

4. In a series of lectures delivered at the Universidad Veracruzana in 1972, and published first in the journal *Texto crítico* (nos. 31–31, January–August 1985) and in book form as *La narrativa de Gabriel García Márquez: Edificación de un arte nacional y popular* (Bogotá: Instituto Colombiano de Cultura, 1991), the Uruguayan critic Ángel Rama, among other topics, discussed the way García Márquez, like the short-story writer Horacio Quiroga, accommodated himself to pre-established models, imported from abroad, but also related to the amount of space a periodical might allow him to shape his narratives.

5. Mario Vargas Llosa, "El jubileo de Carmen Balcells," in *El País* (Madrid), no. 1750, (August 20, 2000).

6. Gabriel García Márquez, *No One Writes the Colonel*: 126–127.

7. Dasso Saldívar, *García Márquez: El viaje a la semilla*. Barcelona: Alfaguara, 1997: 412.

8. José Donoso, *The Boom in Spanish-American Literature: A Personal History*, translated by Gregory Kolovakos. New York: Columbia University Press-Center for Inter-American Relations, 1977: 56.

9. José Donoso, *The Boom in Spanish-American Literature*: 57–58.

10. Rita Guibert, *Seven Voices*: xi.

11. Emir Rodríguez Monegal, "Preface to the Second Volume," in *The Borzoi Anthology of Latin American Literature*, 2 vols., edited by Emir Rodríguez Monegal, with the assistance of Thomas Colchie. New York: Alfred A. Knopf, 1977: vol. 2, xiv.

12. Franz Roh, *Nach-Expressionismus, Magischer Realismus: Probleme der neuesten Europäischen malerei*. Leipzig: Klinkhardt & Biermann, 1925.

13. See the introduction by Lois Parkinson Zamora and Wendy B. Faris in their book *Magical Realism: Theory, History, Community*. Durham, NC: Duke University Press, 1995: 3–4.

14. Alejo Carpentier, "Prologue: *The Kingdom of This World*," reprinted in *The Oxford Book of Modern Latin American Essays*, edited by Ilan Stavans. New York and London: Oxford University Press, 1997: 194–198.

15. Luis Leal, "Magic Realism," in *A Luis Leal Reader*, edited by Ilan Stavans. Evanston, IL: Northwestern University Press, 2007: 324.
16. Gabriel García Márquez, *In Evil Hour*, translated by Gregory Rabassa. New York: Avon Books, 1980: 47.
17. Gregory Rabassa, *If This Be Treason: Translation and Its Discontents*. New York: New Directions, 2005: 103.

6   The Silver Screen

1. Luis Harss and Barbara Dohmann, "Gabriel García Márquez, or the Lost Chord," in *Into the Mainstream: Conversations with Latin-American Writers*. New York: Harper & Row, 1967: 310.
2. Luis Harss and Barbara Dohmann, *Into the Mainstream*: 317.
3. García Márquez, *Living to Tell the Tale*: 83–84.
4. Álvaro Mutis, *Diary of Lecumberri: A Poet Behind Bars*, translated by Jesse H. Lytle, *Hopscotch: A Cultural Review*, vol. 1, no. 3 (1999): 2–37.
5. Dasso Saldívar, *El viaje a la semilla*: 433, 437.
6. Gabriel García Márquez, *"La odisea literaria de un manuscrito,"* published in *El País* (Madrid), July 15, 2001.
7. In chapter nineteen of *One Hundred Years of Solitude* (pages 386–387), the author inserted a prank in which he made reference to his two children: Gastón, a lover of planes, and Amaranta Úrsula "began to love each other at an altitude of fifteen hundred feet in the Sunday air of the moors, and they felt all the closer together as the beings on earth grew more and more minute. She spoke to him of Macondo as the brightest and most peaceful town on earth, and of an enormous house, scented with oregano, where she wanted to live until old age with a royal husband and two strong sons who would be called Rodrigo and Gonzalo, never Aureliano and José Arcadio."
8. Rita Guibert, *Seven Voices: Seven Latin American Writers Talk to Rita Guibert*. New York: Alfred A. Knopf, 1973: 321.
9. Susana Cato, "Soap Operas are Wonderful. I've Always Wanted to Write One," in Gene H. Bel-Villada, *Conversations with Gabriel García Márquez*: 150.

10. Juan Rulfo, *Pedro Páramo*, edited José Carlos González Boixo. Madrid: Cátedra, 1983: 179.
11. Martin Kaplan, "Review of *Innocent Eréndira and Other Stories*," *New Republic*, 179 (August 26, 1978): 46.
12. Luis Harss and Barbara Dohmann, *Into the Mainstream*: *Conversations with Latin-American Writers*: 317.

7 Sleepless in Macondo

1. Alberto Manguel and Gianni Guadalupi, Foreword to the *Dictionary of Imaginary Places*. San Diego: Harcourt Brace Jovanovich, 1980: xi.
2. Ilan Stavans, "García Márquez's Total Novel," *The Chronicle of Higher Education* (June 15, 2007).
3. Edna Van der Walde: "El macondismo como latinoamericanismo," *Cuadernos Americanos*, vol. 12, no. 1, January–February 1998: 223–37.
4. Mario Vargas Llosa, *García Márquez: Historia de un deicidio*: 479.
5. Plinio Apuleyo Mendoza, *The Fragrance of Guava*: 53.
6. Gabriel García Márquez, "'La casa de los Buendía': Apuntes para una novela," listed in *Obra periodística*, vol. 1: *Textos costeños*: 63.
7. Gabriel García Márquez, *Living to Tell the Tale*: 350.
8. The symbol has further echoes: Sor Juana Inés de la Cruz's seventeenth-century play *Los empeños de una casa* uses the image, as does Federico García Lorca, *La casa de Bernarda Alba*. Borges's story *"La casa de Asterión,"* Gilberto Freyre's anthropological study *Casa grande*, Cortázar's story *"Casa tomada,"* and José Donoso's *Casa de campo*. The symbol is also ubiquitous among Latino writers, starting with Sandra Cisneros's *The House on Mango Street*.
9. Peter H. Stone, "Gabriel García Márquez": 185.
10. Dasso Saldívar, *El viaje a la semilla*: 426–427.
11. Pete Hamill, "Love and Solitude": 131.
12. Plinio Apuleyo Mendoza, *La llama y el hielo*. Barcelona: Planeta, 1984: 110–111.

13. Eligio García Márquez, *Tras las claves de Melquíades: Historia de "Cien años de soledad."* Bogotá: Grupo Editorial Norma, 2001: 88–91.

14. Mario Vargas Llosa, *García Márquez: Historia de un deicidio*: 77.

15. Gabriel García Márquez, *Living to Tell the Tale*: 19.

16. Claudia Dreifus, *"Playboy* Interview: Gabriel García Márquez," *Playboy* magazine, (February 1983): 65–77, 172–178, reprinted in Bell-Villada, *Conversations with Gabriel García Márquez*: 123.

17. Miguel Fernández-Bermejo, *La soledad de Gabriel García Márquez*. Barcelona: Planeta, 1972. This portion of the interview appeared in *Triunfo* (Madrid), vol. 25, no. 44 (November 1971): 12–18. Reprinted in *García Márquez habla de García Márquez*, edited by Alfonso Rentería Mantilla. Bogotá: Rentería Editores, 1979: 49–64. The piece is featured as "And Now, Two hundred Years of Solitude," by Ernesto González Bermejo, included in Bell-Villada, *Conversations with Gabriel García Márquez*: 12.

18. Dreifus interview, in Bell-Villada, *Conversations with Gabriel García Márquez*: 122.

19. Rita Guibert, *Seven Voices*: 316–317.

20. Carlos Fuentes, "García Márquez: *Cien años de soledad."* "La Cultura en México," literary supplement of *Siempre!* (Mexico), no. 679 (June 29, 1966).

21. Eduardo García Aguilar, *Celebraciones y otros fantasmas: Una biografía intelectual de Álvaro Mutis*. Bogotá: Tercer Mundo Editores, 1993: 109–110.

22. José Miguel Oviedo, *"Cuarenta, ochenta y cien años,"* in *El arte de leer a García Márquez*, edited by Juan Gustavo Cobo Borda. Bogotá: Grupo Editorial Norma, 2007: 261.

23. Heriberto Fiorillo, *La Cueva*: 346.

24. Gabriel García Márquez, *"La odisea literaria de un manuscrito,"* published in *El País* (Madrid), July 15, 2001.

25. Rita Guibert, *Seven Voices: Conversations with Latin American Writers*: 324–325.

26. Luis Harss was not to follow his instinct. In the Prologue, Harss and Dohmann stated: "Our selection of authors lays no claim to infallibility or exclusiveness. There is a bad habit everywhere nowadays of glorifying certain figures at

the expense of others. Our book tried neither to magnify nor to belittle. Of course there is judgment implicit in every choice. But we insist that ours is personal, and has no wish to be final." *Into the Mainstream*: 34. Of all the authors included, García Márquez was, arguably, the writer who became the biggest revelation to Harss. According to Tomás Eloy Martínez in his syndicated essay "¿Qué se hizo de Luis Harss?" *Diario de las Américas* (February 9, 2008), Harss had only read some short stories by García Márquez as well as *In Evil Hour* when approximately seventy pages of *One Hundred Years of Solitude*, which García Márquez had begun to circulate, reached his hands, although he didn't exactly remember who sent them to him. Harss did remember showing them to Paco Porrúa, the editor in the publishing house Sudamericana. Curiously, after working on an edition of Ricardo Güiraldes' Don Segundo Sombra and a translation of Sor Juana Inés de La Cruz's poem *First Dream*, Harss, born in 1936 and at one time Latin America's most visible cultural chronicler, settled in Mercersburg, Pennsylvania, and beginning the mid-eighties onward all but ceased to produce engaging cultural reflections.

27. Gerald Martin, *Gabriel García Márquez: A Life*. New York: Alfred A. Knopf, 2009: 303–304.

8   *Convergences*

1. The list of active participants in *El Boom* has always been the subject of contention. Some literary historians would hesitate to include writers like Onetti, Guimarães Rosa, and Lezama Lima, born before 1910. Even Juan Rulfo, born in 1917, doesn't make the cut for them. Yet this rule doesn't apply to Cortázar, who, although born in 1914, always presented himself in a youthful manner. Others instead would broaden the parameters to such an extent as to incorporate Borges, who was born in 1899, as well as Miguel Angel Asturias, the Guatemalan writer also born that year. There are also critics who refuse to look at age as the qualifier. To make their argument they point at Cortázar, who

although born in 1914, always presented himself as youthful through his passion for jazz, experimentalism, and a Beatnik-like approach to literature. It is important to emphasize the extent to which *El Boom*, at least during its initial years, was an all boys' club.

2. John King, *El Di Tella y el desarrollo cultural argentino en la década del sesenta*. Buenos Aires: AsuntoImpresoEdiciones and Instituto Torcuato Di Tella, 2007: 13. The translation is mine.

3. John King, *El Di Tella*: 13.

4. Dasso Saldívar, *El viaje a la semilla*: 453.

5. Dasso Saldívar, *El viaje a la semilla*: 454.

6. Eligio García Márquez, *Tras las claves de Melquíades*: 14–15.

7. John King, *El Di Tella*: 14.

8. John King, *El Di Tella*: 14–15.

9. Another one of García Márquez's novels, *The General in His Labyrinth* (1989), about Simón Bolívar's last days, which used as an inspiration a short story by Álvaro Mutis called *"El último rostro,"* is also considered to be part of this canon.

10. Adam Feinstein, *Pablo Neruda: A Passion for Life*. London: Bloomsbury, 2004: 351.

11. Adam Feinstein, *Pablo Neruda*: 352.

12. Mario Vargas Llosa, *García Márquez: Historia de un deicidio*: 80–81.

13. Daniel Samper, *"El novelista García Márquez no volverá a escribir,"* *El Tiempo* [Bogotá] (December 22, 1968): 5.

14. Rita Guibert, *Seven Voices*: 310–311.

15. José Donoso, *The Boom in Spanish-American Literature: A Personal History*: 56.

16. Rita Guibert, *Seven Voices*: 311–312.

17. Alfonso Rentería Mantilla, *"En Moscú con el traductor de "Cien años..."* in *García Márquez habla de García Márquez*, edited by Alfonso Rentería Mantilla. Bogotá: Rentería Editores, 1979: 129.

18. Quoted in Robert G. Mead, Jr. in "For Sustenance: Hope," *Saturday Review*, December 12, 1968: 26.

19. Gregory Rabassa, *If This Be Treason*: 94.

20. Gabriel García Márquez, *"Los peores traductores buenos,"* published on July 21, 1982. Reprinted in *Notas de prensa: 1980–1984*. Bogotá: Grupo Editorial Norma, 1991: 372–373.

21. Gregory Rabassa, interview with the author, New York, April 2003.

22. Gregory Rabassa, *If This Be Treason*: 93.

23. Cass Canfield, Jr., interview with the author, New York, March 2003.

24. Gregory Rabassa, interview with the author, Amherst, MA, November 1999.

25. Gregory Rabassa, *If This Be Treason*: 95–96.

26. Gregory Rabassa, *If This Be Treason*: 99.

27. Gregory Rabassa, *If This Be Treason*: 97–98. Rabassa argues that *was* could have been *would*. But could it? I've always been struck by the use of tense in the first sentence: why use the imperfect pluperfect, *había de recordar*, and not the conditional pluperfect, *habría de recordar*? Is it an error? Or is García Márquez deliberately employing a Colombian modality of the conjugation? Why the imperfect and not the conditional of *haber*? The answer has to do with the varieties of the Spanish language in Latin America, where the conditional perfect is often replaced by the pluperfect. Thus, people say *"Si hubiera tenido dinero, había ido al teatro,"* rather than *había ido*, and, also, *"Si hubiera sido rico, me había comprado un yate,"* instead of *me habría comprado*. In the opening of *One Hundred Years of Solitude*, García Márquez is most probably imitating, consciously or otherwise, the parlance of Colombia's eastern rural region. See Ilan Stavans, *"Gabo y la 'r,'" El Diario* (New York), April 28, 2009.

28. Gregory Rabassa, interview with the author, April 2003.

29. Gregory Rabassa, *If This Be Treason*: 99–100. It is important to note that there have been some "correctives" offered to Rabassa's translation. Gene Dilmore, in his essay *"One Hundred Years of Solitude*: Some Translation Corrections," *Journal of Modern Literature*, vol. 11, num. 2 (July 1984): 311–314, states that upon reading the Spanish original, he "found that several somewhat puzzling or even contradictory phrases were not, as I had assumed, sheer quirkness on the part of García Márquez, but were simply slips of the translation." Some of these are, to be sure, subjective, for example "Lordy!" instead of "Fantastic!" (Harper & Row hardcover edition,

1970, page 26), or else belabored, like "'Jesus Christ,' he explained" instead of "'Shit,' he explained" (page 121). Others seem to me less questionable, as is the case of "that poverty was the servitude of love" instead of "that poverty was the servant of love" (page 345). Dilmore concludes with this statement: "Perhaps, with these few citations. The only remaining problem with the Colombian master's novel will be the insistence of book stores on filing it under "M." Gene Dilmore: *"One Hundred Years of Solitude*: Some Translation Corrections," 314. Chester S. Halka, in *"One Hundred Years of Solitude*: Two Additional Translation Corrections," *Journal of Modern Literature*, vol. 24, num. 1 (Autumn, 2000): 173–175, offers two further correctives. The most enlightening of them involved a reference to the title phrase of the novel and becomes clear in the following exmplanation: "When Aureliano Segundo, at age twelve, becomes interested in the literature in Melquíades' room, he tries to decipher the manuscripts left by the gypsy. We are told that "Melquíades talked to him about the world, tried to infuse him with the old wisdom, but refuse to translate the manuscripts. 'No one must know their meaning until he has reached one hundred years of age,' he explained." In the Spanish, however, it is clear that it is the *manuscript*, and not the translator, that must reach one hundred years of age before they can be deciphered. The same quotation in the Spanish original reads: "Melquíades le hablaba del mundo, trataba de infundirle su vieja sabiduría, pero se negó a traducir los manuscritos. 'Nadie debe conocer su sentido mientras no hayan cumplido cien años,' explicó." The plural "hayan" can refer only *manuscritos*, which is plural, and not to *nadie*, which is singular (and is, therefore, in proper agreement with its third person, singular verb, "debe"). Chester S. Halka: *"One Hundred Years of Solitude*: Two Additional Translation Corrections": 173–174.

30. John Leonard, "Myth Is Alive in Latin America," *New York Times*, March 3, 1970: 39.
31. Robert Kiely, "Review of *One Hundred Years of Solitude*," *New York Times Book Review*, March 8, 1970: 5.
32. V. S. Pritchett, "The Myth Makers," *The Myth Makers: European and Latin American Writers*. New York: Random House, 1979: 164–173.

33. Anonymous: "Orchids and Bloodlines," *Time* (March 16, 1970): 96.

34. Peter H. Stone, "Gabriel García Márquez": 198.

35. Raymond Leslie Williams: "The Visual Arts, the Poetization of Space and Writing: An Interview with Gabriel García Márquez," *PMLA*, vol. 104, num. 2 (March 1989): 138–139.

36. Gabriel García Márquez, *"Una tontería de Anthony Quinn,"* first published on April 21, 1982, included in *Gabriel García Márquez: Notas de Prensa, 1980–1984*. Bogotá: Grupo Editorial Norma, 1995: 318–21.

Bibliography

Since the publication of *One Hundred Years of Solitude*, the work of Gabriel García Márquez has generated enormous international interest. His books have been translated into almost three dozen languages. These are the titles, in the original Spanish, of novels, essays, stories, reportage, film workshops, and plays. There are several valuable bibliographical resources, up to 2003, before the release of *Memoirs of My Melancholy Whores* and excluding the autobiography *Living to Tell the Tale*. These are *Gabriel García Márquez: An Annotated Bibliography, 1947–1979*, compiled by Margaret Eustella Fau (Westport, Conn.: Greenwood, 1980); *Bibliographic Guide to Gabriel García Márquez: 1986–1992*, compiled by Nelly Sfeir de González (Westport, Conn.: Greenwood, 1994); *Gabriel García Márquez: Crítica y bibliografía*, compiled by Juan Gustavo Cobo Borda (Madrid: Embajada de Colombia en España, 1994); and *Gabriel García Márquez: Una bibliografía descriptiva*, 2 vols., compiled by Don Klein (Bogotá: Grupo Editorial Norma, 2003).

Works by Gabriel García Márquez

Books

Los funerales de la Mamá Grande. Jalapa, Veracruz: Editorial de la Universidad Veracruzana, 1962. Includes "La siesta del martes,"

"Un día de estos," "En este pueblo no hay ladrones," "La prodigiosa tarde de Baltazar," "La viuda de Montiel," "Un día después del sábado," "Rosas artificiales," and "Los funerales de la Mamá Grande."

La hojarasca. Montevideo: Arca, 1965.

El coronel no tiene quien le escriba. México: Ediciones Era, 1966.

Cien años de soledad. Buenos Aires: Editorial Losada, 1967.

Relato de un náufrago que estuvo diez días a la deriva en una balsa sin comer ni beber, que fue proclamado héroe de la patria, besado por las reinas de la belleza y hecho rico por la publicidad, y luego aborrecido por el gobierno y olvidado para siempre. Barcelona: Tusquets, 1970.

La increíble y triste historia de la cándida Eréndira y su abuela desalmada. México: Ediciones Era, 1972. Includes "Un señor muy viejo con unas alas enormes," "El mar del tiempo perdido," "El ahogado más hermoso del mundo," "Muerte constante más allá del amor," "El último viaje del buque fantasma," "Blacamán el bueno vendedor de milagros," and "La increíble y triste historia de la cándida Eréndira y su abuela desalmada."

Ojos de perro azul. México: Secretaría de Obras y Servicios, 1973. Includes "La tercera resignación," "La otra costilla de la muerte," "Eva está dentro de su gato," "Amargura para tres sonámbulos," "Diálogo del espejo," "Ojos de perro azul," "La mujer que llegaba a las seis," "Nabo, el negro que hizo esperar a los ángeles," "Alguien desordena las rosas," and "La noche de los alcaravanes."

Cuando era feliz e indocumentado. Barcelona: Plaza & Janés, 1975.

El otoño del patriarca. Buenos Aires: Editorial Sudamericana, 1975.

Todos los cuentos: 1947–1972. Barcelona: Plaza y Janés, 1975. Includes "La tercera resignación," "La otra costilla de la muerte," "Eva está dentro de su gato," "Amargura para tres sonámbulos," "Diálogo del espejo," "Ojos de perro azul," "La mujer que llegaba a las seis," "Nabo, el negro que hizo esperar a los ángeles," "Alguien desordena las rosas," "La noche de los alcaravanes," "La siesta del martes," "Un día de estos," "En este pueblo no hay ladrones," "La prodigiosa tarde de Baltazar," "La viuda de Montiel," "Un día después del sábado," "Rosas artificiales," "Los funerales de la Mamá Grande," "Un señor muy viejo con unas alas enormes," "El mar del tiempo perdido," "El ahogado más hermoso del mundo," "Muerte constante más allá del amor," "El último viaje del buque fantasma," "Blacamán el bueno vendedor de milagros," and "La increíble y triste historia de la cándida Eréndira y su abuela desalmada."

Crónicas y reportajes. Bogotá: Instituto Colombiano de Cultura, Subdirección de Comunicaciones Culturales, División de Publicaciones, 1976.

De viaje por los países socialistas: 90 días en la "Cortina de hierro." Cali: Ediciones Macondo, 1978.

La mala hora. Buenos Aires: Editorial Sudamericana, 1979.

Crónica de una muerte anunciada. Bogotá: Oveja Negra, 1981.

Obra periodística: vol. 1: *Textos costeños,* edited by Jacques Gilard. Barcelona. Bruguera, 1981. *El secuestro: Guión cinematográfico.* Bogotá: Oveja Negra, 1982.

Obra periodística: vol. 2: *Entre cachacos I,* edited by Jacques Gilard. Barcelona: Bruguera, 1982.

Obra periodística: vol. 3: *Entre cachacos II,* edited by Jacques Gilard. Barcelona: Bruguera, 1982.

Viva Sandino. Managua: Nueva Nicaragua, 1982.

El coronel no tiene quien le escriba, Cien años de soledad, La soledad de América Latina and *Brindis por la poesía,* prologue by Agustín Cueva. Caracas: Biblioteca Ayacucho 1989.

Obra periodística: vol. 4: *De Europa y América: 1955–1960,* edited by Jacques Gilard. Barcelona: Bruguera, 1983.

El amor en los tiempos del cólera. Bogotá: Oveja Negra, 1985.

El cataclismo de Demóstenes. Bogotá: Oveja negra, 1986.

Miguel Littín, clandestino en Chile. Bogotá: Oveja Negra, 1986.

El general en su laberinto. Bogotá: Oveja Negra, 1989.

Notas de prensa: 1980–1984. Bogotá: Grupo Editorial Norma, 1991.

Doce cuentos peregrinos. Bogotá: Oveja Negra, 1992. Includes "Prólogo: Porqué doce, porqué cuentos y porqué peregrinos," "Buen viaje, señor presidente," "La santa," "El avión de la bella durmiente," "Me alquilo para soñar," "Sólo vine a hablar por teléfono," "Espantos de agosto," "María dos Prazeres," "Diecisiete ingleses envenenados," "Tramontana," "El verano feliz de la señora Forbes," "La luz es como el agua," and "El rastro de tu sangre en la nieve."

Diatriba de amor contra un hombre sentado: Monólogo en un acto. Bogotá: Arango Editores, 1994.

Del amor y otros demonios. Bogotá: Oveja Negra, 1994.

Me alquilo para soñar: Taller de guión. Bogotá: Editorial Voluntad, Escuela Internacional de Cine y TV San Antonio de los Baños, 1995.

Cómo se cuenta un cuento: Taller de guión. Bogotá: Editorial Voluntad, Escuela Internacional de Cine y TV San Antonio de los Baños, 1995.

Noticia de un secuestro. Bogotá: Oveja Negra, 1996.

Por la libre: 1974–1995. Bogotá: Grupo Editorial Norma, 1999.

Vivir para contarla. Barcelona: Mondadori, 2002.

Memorias de mis putas tristes. Bogotá: Oveja Negra, 2004.

Cien años de soledad. Commemorative edition revised by the author. Madrid: Alfaguara y Real Academia Española de la Lengua, 2007.

English Translations

No One Writes to the Colonel and Other Stories, translated by J. S. Bernstein. New York: Harper & Row, 1968. Includes "No One Writes to the Colonel," "Big Mama's Funeral," "Tuesday Siesta," "One of These Days," "There Are No Thieves in This Town," "Balthazar's Marvelous Afternoon," "Montiel's Widow," "One Day After Saturday," "Artificial Roses," and "Big Mama's Funeral."

One Hundred Years of Solitude, translated by Gregory Rabassa. New York: Harper & Row, 1970.

Leaf Storm and Other Stories, translated by Gregory Rabassa. New York: Harper & Row, 1972. Includes "Leaf Storm," "The Handsomest Drowned Man in the World," "A Very Old Man With Enormous Wings," "Blacamán the Good, Vendor of Miracles," "The Last Voyage of the Ghost Ship," "Monologue of Isabel Watching It Rain in Macondo," and "Nabo: The Black Man Who Made the Angels Wait."

The Autumn of the Patriarch, translated by Gregory Rabassa. New York: Harper & Row, 1976.

Innocent Erendira and Other Stories, translated by Gregory Rabassa. New York: Harper & Row, 1978. Includes "A Very Old Man with Enormous Wings," "The Sea of Lost Time," "The Handsomest Drowned Man in the World," "Death Constant Beyond Love," "The Last Voyage of the Ghost Ship," "Blacamán the Good,

Bibliography 205

Vendor of Miracles," and "The Incredible and Sad Tale of
Innocent Erendira and Her Heartless Grandmother."

In Evil Hour, translated by Gregory Rabassa. New York: Harper &
Row, 1979.

Chronicle of a Death Foretold, translated by Gregory Rabassa. New
York: Alfred A. Knopf, 1983.

Collected Stories, translated by Gregory Rabassa. New York:
Harper & Row, 1984. Includes "The Third Resignation," "The
Other Side of Death," "Eva Is Inside Her Cat," "Bitterness for
Three Sleepwalkers," "Dialogue with the Mirror," "Eyes of a
Blue Dog," "The Woman Who Came at Six O'clock," "Nabo:
The Black Man Who Made the Angels Wait," "Someone Has
Been Disarranging the Flowers," "The Night of the Curlews,"
"Monologue of Isabel Watching It Rain in Macondo," "Tuesday
Siesta," "One of These Days," "There Are No Thieves in This
Town," "Balthazar's Marvelous Afternoon," "Montiel's Widow,"
"One Day After Saturday," "Artificial Roses," "Big Mama's
Funeral," "A Very Old Man with Enormous Wings," "The Sea
of Lost Time," "The Handsomest Drowned Man in the World,"
"Death Constant Beyond Love," "The Last Voyage of the Ghost
Ship," "Blacamán the Good, Vendor of Miracles," and "The
Incredible and Sad Tale of Innocent Erendira and Her Heartless
Grandmother."

*The story of a shipwrecked sailor who drifted on a life raft for ten days without
food or water, was proclaimed a national hero, kissed by beauty queens,
made rich through publicity, and then spurned by the government and
forgotten for all time*, translated by Randolph Hogan. New York:
Vintage, 1986.

Clandestine in Chile: The Adventures of Miguel Littín, translated by Asa
Zatz. New York: Henry Holt, 1987.

Love in the Time of Cholera, translated by Edith Grossman. New York:
Alfred A. Knopf, 1988.

The General in His Labyrinth, translated by Edith Grossman. New
York: Alfred A. Knopf, 1990.

Collected Novellas. New York: HarperCollins, 1990. Includes "Leaf
Storm," "No One Writes to the Colonel," and "Chronicle of a
Death Foretold."

Strange Pilgrims, translated by Edith Grossman. New York: Alfred A.
Knopf, 1993. Includes "Prologue: Why Twelve, Why Stories, Why

Pilgrims," "Bon Voyage, Mr. President," "The Saint," "Sleeping
Beauty and the Airplane," "I Sell My Dreams," "'I Only Came
to Use the Phone,'" "The Ghost of August," "Maria dos Prazeres,"
"Seventeen Poisoned Englishmen," "Tramontana," "Miss Forbes'
Summer of Happiness," "Light Is Like Water," and "The Trail of
Your Blood in the Snow."
Of Love and Other Demons, translated by Edith Grossman. New York:
Alfred A. Knopf, 1995.
News of a Kidnapping, translated by Edith Grossman. New York:
Alfred A. Knopf, 1997.
Living to Tell the Tale, translated by Edith Grossman. New York:
Alfred A. Knopf, 2003.
Memoirs of My Melancholy Whores, translated by Edith Grossman. New
York: Alfred A. Knopf, 2005.

Conversations

García Márquez has given numerous interviews during his career.
The most important ones are either singled out in this section or else
included in the volumes listed in chronological order.

Harss, Luis, with Barbara Dohmann. "Gabriel García Márquez, or The
Lost Chord," in *Into the Mainstream: Conversations with Latin American
Writers.* New York: Harper & Row, 1967: 310–341. In Spanish, *Los
Nuestros.* Buenos Aires: Editorial Sudamericana, 1969.
Durán, Armando. "Conversaciones con Gabriel García Márquez,"
Revista Nacional de Cultura [Caracas], vol. 24, no. 185 (July–
September 1968): 23–34.
*La novela en América Latina: Diálogo entre Gabriel García Márquez y Mario
Vargas Llosa.* Lima: C.M. Batres and Universidad Nacional de
Ingeniería, 1968.
Kennedy, William. "The Yellow Trolley Car in Barcelona and Other
Visions: A Profile of Gabriel García Márquez," *The Atlantic,*
vol. 231, no. 1 (January 1973): 50–58. Included in *Riding the
Yellow Trolley Car.* New York: Viking, 1993.
Guibert, Rita. *Seven Voices: Seven Latin American Writers Talk to Rita
Guibert.* New York: Alfred A. Knopf, 1973: 306–337.

Rodman, Seiden. *Tongues of Fallen Angels*. New York: New Directions, 1974.

Rentería Mantilla, Alfonso, ed. *García Márquez habla de García Márquez*. Bogotá: Rentería Mantilla Ltd., 1979.

Stone, Peter H. "Gabriel García Márquez: The Art of Fiction," in *Paris Review* 82 (1981). Reprinted in *The Paris Review Interviews*, vol. II, introduction by Orhan Pamuk. New York: Picador, 2007: 178–206.

Prego, Omar. "Conversaciones con Gabriel García Márquez," *Cuadernos de Marcha* (Mexico City) 3, no.15 (September–October 1981): 69–77.

Fernández-Braso, Miguel. *La soledad de Gabriel García Márquez: Una conversación infinita*. Barcelona: Planeta, 1969, 1972, 1982.

Dreifus, Claudia. "*Playboy* Interview: Gabriel García Márquez," *Playboy* (February 1983): 65–77, 172–78.

Mendoza, Plinio Apuleyo. *El olor de la guayaba*. Bogotá: Oveja Negra, 1982. In English: *The Fragrance of Guava: Conversations with Gabriel García Márquez*, translated by Ann Wright. London: Verso, 1983.

Simmons, Marlisse. "Love and Age: A Talk with García Márquez," in *New York Times Book Review*, April 7, 1985: 1, 18–21.

Hamill, Pete. "Love and Solitude," *Vanity Fair*, March 1988: 124–131, 192.

Williams, Raymond Leslie. "The Visual Arts, the Poetization of Space and Writing: An Interview with Gabriel García Márquez," *PMLA, vol. 104, num. 2* (March 1989): 131–40.

Anderson, Jon Lee. "The Power of Gabriel García Márquez," *New Yorker*, September 27, 1999: 56–70.

Bell-Villada, Gene H., ed. *Conversations with Gabriel García Márquez*. Jackson, MS.: University Press of Mississippi, 2006.

Documentaries

Tales Beyond Solitude: Profile of a Writer: Gabriel García Márquez. Dir. Holly Aylett. London: South Bank Shows, 1989.

García Márquez: A Witch Writing. Dir. Yves Billon. Paris: Zarafa Films, France 3, 1998.

Buscando a Gabo. Dir. Pancho Bottía. Colombia, 2007.

Films

This is a list of movies based on, or related to, García Márquez's work, as well as companions to the shooting of those films. A film series called *Amores difíciles*, co-produced by Televisión Española, based on several of his stories and directed by various Latin American filmmakers, was released in 1988–1989. The titles included in it are marked with an [AD].

La langosta azul. Story by Gabriel García Márquez. Dir. Álvaro Cepeda Samudio, Enrique Grau Araújo, and Luis Vicens. 1954.

El gallo de oro. Story by Juan Rulfo, screenplay done in collaboration between Carlos Fuentes, Gabriel García Márquez, and Roberto Gavaldón. Dir. Roberto Gavaldón. 1964.

Lola de mi vida. Adaptation by Miguel Barbachano Ponce and Gabriel García Márquez, screenplay by Juan de la Cabada and Carlos A. Figueroa. Dir. Miguel Barbachano Ponce. 1965.

En este pueblo no hay ladrones. Story by Gabriel García Márquez. Screenplay by Emilio García Riera and Alberto Isaac. Dir. Jorge Isaac. 1965.

Tiempo de morir. Story by Gabriel García Márqiuez. Adapted by Carlos Fuentes and Gabriel García Márquez. Dir. Arturo Ripstein. 1966. Remake directed by Jorge Ali Triana. 1985.

Juegos peligrosos. Story by Gabriel García Márquez. Part I: *H.O.*, dir. Arturo Ripstein. Part II: *Divertimento.* Dir. Luis Alcoriza. 1966.

Patsy mi amor. Story by Gabriel García Márquez. Screenplay by Manuel Michel. Dir. Manuel Michel. 1969.

La viuda de Montiel. Story by Gabriel García Márquez. Screenplay by José Agustín. Dir. Miguel Littín. 1979.

La viuda de Montiel. Text by Jorge Ruffinelli on the filming of Miguel Littín's movie, photos by Julio Jaimes. Xalapa: Universidad Veracruzana, 1979.

María de mi corazón. Screenplay by Gabriel García Márquez and Jaime Humberto Hermosillo. Dir. Jaime Humberto Hermosillo. 1979.

El año de la peste. Screenplay by Gabriel García Márquez and Juan Arturo Brennan. Dialogue by José Agustín. Dir. Felipe Cazals. 1979.

Eréndira. Screenplay by Gabriel García Márquez. Dir. Ruy Guerra. 1983.

Saraba hakobune. Story by Gabriel García Márquez. Screenplay by Rio Kishida and Shuji Terayama. Dir. Shuji Terayama. 1984.

Cronaca di una morte annunciata. Story by Gabriel García Márquez. Screenplay by Tonino Guerra and Francesco Rosi. Dir. Francesco Rosi. 1987.

La tercera muerte de Santiago Nasar. Chronicle by Eligio García Márquez on the filming of Francesco Rosi's movie. Bogotá: Oveja Negra, 1987.

Yo soy el que tú buscas. Story by Gabriel García Márquez. Screenplay by Jaime Chávarri and Juan Tébar. Dir. Jaime Chávarri. 1988. [AD]

Un señor muy viejo con unas alas enormes. Screenplay by Gabriel García Márquez and Fernando Birri. Dir. Fernando Birri. 1988. [AD]

Fábula de la Bella Palomera. Screenplay by Gabriel García Márquez and Ruy Guerra. Dir. Ruy Guerra. 1988. [AD]

Milagro en Roma. Screenplay by Gabriel García Márquez and Lisando Duque Naranjo. Dir. Lisandro Duque Naranjo. 1988. [AD]

Un domingo feliz. Story by Gabriel García Márquez. Screenplay by Eliseo Alberto and Olegario Barrera. Dir. Olegario Barrera. 1988. [AD]

El verano de la Señora Forbes. Story by Gabriel García Márquez. Screenplay by Jaime Humberto Hermosillo. Dir. Jaime Humberto Hermosillo. 1988. [AD]

Cartas del parque. Screenplay by Gabriel García Márquez. Dialogue by Eliseo Alberto. Dir. Tomás Gutiérrez Alea. 1989. [AD]

La mujer que llegaba a las seis. Story by Gabriel García Márquez. Screenplay by Arturo Flores, Rogelio Jaramillo, and María Andrea de León. Dir. Arturo Flores and Rogelio Jaramillo. 1991.

Contigo a la distancia. Screenplay by Gabriel García Márquez and Eliseo Alberto. Dir. Tomás Gutiérrez Alea. 1991.

Oedipo alcalde. Story by Gabriel García Márquez. Screenplay by Stella Malagón. Dir. Jorge Ali Triana. 1996.

The Two-Way Mirror. Screenplay by Gabriel García Márquez and Susana Cato. Dir. Carlos García Agraz. 1996.

El coronel no tiene quien le escriba. Story by Gabriel García Márquez. Screenplay by Paz Alicia Garciadiego. Dir. Arturo Ripstein. 1999.

Los niños invicibles. Screenplay by Gabriel García Márquez and Lisandro Duque Naranjo. Dir. Lisandro Duque Naranjo. 2001.

O veneno da madrugada. Story by Gabriel García Márquez. Screenplay by Tairone Feitosa and Ruy Guerra. Dir. Ruy Guerra. 2004.

Love in the Time of Cholera. Story by Gabriel García Márquez. Screenplay by Ronald Harwood. Dir. Mike Newell. 2007.

Del amor y otros demonios. Story by Gabriel García Márquez. Screenplay by Hilda Hidalgo. Dir. Hilda Hidalgo. 2009.

Secondary Sources

This list of secondary sources includes material decisive in the making of this biography, referring not only to García Márquez but his entourage and, in general, to Latin American history, politics, and literature. I have limited the inclusion of scholarly articles to those quoted in, or which inspired, this biography.

Andrade, María Mercedes. "Latin America's Solitude: Gabriel García Márquez Reviewed in English," *Translation Review*, vol. 60, 2000: 32–36.

Anonymous: "Stranger in Paradise (Review of *Cien años de soledad*)," *Times Literary Supplement*, November 9, 1967.

Anonymous: "Orchids and Bloodlines," in *Time* (March 16, 1970): 96.

Arango, Gustavo. *Un ramo de nomeolvides: Gabriel García Márquez en "El Universal."* Cartagena: Ediciones El Universal, 1995.

Arciniegas, Germán. "Macondo, primera ciudad de Colombia," in *Panorama* (Maracaibo), (January 28, 1968).

Arévalo, Guillermo Alberto. *"Cien años de soledad": Novela de la palabra.* Bogotá: Colcultura and Biblioteca Nacional de Colombia, 1993.

Armas Marcelo, J. J. *Vargas Llosa: El vicio de escribir.* Madrid: Alfaguara, 2002.

Arnau, Carmen. *El mundo mítico de Gabriel García Márquez.* Barcelona: Ediciones Península, 1971.

Bell, Michael. *Gabriel García Márquez: Solitude and Solidarity.* New York: St. Martin's Press, 1993.

Bell-Villada, Gene H., ed. *García Márquez: The Man and His Work.* Chapel Hill: University of North Carolina Press, 1990.

——, ed. *Gabriel García Márquez's "One Hundred Years of Solitude": A Casebook.* New York and London: Oxford University Press, 2002.

Benet, Juan. "De Canudos a Macondo," *Revista de Occidente,* Tomo XXIV (Segunda Epoca), no. 70 (January 1969).

Benson, John. "Gabriel García Márquez en *Alternativa,* 1974–1979: Una bibliografía comentada," *Chasqui,* vol. 8, no. 3 (May 1979): 69–81.

——. "Notas sobre *Notas de prensa: 1980–1984,*" *Revista de Estudios Colombianos* 18 (1998): 27–37.

Bloom, Harold, ed. *Gabriel García Márquez.* New York: Chelsea House, 1989.

Bodtorf Clark, Gloria Jean. *A Synergy of Styles: Art and Artifact in Gabriel García Márquez.* Lanham, MD: University Press of America, 1999.

Bolletinno, Vincenzo. *Breve estudio de la novelística de García Márquez.* Madrid: Playor, 1974.

Braum, Herbert. *The Assassination of Gaitán: Public Life and Urban Violence in Colombia.* Madison: University of Wisconsin Press, 1985.

Bravo Mendoza, Víctor. *La Guajira en la obra de Gabriel García Márquez.* Riohacha, Colombia: Gobernación de La Guajira, 2007.

Brotherston, Gordon. "An End to Secular Solitude: Gabriel García Márquez," *The Emergence of the Latin American Novel.* New York: Cambridge University Press, 1977: 122–135.

Brunner, José Joaquín. "Traditionalism and Modernity in Latin American Culture," in *Latin America Writes Back: Postmodernity in the Periphery, Hispanic Issues* vol. 28, edited by Emil Volek. New York and London: Routledge, 2002: 3–31.

Carpentier, Alejo. "*Lo barroco y lo real maravilloso,*" *La novela hispanoamericana en vísperas de un nuevo siglo.* Mexico: Siglo XXI, 1981.

Carpentier, Alejo. "Prologue," *The Kingdom of This World,* translated by Harriet de Onís. New York: Alfred A. Knopf, 1957.

Cebrián, Juan Luis. *Retrato de Gabriel García Márquez.* Barcelona: Galaxia Gutenberg / Círculo de Lectores, 1997.

Cepeda Samudio, Álvaro. *La Casa Grande,* translated by Seymour Menton, forward by Gabriel García Márquez. Austin: University of Texas Press, 1991.

——. *Antología.* Edited by Daniel Samper Pizano. Bogotá: El Áncora Editores, 2001.

Christ, Ronald, ed. Supplement of *Gabriel García Márquez, Review 70.* New York: Center for Inter-American Relations, 1971: 99–191.

Clark, Jon R. "'The Biblical Hurricane' in *One Hundred Years of Solitude*: Bang or Whimper?" *Studies in Contemporary Satire: A Creative and Critical Journal*, vol. 19 (1995): 118–123.

Cobo Borda, Juan Gustavo, ed. ...*para que mis amigos me quieran más: Homenaje a Gabriel García Márquez*. Bogotá: Siglo del Hombre, 1992.

——, ed. *Repertorio crítico sobre Gabriel García Márquez*. 2 vols. Bogotá: Instituto Caro y Cuervo, 1995.

——. *Para llegar a García Márquez*. Bogotá: Ediciones Temas de Hoy, 1997.

——. *Lecturas convergentes*. Bogotá: Taurus, 2006.

——, ed. *El arte de leer a García Márquez*. Bogotá: Grupo Editorial Norma, 2007.

Collazos, Oscar. *García Márquez, la soledad y la gloria: Su vida y su obra*. Barcelona: Plaza & Janés, 1983.

Cortázar, Julio. *Cartas*. Vol. 1: 1937–1963. Vol. 2: 1964–1968. Vol. 3: 1969–1983. Edited by Aurora Bernárdez. Buenos Aires: Alfaguara, 2000.

Cristóbal, Juan, ed. *García Márquez y los medios de comunicación*. Jesús María, Peru: Editorial San Marcos, 1999.

Dilmore, Gene. *"One Hundred Years of Solitude:* Some Translation Corrections," *Journal of Modern Literature*, vol. 11, no. 2 (July 1984): 311–314.

Donoso, José. *The Boom in Spanish American Literature: A Personal History*, translated by Gregory Kolovakos. New York: Columbia University Press, in association with the Center for Inter-American Relations, 1977.

Earle, Peter G., ed. *Gabriel García Márquez*. Madrid: Taurus, 1981.

Esteban, Ángel, with Stéphanie Panichelli. *Gabo y Fidel: El paisaje de una amistad*. Madrid: Espasa, 2004.

Fiddian, Robin, ed. *García Márquez*. London: Longman, 1995.

Fiorillo, Heriberto. *La Cueva: Crónica de El grupo de Barranquilla*. Photographs by Nereo López. Barranquilla: Ediciones La Cueva, 2006.

Fuenmayor, Alfonso. *Crónica sobre "El grupo de Barranquilla."* Bogotá: Instituto Colombiano de Cultura, 1978.

Fuentes, Carlos. "García Márquez: *Cien años de soledad*," *"La cultura en México,"* supplement of *Siempre!* (Mexico) no. 228 (June 29, 1966): vii.

——. *La nueva novela hispanoamericana*. México: Joaquín Mortiz, 1969.

——. *Gabriel García Márquez and the Invention of America*. Liverpool: Liverpool University Press, 1987.

——. *Myself with Others*. New York: Farrar, Straus and Giroux, 1988.

——. *Valiente mundo nuevo: Épica, utopía y mito en la novela hispanoamericana*. México: Fondo de Cultura Económica, 1990.

——. *Geografía de la novela*. México: Fondo de Cultura Económica, 1993.

Galvis, Silvia. *Los García Márquez*. Bogotá: Océano and Arango Editores, 1996.

García Aguilar, Eduardo. *García Márquez: La tradición cinematográfica*. México: UNAM, 1985.

——. *Celebraciones y otros fantasmas: Una biografía intelectual de Álvaro Mutis*. Bogotá: Tercer Mundo Editores, 1993.

——. *García Márquez: La tentación cinematográfica*. Mexico: Filmoteca de la UNAM, 1985.

García Ascot, Jomí. *"Cien años de soledad:* Una novela de Gabriel García Márquez sólo comparable a *Moby Dick," "La cultura en México,"* supplement of *Siempre!* (Mexico), no. 732 (July 1967).

García Márquez, Eligio, *Tras las claves de Melquíades: historia de "Cien años de soledad,"* edited by Roberto Burgos. Bogotá: Grupo Editorial Norma, 2001.

García Usta, Jorge. *García Márquez en Cartagena: Sus inicios literarios*. Bogotá: Editorial Planeta Colombiana, 2007.

Garman, A. A. "'Yes! We Have No Bananas': A Marxist Literary Critique on Capitalism in Gabriel García Márquez' *One Hundred Years of Solitude," Lamar Journal of the Humanities*, vol. 27, no. 1 (Spring 2002): 5–11.

Giacomán, Helmy F., ed. *Homenaje a Gabriel García Márquez; Variaciones interpretativas en torno a su obra*. Long Island City: Las Américas, 1972.

Gilard, Jacques. *Veinte y cuarenta años de algo peor que la soledad*. Paris: Editions du Centre Culturel Colombien, 1989.

Giraldo, Luz Mary. *Más allá de Macondo: Tradición y rupturas literarias*. Bogotá: Universidad Externado de Colombia, 2006.

González Bermejo, Ernesto. *Cosas de escritores; Gabriel García Márquez, Mario Vargas Llosa, Julio Cortázar*. Montevideo: Biblioteca de Marcha, 1971.

Grossman, Edith. "Truth Is Stranger than Fact," *Review* 30 (September–December, 1981): 71–73.

Gullón, Ricardo. *García Márquez; o, El olvidado arte de contar.* Madrid: Taurus, 1970.

Haberly, David T. "Bags of Bones: A Source for *One Hundred Years of Solitude*," *MLN*, vol. 105, no. 2 (March 1990): 392–3.

Hahn, Hannelore. *The Influence of Franz Kafka on Three Novels by Gabriel García Márquez.* New York: P. Lang, 1993.

Halka, Chester S: *"One Hundred Years of Solitude:* Two Additional Translation Corrections," *Journal of Modern Literature,* vol. 24, no. 1 (Autumn, 2000): 173–175.

Hargrave, Nelly, with Georgina Smith Seminet. "De Macondo a *McOndo*: Nuevas voces en la literatura latinoamericana," *Chasqui,* vol. 2 (November 1998): 14–26.

Hart, Stephen M. *Gabriel García Márquez: Crónica de una muerte anunciada.* London: Grant & Cutler, 2005.

Henríquez Torres, Guillermo. *El misterio de los Buendía: El verdadero trasfondo histórico de "Cien años de soledad."* Bogotá: Editorial Nueva América, 1996, 2003.

Hernández de López, Ana María, ed. *En el punto de mira: Gabriel García Márquez.* Madrid: Editorial Pliegos, 1985.

Janes, Regina. *Gabriel García Márquez: Revolutions in Wonderland.* Columbia and London: University of Missouri Press, 1981.

Joset, Jacques. *Gabriel García Márquez: Coetáneo de la eternidad.* Amsterdam, Holland: Rodolpi, 1984.

——, ed. *Cien años de soledad.* Madrid: Cátedra, 1984. 17th printing, 2005.

Kaplan, Martin. Review of *Innocent Erendira and Other Stories, New Republic,* 179 (August 26, 1978): 44–46.

Kazin, Alfred. Review of *Leaf Storm and Other Stories, New York Times Book Review,* February 20, 1972: 1, 14–16.

Kiely, Robert. Review of *One Hundred Years of Solitude, New York Times Book Review,* March 8, 1970: 5, 24.

King, John, ed. *On Modern Latin American Fiction.* New York: Hill and Wang, 1987.

——. *El Di Tella y el desarrollo cultural argentine en la década del sesenta.* Buenos Aires: Asunto Impreso Ediciones, 2007.

Kristal, Efraín. *The Cambridge Companion to the Latin American Novel.* Cambridge: Cambridge University Press, 2005.

Kulin, Katain. *Crónica mítica en la obra de García Márquez.* Budapest: Editorial de la Academia de Ciencias de Hungría, 1980.

Leal, Luis. "Magic Realism," *A Luis Leal Reader,* edited by Ilan Stavans. Evanston, IL: Northwestern University Press, 2007.

Leante, César. *Gabriel García Márquez: El hechicero.* Madrid: Piegos, 1996.

Leonard, John: "Myth Is Alive in Latin America," *New York Times,* March 3, 1970: 39.

Levine, Suzanne Jill. *El espejo hablado: Un estudio de "Cien años de soledad."* Caracas: Monte Avila Editores, 1975.

Ludmer, Josefina. *"Cien años de soledad": Una interpretación.* Buenos Aires: Bibliotecas Universitarias, Centro Editor de América Latina, 1985.

Manguel, Alberto, with Gianni Guadalupi. *Dictionary of Imaginary Places.* New York: Harcourt Brace Jovanovich, 1980, 1987.

Martin, Gerald. *Gabriel García Márquez: A Life.* New York: Alfred A. Knopf, 2009.

Martínez, Pedro Simón. *Sobre García Márquez.* Montevideo: Biblioteca de Marcha, 1971.

Martínez, Tomás Eloy. "América: la gran novela. Gabriel García Márquez: *Cien años de soledad,*" *Primera Plana* (Buenos Aires), vol. 234, (July 20–26, 1967): 54–55.

Maturo, Graciela. *Claves simbólicas de García Márquez.* Buenos Aires: F. García Cambeiro, 1972.

McGuirk, Bernard, with Richard Cardwell, ed. *Gabriel García Márquez: New Readings.* Cambridge and New York: Cambridge University Press, 1987.

McMurray, George R. *Gabriel García Márquez.* New York: F. Ungar, 1977.

——. *Gabriel García Márquez: Life, Work, and Criticism.* Fredericton, Canada: York Press, 1987.

——, ed. *Critical Essays on Gabriel García Márquez.* Boston: G.K. Hall, 1987.

Mead, Jr., Robert G. "For Sustenance: Hope," *Saturday Review,* December 12, 1968: 26.

Mejía Duque, Jaime. *Mito y realidad en Gabrcel García Márquez.* Bogotá: Oveja Negra, 1971.

Mendoza, Plinio Apuleyo. *La llama y el hielo.* Barcelona: Planeta, 1984.

——. *Aquellos tiempos con Gabo.* Barcelona: Plaza & Janés, 2000.

Menton, Seymour. *La novela colombiana: planetas y satélites.* Bogotá: Plaza & Janés, 1978.

——. *Caminata por la narrativa latinoamericana.* Mexico: Universidad Veracruzana and Fondo de Cultura Económica, 2002.

Mera, Aura Lucía, ed. *Aracataca/Estocolmo.* Reports and recollections by Ana Lucía Mera, Álvaro Castaño Castillo, Germán Vargas, Alfonso Fuenmayor, Guillermo Angulo, and Nereo López. Bogotá: Instituto Colombiano de Cultura, 1983.

Minta, Stephen. *García Márquez: Writer of Colombia.* New York: Harper & Row, 1987.

Montaner, María Eulalia. *Guía para la lectura de "Cien años de soledad."* Madrid: Editorial Castalia, 1987.

Moretti, Franco. *Modern Epic: The World System from Goethe to García Márquez.* London: Verso, 1996.

Mutis, Álvaro. *"El último rostro,"* in *Cuatro relatos.* Bogotá: Grupo Editorial Norma, 1978.

——. *Diary of Lecumberri: A Poet Behind Bars,* translated by Jesse H. Lytle, *Hopscotch: A Cultural Review,* vol. 1, no. 3 (1999): 2–37.

Oberhelman, Harley D. *Gabriel García Márquez: A Study of the Short Fiction.* Boston: Twayne, 1991.

——. *The Presence of Hemingway in the Short Fiction of Gabriel García Márquez.* Fredericton, Canada: York Press, 1994.

——. *García Márquez and Cuba: A Study of Its Presence and the Powers of Fiction.* Fredericton, Canada: York Press, 1995.

Ochoa, Ana María. *"*García Márquez, Macondismo, and the Soundscape of Vallenato,*"* *Popular Music,* vol. 24, no. 2 (May 2005): 207–222.

Onetti, Juan Carlos. *Confesiones de un lector.* Madrid: Alfaguara, 1995.

Ortega, Julio. *Gabriel García Márquez and the Powers of Fiction.* Austin: University of Texas Press, 1988.

——, ed. *Gaborio: Artes de releer a Gabriel García Márquez.* Mexico: Jorale Ediciones, 2003.

Ovideo, José Miguel, with Hugo Achugar and Jorge Areleche, eds. *Aproximaciones a Gabriel García Márquez.* Montevideo: Fundación de Cultura Universitaria, 1969.

Oyarzún, Kemy, with William W. Magenny, eds. *Essays on Gabriel García Márquez.* Riverside: University of California-Riverside, 1984.

Palencia-Roth, Michael. *Gabriel García Márquez: La línea, el círculo y las metamorfosis del mito.* Madrid: Gredos, 1983.

——, ed. *Myth and the Modern Novel: García Márquez, Mann, and Joyce.* New York: Garland, 1987.

Parkinson Zamora, Lois, with Wendy B. Faris, eds. *Magical Realism: Theory, History, Community.* Durham: Duke University Press, 1995.

Pelayo, Rubén. *Gabriel García Márquez: A Critical Companion.* Westport, CT: Greenwood, 2001.

Posada-Carbo, Eduardo. "Fiction as History: The Bananeras and Gabriel Garcia Marquez's *One Hundred Years of Solitude*," *Journal of Latin American Studies,* vol. 30, no. 2 (May 1998): 395–414.

Pritchett, V. S. "The Myth Makers," *The Myth Makers: European and Latin American Writers.* New York: Random House, 1979: 164–173.

Rabassa, Gregory. *If This Be Treason: Translation and Its Discontents.* New York: New Directions, 2005.

Rama, Angel, with Mario Vargas Llosa. *García Márquez y la problemática de la novela: Una polémica.* Buenos Aires: Corregidor-Marcha, 1973.

——. *Los dictadores latinoamericanos.* Mexico: Fondo de Cultura Económica, 1976.

——. *García Márquez: Edificación de un arte nacional y popular.* Montevideo: Universidad de la República, Facultad de Humanidades y Ciencias, Departamento de Publicaciones, 1987.

Ramírez Molas, Pedro. *Tiempo y narración: Enfoques de la temporalidad en Borges, Carpentier, Cortázar y García Márquez.* Madrid: Editorial Gredos, 1978.

Robinson, Lorna: "The Insomnia Plague in *One Hundred Years of Solitude*," *Neophilologus,* vol. 90 (April 2006): 249–269.

Rodríguez Monegal, Emir. "Novedad y anacronismo en *Cien años de soledad*," *Revista Nacional de Cultura* (Caracas), no. 185 (July–September, 1968): 3–21.

——. *El Boom de la novela latinoamericana.* Caracas: Editorial Tiempo Nuevo, 1972.

Roh, Franz. *Nach-Expressionismus, Magischer Realismus: Probleme der neuesten Europäischen Malerei.* Leipzig: Klinkhardt & Biermann, 1925.

Richardson, Jack. "Master Builder: *One Hundred Years of Solitude*," *New York Review of Books,* March 26, 1970.

Rufinelli, Jorge. "*Cien años de soledad: ¿un plagio?*" *Marcha* (Montevideo), vol. 33, no 1550, July 2, 1971: second scetion, page 3.

Saldívar, Dasso. *García Márquez: El viaje a la semilla*. Madrid: Alfaguara, 1997.

Samper, Daniel. "El novelista García Márquez no volverá a escribir," *El Tiempo* (Bogotá), December 22, 1968.

Seguí, Agustín Francisco. *La verdadera historia de Macondo*. Madrid: Iberoamericana, 1994.

Sghirlanzoni, A., with F. Carella. "The Insomnia Plague: A Gabriel García Márquez Story," *Neurological Sciences*, vol. 21, no. 4 (Dec. 2000): 251–258.

Shaw, Bradley A., with Nora Vera-Godwin, eds. *Critical Perspectives on Gabriel García Márquez*. Lincoln, NE: Society of Spanish and Spanish-American Studies, 1986.

Sims, Robert L. *The First García Márquez: A Study of His Journalistic Writing from 1948 to 1955*. Lanham, MD: University Press of America, 1992.

Sorela, Pedro. *El otro García Márquez: Los años difíciles*. Madrid: Mondadori, 1988.

Stanion, Charles.: "A Lingering Mystery in *One Hundred Years of Solitude*," *Romance Notes*, vol. 31, no. 1 (Fall 1995): 69–73.

Stavans, Ilan. "Gabo in Decline," *Transition* 62 (1993): 58–78. Reprinted in *The Essential Ilan Stavans*. New York and London: Routledge, 2000.

——. "García Márquez's 'Total Novel.'" *The Chronicle of Higher Education* (June 15, 2007). Reprinted as "Macondo Turns 40," in *A Critic's Journey*. Ann Arbor: University of Michigan Press, 2009.

——. "Macondo Magic," *Toronto Globe and Mail*, April 26, 2008.

——. "A Mode of Truth: A Conversation on Biography Between Ilan Stavans and Donald Yates," *Michigan Quarterly Review*, volume 48, number 4 (Fall 2009): 577–606.

Stavans, Ilan, ed. *The Oxford Book of Latin American Essays*. New York and Oxford: Oxford University Press, 1997.

——, ed. *Mutual Impressions: Writers of the Americans Reading One Another*. Durham: Duke University Press, 1999.

——, ed. *Gabriel García Márquez: Critical Insights*. Pasadena, CA: Salem Press, 2009.

——, ed. *"One Hundred Years of Solitude": Critical Insights*. Pasadena, CA: Salem Press, 2010.

Valdés, María Elena de, with Mario J. Vadlés, eds. *Approaches to Teaching García Márquez's "One Hundred Years of Solitude."* New York: Modern Language Association of America, 1990.

Van der Walde, Erna. "El macondismo como latinoamericanismo," *Cuadernos Americanos*, vol 12, no. 1 (January–February 1998): 223–37.

Vargas Llosa, Mario. *García Márquez: Historia de un deicidio*. Barcelona: Barral Editores, 1971.

———. "El jubileo de Carmen Balcells," *El País* (Madrid), no. 1750 (August 20, 2000).

Volkening, Ernesto. *Gabriel García Márquez: Un triunfo sobre el olvido*, edited by Santiago Mutis. Bogotá: Arango Ediciones, 1998.

Wallrafen, Hannes. *The World of García Márquez*. London: Ryan, 1991.

Williams, Raymond Leslie. *Gabriel García Márquez*. Boston: Twayne, 1984.

———. *The Colombian Novel: 1844–1987*. Austin: University of Texas Press, 1991.

Wood, Michael. *Gabriel García Márquez: "One Hundred Years of Solitude."* Cambridge and New York: Cambridge University Press, 1990.

Zapata, Juan Carlos. *Gabo nació en Caracas, no en Aracataca*. Caracas: Editorial Alfa, 2007.

Zuluaga Osorio, Conrado. *Puerta abierta a Gabriel García Márquez: Aproximaciones a la obra del Nobel colombiano*. Barcelona: Editorial Casiopea, 2001.

———. *Gabriel García Márquez: El vicio incurable de contar*. Bogotá: Panamericana, 2005.

About the Author

Ilan Stavans is Lewis-Sebring Professor in Latin American and Latino Culture at Amherst College.

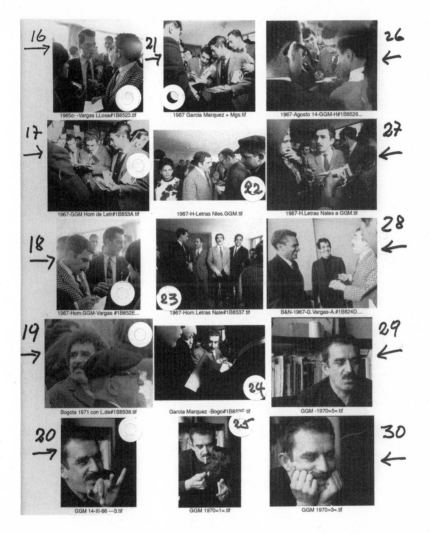

16 →
21 →
26 ←
17 →
22
27 ←
18 →
23
28 ←
19 →
24
29 ←
20 →
25
30 ←

1965c- -Vargas LLosa#1B6523.tif

1967 García Marquez + Mgs.tif

1967-Agosto 14-GGM-H#1B8526...

1967-GGM Hom de Letr#1B853A.tif

1967-H-Letras Nles.GGM.tif

1967-H.Letras Nales a GGM.tif

1967-Hom.GGM-Vargas #1B852E...

1967-Hom.Letras Nale#1B8537.tif

B&N-1967-G.Vargas-A.#1B824D...

Bogota 1971 con L.de#1B8538.tif

Garcia Marquez -Bogo#1B853F.tif

GGM -1970=5=.tif

GGM 14-III-66 ---3.tif

GGM 1970=1=.tif

GGM 1970=3=.tif

$\mathcal{I}ndex$

"En este pueblo no hay ladrones"
(There Are No Thieves
in This Town), 13–14,
127, 129
Estudios Churubusco, 118
Europe, 79–87
"Eva está dentro de su gato"
(Eve Is Inside Her Cat), 53

Fallas, Carlos Luis, 21
Fanon, Franz, 80
Faulkner, William, 8, 51–2,
60–1, 92–3, 120, 129, 132,
140, 178
See Yoknapatawpha County
Félix Fuenmayor, José, 68
Fernández, Emilio ("El Indio"),
119–20
Fernández-Bermejo, Miguel, 148
Fernández-Braso, Miguel, 131
Fernández Renowitsky, Juan B.,
43
Figueroa, Carlos A., 126–7
Figueroa, Gabriel, 119, 130
Fin del mundo, 162
Finnegans Wake, 98
Fiorillo, Heriberto, 152
Flaubert, Gustave, 34
Flores, Ángel, 109
Fondo de Cultura Económica,
101
French New Wave, 120
French Parnassianism, 96
Freud, Sigmund, 110, 113, 168
Fuenmayor, Alfonso, 65, 67–9,
79, 152–3
Fuentes, Carlos, 8, 41, 80, 92–3,
100, 103- 4, 118, 122–5, 128,
130, 147, 151, 155–7, 162–3

Fuentes, Fernando de, 118
Fuguet, Alberto, 10
Los funerals de la Mamá Grande
(Big Mama's Funeral),
88–9, 169, 182

Gaitán, Jorge Eliécer, 5, 35, 52,
54–7, 63
See El Bogotazo
Gallimard, 104
El gallo de oro, 8–9, 130, 211
Galvis, Silvia, 27
Gambaro, Griselda, 161
García Ascot, Jomí, 123,
125–6, 151
García Barcha, Gonzalo (son),
126, 194n7
García Barcha, Rodrigo (son),
89, 91, 115, 123, 194n7
"García Márquez" (poem),
162–3
García Márquez, Aida Rosa
(sister), 27, 39
García Márquez, Gabriel
birth of, 15–16
as book salesman, 72
on the Caribbean, 18–19
childhood of, 29–37, 39–43
on communism, 82, 85
on critics, 178–80
descriptions of, 115, 160
and drawing, 40
education of, 42–4, 46–7,
54, 82
and Europe, 79–87
and fame, 7, 160–7, 182
film criticism, 73, 81, 120
historical influence of, 4–5
and love, 45